Samuel Taylor Coleridge

and the Anglican Church

Samuel Taylor
COLERIDGE

and the Anglican Church

LUKE SAVIN HERRICK WRIGHT

University of Notre Dame Press

Notre Dame, Indiana

PR
4487
.R4
W75
2010

Library of Congress Cataloging-in-Publication Data

Wright, Luke S. H.
Samuel Taylor Coleridge and the Anglican Church /
Luke Savin Herrick Wright.
p. cm.
Includes bibliographical references and index.
ISBN-13: 978-0-268-04418-3 (pbk. : alk. paper)
ISBN-10: 0-268-04418-X (pbk. : alk. paper)
1. Coleridge, Samuel Taylor, 1772–1834—Religion. 2. Coleridge,
Samuel Taylor, 1772–1834—Political and social views. 3. Church and state
in literature. 4. Church and state—England—History—19th century.
5. Christianity and politics—History of doctrines—19th century.
6. England—Intellectual life—19th century. I. Title.
PR4487.R4W75 2010
821'.7—dc22

2010008788

for

JERRY SMITH and JIM CLAYTON

CONTENTS

Part One

Coleridge as a Young Man

I

Coleridge's Political Milieu

THIS PROJECT BEGAN AS AN INVESTIGATION OF THE INFLUENCE of Richard Hooker's *Laws of Ecclesiastical Polity* (1593/1594) upon the thought of Samuel Taylor Coleridge. It expanded into a study of the relationship of Coleridge to the Church of England throughout his life. During this expansion it became more focused upon placing Coleridge in his political context and on demonstrating the immense influence that his years at Jesus College, Cambridge, had on the structure of his thought. As a detailed picture of Coleridge the churchman and political pundit emerged, it became more and more clear that Coleridge's Hookerianism was a part of a larger dialogue. Undoubtedly Hooker's influence was pervasive in Coleridge's later works. Yet although Coleridge was drawn to Hooker's works for their own merit and beauty, rather than because any other thinker sent him there, and although Coleridge's respect for and belief in Hooker's theological position were utterly genuine and deep, his interest in Hooker was nevertheless an integral part of a greater project. He adopted Hooker's ideas and arguments, partly because they provided him an authoritative position to speak from, and partly as a rhetorical tool in a debate in which he participated from 1809 until his death in 1834.

A major (if at times subtle) focus of Coleridge's lifetime work was his dissent from the standard public and political doctrines of his day. This dissent did not coalesce into a long-term project until about 1809 (the period when *The Friend* was published), but even in his early radical period he had rejected political orthodoxy. His mature project was reactionary in nature, while his young mind had taken a radical path, but

3

in both cases Coleridge attacked the ruling political conceptions of the day. He saw Hooker as part of an "old order" intellectual tradition that, from 1809 onwards, he carefully began to access in order to give his own political views authority. The young romantic of the period that produced *The Watchman,* who had once taken up a position of radical dissent because he found Pitt's and Addington's administrations too arid and staid in their beliefs, in later life adopted a position of reactionary dissent because he found the Portland, Perceval, and Liverpool administrations utilitarian in their political philosophy—too untheological, in other words. In the discussion that follows, the political and religious orthodoxy of the day will be described as "Whig." It might seem strange to use this term to describe an orthodoxy, given that the political party that appropriated the name *Whig* was out of office for all but a handful of months during 1783–1830. It must be borne in mind, however, that *all* politicians (including the younger Pitt and his ministers) thought of themselves as Whigs, at least until the 1810s, while hardly any thought of themselves as Tories. *Whig* here refers, not to any one political party, but to the political establishment as a whole and to their assumptions and preconceptions.

Therefore, by its very nature, this project never sought to undertake an examination of Coleridge's poetry. This choice was made for two substantive reasons. First, although there are some unpublished later poems and fragments in the Notebooks, Coleridge stopped writing poetry that he published by 1806: three full years before he wrote *The Friend* in its serial incarnation. This work argues that *The Friend* marks the outset of Coleridge's mature project. Since the aim of this book is to examine Coleridge's mature project (and to examine his early politics and theological convictions in an ancillary way in order to set the mature material in its context), the poems are simply not relevant. This might not have been the case were the poems written about theological or political themes and issues, but they are not—and this is the second substantive reason that they are not examined. Coleridge's poetry is profoundly untheological and apolitical—though the final third of "Frost at Midnight" constitutes the exception that proves the rule to the former, and "France: An Ode" the exception that proves the rule to the latter. Within the parameters of the examination of Coleridge's mature project that this book undertakes, it would therefore have been wrongheaded, not to mention cumbersome to the reader, to attempt to key this discussion of Coleridge's theology and polity to his poetry and aesthetic writings—the text would have become bloated and unwieldy.

The common thread that bound Coleridge's life's project together was theology. His perennial standpoint in any political debate was to ask whether or not the participants in the debate—and the actions taken as a result—lived up to the expectations of a Christian nation and a Christian society. Time and again he began his examination of polity by asking whether the government took due note of the *responsibilities* that the establishment of the Church of England brought with it. Theology, or a theological perspective, is one (and often the only) congruent theme within the many independent works that make up Coleridge's eclectic corpus. But any attempt to illuminate the way in which he revived "old order" political ideas and beliefs first requires that the Whig orthodoxy of Coleridge's era be clearly defined. Fortunately this is not a difficult task: for Whig political and theological orthodoxy was embodied almost entirely in the work of one person. That man was William Warburton, and the philosophy that bears his name was the solidly entrenched perspective against which Coleridge would wage intellectual war. Subsequent chapters of this work seek to demonstrate how and where Coleridge dissented from Whig political orthodoxy and also to explain how he fitted into what Colin Matthew describes as the gathering forces of Toryism.[1] This will necessitate making links between Coleridge and other theologians, both those who preceded him and those who continued his project into the mid-nineteenth century.

Court Whig Ideology and Coleridge's Radicalism

First, however, it is necessary to explain the paradigm of Whig political orthodoxy from which Coleridge was to dissent. The remainder of this chapter will therefore concentrate on Warburtonian philosophy and its reception. It will set it in the context of other Whig political thought, as well as introducing Coleridge's dissent from it and his adoption of "old order" philosophy.

---

1. H. C. G. Matthew, "Noetics, Tractarians, and the Reform of the University of Oxford in the Nineteenth Century," *History of Universities* 9 (1990): 195–225.

There is general agreement that the Glorious Revolution was caused by the concern of centrist English Protestants, once again in the political ascendancy following the Restoration, that the birth of a Catholic heir threatened to perpetuate a Catholic dynasty and that this danger required a forced change in the succession of the monarchical line. The Glorious Revolution of course led to immense complications for Anglican divine right theory—though these were resolved largely through the fact that post-Restoration political divine right theory (which was fully endorsed by Church of England divines) was based upon pure theology deriving from natural law theory, rather than upon contemporary perception of biblical doctrine, and began with the concept of Adam as steward of the earth. Because this theory was based on speculative systematic theology, it was possible to massage it into one dictating that a Protestant monarch could hold the English (later British) throne by divine right and to employ a concept of the ancient English constitution—a concept plastic enough to be molded to suit different political concerns throughout history. Also integral to this new divine right theory was the idea of a partly devolved monarchy that ruled through the three-tier system of Crown, Lords, and Commons.

Although it was Tory theorists who worked out this new (and quite literally revolutionary) theory of divine right, the Glorious Revolution also laid the foundation for the hegemony of power that the Whig party would hold for over two-thirds of the eighteenth century. Because of the circumstances in which the Whigs rose to hegemonic power (i.e., the fact that the Glorious Revolution was a landed and Anglican settlement) the protection of Church of England Protestantism became a necessary and important part of their political ideology. Until quite recently historians failed to emphasize this platform, partly because of the cynicism prevalent in the Namierite method that so dominated the twentieth century until the work of J. G. A. Pocock, H. T. Dickinson, and Quentin Skinner. Such an emphasis would have been obvious to historians working in either the eighteenth century or the nineteenth. Pocock summarized the historiographical landscape on this issue in 1985:

> Who the First Whigs were and what they were attempting is a question notoriously hard to resolve; interpretation is currently turning back toward the view that the central facts of Restoration politics were the reestablishment of the church and the institutionaliza-

tion of dissent, and that the First Whigs were a faction of former Presbyterians seeking to put together an alliance of Anglicans and Dissenters aimed at preempting the policy of indulgence, whereby the crown sought to make itself the patron of dissent and lessen its dependence on the church and church party. If the religious rather than the constitutional establishment is to be made the central issue, we must downgrade (though we cannot ignore) the tradition of seeing the Whigs as primarily concerned with safeguarding whatever gains Parliament could be supposed to have inherited from the years of civil war and interregnum; religion was the issue on which Parliament was dragged back into self-assertion, and the Test Act was to stand beside the Toleration Act as pillars of the central pier of the Whig edifice—a perception quite generally held in the first half of the nineteenth century. . . .

We must now place at the center of the picture a phenomenon that in the years following the Restoration certainly could not have been called Whig, though it was later to form a part of what we call an "Augustan" ethos and think of as an ideological buttress of the "Whig supremacy." This is the emergence of a latitudinarian churchmanship, a rational religion aimed at repressing, moderating, or replacing the "enthusiasm" now thought of as the essential characteristic of Puritanism. . . .[2]

J. C. D. Clark also stresses the importance of the concept of divine right as a political strategy. He argues that politicians of the period were speaking to a religiously conscious electorate and that this electorate believed strongly in the activity of divine providence. Providence was used as an explanation for political action and as an explanation for historical circumstance.

Providence was still "the age's leading concept of natural and historical causation." It was invoked to explain both events in the natural world, from harvests and sickness to earthquakes, and events in the life of man. Incidents like the minor earthquake of 1692 allowed

---

2. J. G. A. Pocock, "Varieties of Whiggism," in *Virtue, Commerce, and History* (Cambridge: Cambridge University Press, 1985), 219.

commentators to draw the two closely together; and the Revolution of 1688 took its place beside other episodes in English history—the Armada, the Gunpowder Plot, the Restoration—which were celebrated as obvious interventions of the Deity in advancing the interests of Protestant England. The Hanoverian accession in due course was hailed by some as just such a national deliverance. Almost all churchmen joined in endorsing and preaching the notion of Providence, to the point where the victory of William III, significantly landing at Torbay on that fraught anniversary, 5th November, could be argued by Whigs to show as direct a divine commission and mandate as anything James II could claim.[3]

A Christian consciousness was more than a buttress of Whig ideology, it was an organic part of the architecture of eighteenth-century thought. The concept of secular politics did not exist.

Important though a broad and tolerant Church of England was in the eighteenth century (as integral to Whig ideology), it did not entirely overshadow the existence of another tradition: that of the contract theory of government, which grew out of late seventeenth-century English philosophy and principally out of the work of Locke—though Warburton tended to cite Hobbes more than Locke in *The Alliance between Church and State* (1736).[4] What Warburton achieved—and it was this achievement that allowed him to be propelled from obscurity to a position of influence and eventually a bishopric—was to create a systematic political theology that took contract theory as its basis and incorporated the post-Glorious Revolution divine right theory of monarchy, while at the same time he went to extreme lengths to avoid Erastianism, though seeming to give an actual supremacy within the contract to the church. The Whig party could not have obtained a theological work more cogently suited to its political ideology if it had commissioned one explicitly. Warburton's theory was congenial to the political ideologues of the eighteenth century, even if some clerical voices chose to dissent from his idea of a con-

---

3. J. C. D. Clark, *English Society, 1688–1832* (Cambridge: Cambridge University Press, 1985), 124.

4. See chapter 2 for a discussion of the question of tolerance in the late eighteenth century.

tract between church and state—and by far the majority of clerics did not; it became an organic part of the public doctrine prevalent during what proved to be one of the most stable periods of government in British history.

Although the Tory party was in a shambles during the reigns of George I and George II, and so unable to form a viable opposition, and although it went into abeyance under George III, individual Tories remained in the nooks and crannies of public life; however, for stability to be achieved, it was necessary for both Whigs and Tories to moderate their ideological positions. Though the political landscape of the period was dominated by the ideological differences between Court and Country members of Parliament, the Court Whigs dominated government in this period, and it is Court Whiggery to which I refer (again broadly speaking) when I speak of "Whig orthodoxy." H. T. Dickinson describes the ideology:

> Court Whigs no longer required an ideology designed to oppose those in power, but an ideology which would defend and justify the *status quo.* They were therefore careful not to endorse all of Locke's political views, though they did recognize the conservative side of Locke's work and did realize that this could be exploited to support the Whig supremacy. They appreciated that Locke had gone to great lengths to justify private property and the unequal distribution of wealth. Indeed, he had insisted that civil government was established in order to protect the individual's right to his property and to preserve the unequal division of wealth which had arisen in the state of nature. The Court Whigs did not therefore have to abandon all support for Locke's political ideology. What they had to do was to appropriate and endorse the conservative elements in Locke's work while rejecting the more radical implications of some of his views.
>
> The Court Whigs fully endorsed Locke's view that property had been divided unequally in the state of nature, that civil government was erected to protect this natural right to private property, and that no authority could infringe the rights of property without the consent of the owner. Government was still regarded as an artificial creation which had only become necessary when men had acquired private property and needed to defend it. Locke had therefore been right to argue that an equal division of the fruits of the earth or a system

of communal ownership were both inconsistent with human nature. To allow such claims would create far more problems than the existence of an unequal distribution of private property. Since, the Court Whigs insisted, Locke was therefore right to claim that civil government was deliberately set up to protect the rich from the envy and violence of the poor, no government could possess the authority to infringe the rights of private property without the consent of the owner.[5]

Government was viewed as ordained by God, but different *forms* of government were left to humanity to organize. In this scheme no particular form, or system, of government could be said to be ordained as necessarily correct, and systems evolved over time. The Whig view was that the English constitution of limited monarchy had evolved over time and had proven to be the most appropriate to both England and, indeed, the world.[6] All Whig ideology, even Country Whiggery, held that government was a contract with the populace (though granted it was a contract that once entered into could not be dissolved by the lesser party: the governed masses) and that this contract had become necessary only with the creation and institution of private property; once private property had come into existence, the creation of a government had become necessary in order to protect it. This emphasis upon the concept of property as fundamental both to democracy and to government was absolutely inseparable from both the Court and Country ideologies of the final decades of the eighteenth century.[7]

Most establishment Whigs believed that God had ordained government for the benefit of man, but they insisted that he had allowed the various races and nations to devise different constitutions to suit their particular circumstances. Thus, while the authority of government in general came from God, the precise form of any government came from man. No particular form of government could claim to be

---

5. H. T. Dickinson, *Liberty and Property: Political Ideology in Eighteenth-Century Britain* (London: Weidenfeld and Nicolson, 1977), 127–28.
6. Dickinson, *Liberty,* 129.
7. Dickinson, *Liberty,* 127 ff.

divinely ordained and hence unalterable by man. Each government must be tested by experience before it could be regarded as appropriate to the needs of a particular society. Over many centuries the English had recognized the merits of a limited monarchy in which the legislative sovereignty was shared by Crown, Lords and Commons. England's ancient constitution enshrined the principle of government by consent, but this was not the same as the radical claim that all legitimate civil governments were based on original contract or on the sovereignty of the people. The Court Whigs readily accepted that governments might have originated in conquest or through a gradual extension of the patriarchal family, but, nonetheless, their authority was limited by the subsequent need to secure at least the tacit consent of their subjects. Originally certain leaders may have imposed their authority on other men, but no exercise of authority could be legitimate unless it was for the benefit of the whole community, and hence all power had to be held in trust. The need to safeguard the welfare of society placed limits on the authority of every government and also defined the subject's duty to obey. Civil society was undoubtedly created to protect life, liberty and property. Any government which sacrificed these ends betrayed the trust placed in it. When that happened the people had the right to resist.[8]

This is exactly the sort of contract theory that Warburton employed in the 1730s when writing *The Alliance between Church and State*; his voice was extremely characteristic of the Court Whig position, though he would never have gone so far as to acknowledge any truth in the position that would later be argued by radicals: that resistance was acceptable if the government had ceased to perform its functions of preserving life and property, since the contract had been rendered null and void by the greater party (the government).

Now, it *is* true that by the 1760s Whig theorists were beginning to abandon contract theory, and the idea of an ancient constitution brought into its current form by successive governments over time, but *The Alliance* was written some twenty years earlier when these subjects were very much at the fore of Court ideology. In fact it was precisely the

---

8. Dickinson, *Liberty*, 129.

moves *towards* abandoning contract theory (and the idea of an ancient constitution) that would herald the rebirth of radicalism—though there would be no fully fledged radicals until the 1780s and no full-throated radical voices until the 1790s.

It is noteworthy, though, that both the Court and Country Whigs (and Country Tories) were absolutely wedded to the concept that only men of property could govern adequately. One manifestation of this emphasis on property was the form it took in early eighteenth-century Tory ideology: only men whose wealth resided in land were tied to the kingdom by their own interests and so could not flee with transportable wealth as could the merchant class and financiers; therefore the interests of the kingdom were by necessity tied to the interests of the landed class as they were by nature coterminous.[9] This particular description of the property qualification may have been made by the Tories of the 1720s, but the general idea was not foreign to either Country Whigs or their Court counterparts. When radicalism began to develop in the 1780s, it began shifting the opposition's traditional Country focus (on restricting the opportunity for corruption and nepotism in government) to a "platform" from which it would seek to exercise the democratic nature of the British constitution.[10] "The Country idea had been an independent House of Commons, free from the corruption of the Court and instructions of the people. The radicals appealed to a different concept of a pure House of Commons. They still wished to see it independent of the Court but they wanted it to be representative of the people at large and more responsive to public opinion."[11] Here "instructions of the people" refers to the practice of electors sending their member of Parliament written instructions on how to vote on a given issue before the House. It was thought by the Country element that this was a violation of the trust that had been placed in the representatives by the electors; they believed that an MP must use his own disinterested judgment to come to a decision and that he represented the interests of the country as a whole, which he represented virtually. Also he must put this general interest above the specific interests of the electors. It should be noted, however,

---

9. Dickinson, *Liberty,* 50–56.

10. *Focus* is perhaps a better word but not strong enough; *platform*, however, implies too much coordinated effort.

11. Dickinson, *Liberty,* 221.

that certain Country elements did advocate using instructions as a way to rein in corruption at the Court, and from time to time there were moves both to force Country politicians to appear in the House for important votes (which their rural locations and agrarian interests often prevented them from doing) and to persuade them to vote in a particular way by sending them written "instructions," which were effectively threats of refusing to reelect them.

Contract theory was, however, not entirely eschewed by radical elements. Richard Price (a leading radical Whig) argued for democratization through a claim of popular sovereignty based on an original contract to which all men had subscribed. "Parliament therefore only possessed a delegated trust for ultimate sovereignty was retained by the people."[12] Price, though, was a Whig on the fringes of radicalism only. On the whole the radicals were more centrist: they wished to make the House of Commons more representative, but they did not wish to democratize the entire constitution—they still believed strongly in a mixed government of monarch, lords, and a democratized commons. Even Price, along with other leading radicals such as James Burgh, explicitly denied that he wished to undermine the sovereignty of the Crown. Radicals might deplore the horrible living circumstances of the poor, but this concern rarely led to demands for political action, let alone direct action.[13] On the whole, even the radicals felt that education and some leisure were necessary qualifications for a man to hold a seat in Parliament. For instance, even John Thelwall (generally agreed to be one of the most determined radicals of the 1790s) had reservations about changing the system of government to make it absolutely democratic; though he wished to restore the poor to their rights, which he believed they would soon learn to exercise properly, he never expected the poor to "become sufficiently qualified" to govern. "Thelwall never envisaged a government by the people. He expected the lower orders to follow the lead of enlightened men from the middle and upper ranks of society. Indeed, at times he feared that democracy might obstruct progress."[14] Universal manhood suffrage was not in any way a telos of the radical plan (let alone women's suffrage; among radicals Catherine Macaulay and Mary Wollstonecraft

---

12. Dickinson, *Liberty*, 222.
13. Dickinson, *Liberty*, 230.
14. Dickinson, *Liberty*, 251.

were virtually alone in their concern for the rights and suffrage of women). All of this is relevant because, with the Pantisocratic scheme, Coleridge envisioned precisely what the vanguard of radicalism was being exceptionally careful to make clear it did not want: the abolition of property.[15] Furthermore, the idea of Pantisocracy—a utopian society where property was abolished and intellectual activity was the focus of life—was a direct departure from Court Whig ideology in that it was *utopian.*

In other words, the radicals were not even advocating universal suffrage, let alone redistribution of property or its abolition. The abolition of property found no support from radical philosophy either. Bentham, for instance, argued that equal distribution of property would remove all impetus for diligent work. The abolition of property was in fact so abhorrent to the Whig ethos that most radical groups felt the need to issue statements explicitly denying any plans to effect or even merely to advocate it. The Manchester Reformation Society stated that it wished equality of rights but *specifically denied* that it wanted equality of property. The radicals of Sheffield went further: publishing that "we demand equality of rights, in which is included equality of representation; . . . We are not speaking of that visionary equality of property, the practical assertion of which would desolate the world, and replunge it into the darkness and wildest barbarism. . . ."[16]

---

15. Pantisocracy was a scheme envisioned first by both Coleridge and Southey, but soon only by Coleridge, as Southey became disillusioned with the impracticality of the project. The scheme was to create a utopian society of intellectual activity and perfect justice. Coleridge, Southey, and several intellectual friends would move en masse to the banks of the Susquehanna River in the newly founded nation of America. There the community would abolish private property and all items would be owned communally. Work would likewise be shared out absolutely equally within the community; it was posited that a mere two hours of manual labor a day undertaken together would provide enough man-hours to cultivate sufficient produce for the group's subsistence. The remainder of the waking hours would be spent in purely intellectual pursuits—effectively creating a permanent salon. Presumably it was expected that the proceeds from the sale of any work published by any of the members of the community would be used to buy manufactured goods such as milled cloth for the benefit of the entire community.

16. Dickinson, *Liberty,* 255.

Reed Browning has identified three fundamental assertions that constituted the "axiomatic framework within which the Court Whig view took on plausibility": (1) government (and politics) were fundamentally nonutopian in nature, (2) liberty in excess became licentiousness, and (3) Court Whigs held the middle ground between factions that sought to return to royal authoritarianism of the period preceding the Glorious Revolution and those that sought to transfer all power to the House of Commons.[17] The claim that some politicians wished to house all power in the House of Commons seems to be denying Dickinson's interpretation that virtually all politicians of the period, including radicals, envisioned reforming the House of Commons to make a stronger organ of government in a three-part system. This is not the case, though, because Browning identifies this third assertion as "blatantly self-serving, violently distorting the real views of their opponents."[18]

Browning argues that the first of these assertions was the most fundamental:

> The first general assertion posited the essentially nonutopian nature of politics. It has already been noted how Hervey, Hoadly, Herring, Squire, and Hardwicke to a man denounced utopianism. All Court Whigs concurred. The perfect regime, they declared, was unattainable.... Moreover, this Court Whig assertion embraced the sobering notion that many problems lay beyond the capacity of human government to rectify or ameliorate.... These were consistent themes in Court Whig writing, and their purpose is obvious. If the exercise of power invariably entailed errors and difficulties, and if many of the trials of civil life were irremovable, then the responsibility of the ministers presiding over affairs for the problems arising during their ministry was thereby diminished.[19]

The Pantisocratic scheme, which receives its fullest presentation in *The Lectures on Revealed Religion* (1795), constitutes the most carefully

---

17. Reed Browning, *Political and Constitutional Ideas of the Court Whigs* (Baton Rouge: Louisiana State University Press, 1982), 176–78; quotation from 176.

18. Browning, *Political and Constitutional Ideas,* 178.

19. Browning, *Political and Constitutional Ideas,* 176–77.

worked out early systematic theology Coleridge wrote, as well as his most intricate early discussion of civil government. Pantisocracy advocated the abolition of property, and this made it a scheme of radicalism different from nearly every other piece of radical thought in the 1790s; furthermore, its Utopian vision made it a stronger departure from the Court Whig (Warburtonian) position that the state required the church to provide incentives that the state could not provide itself—other radical thinkers of the period were as a rule less utopian.

Admittedly, Coleridge was not the only person to advocate the abolition of property. He was one of two. Thomas Spence was the other. Interestingly, Spence also pushed this argument along agrarian lines, as did the tiny handful of radicals who suggested a somewhat less substantial redistribution of wealth.

> A few radicals did suggest economic ways of improving the lot of the poor. James Oswald and an anonymous contributor to *The Cabinet* proposed that waste and common land should be divided among the poor while Mary Wollstonecraft suggested that large estates might be divided into small farms. Only Thomas Spence however advocated a truly revolutionary scheme for redividing all the available land of the country equally among the entire adult male population. He was the only radical whose concept of natural rights led him to advocate a return to the state of nature when all men had enjoyed an equal claim to the fruits of the earth. Nonetheless, while Spence's ideas were revolutionary they were also hopelessly visionary. . . . Moreover Spence, like the other radicals, had little grasp of the economic realities of the late eighteenth century. He concentrated all his attention on the agricultural sector of the economy just at a time when Britain was undergoing rapid commercial and industrial development. He believed that landed property was the sole basis of wealth and utterly failed to recognize that industry could produce wealth far more rapidly than agriculture. . . .
>
> Spence's plan for the redistribution of property showed no appreciation of economic realities or of the economic means which might be at the disposal of the labouring masses.[20]

---

20. Dickinson, *Liberty,* 267–68.

One might well have called Spence a Romantic. There is no indication that Coleridge read or was influenced by Spence; his ideas on the redistribution of property and its abolition came from another source: the Bible.[21]

COURT WHIG IDEOLOGY AND WARBURTON

The general lay of the philosophical and political land having been surveyed, a more detailed discussion of Warburton's thought is now appropriate. Warburtonianism was a social theory expounded in his book *The Alliance between Church and State, or the Necessity of an Established Religion and a Test Law Demonstrated* (1736). At its most basic, Warburtonian theory can be summarized as a belief that church and state cooperate because each recognizes a mutual benefit in such a relationship— Warburton was, broadly speaking, a utilitarian. The first few lines of A.W. Evans's *Warburton and the Warburtonians* aptly and concisely summarize the received critical wisdom on Warburton's contribution to English ecclesiology:

> It has been Warburton's fate to be over-estimated during his lifetime and to be under-estimated since his death. He touched the intellectual life of his time at many points; and, in Gibbon's phrase, "he reigned the dictator and the tyrant of literature." He edited Pope, and he edited Shakespeare. He wrote the preface to Richardson's *Clarissa* and the dissertation on chivalry and romance at the beginning of Jarvis's translation of *Don Quixote*. He was the author of one of the most famous theological treatises of his generation. He propounded a theory of the relations between Church and State to which Coleridge was indebted and with the greater part of which Macaulay agreed.[22]

This is on the whole a fair and accurate statement—though the reference to Coleridge's debt to Warburton is true only in the sense that

---

21. See below.
22. A.W. Evans, *Warburton and the Warburtonians: A Study in Some Eighteenth-Century Controversies* (London: Oxford University Press, 1932), 1.

Warburton gave Coleridge a target against which to react. Certainly Warburton was "over-estimated" in his own lifetime (this is evident from the currency of his works among his contemporaries) and "underestimated since his death," yet he was certainly not completely forgotten. Evans continues:

> If he upholds what is "surely, the most utilitarian theory of the English church ever advanced by a representative churchman," and, if, in consequence, his theory was denounced by Cardinal Newman as making religious doctrine depend upon political expedience, and charged for the same reason by Gladstone with possessing "great moral defects," it is at least consistently held and without any skeptical intention in Warburton's mind. Early in his book he takes up the position that "TRUTH and PUBLIC UTILITY coincide," that "truth is productive of utility, and utility indicative of truth"; and, towards the end, he adds the deduction that "to provide for utility is, at the same time, to provide for truth, its inseparable associate."[23]

Warburton had a lasting and pervasive influence through *The Alliance* and was the figure with whom subsequent theorists of ecclesiology would have to contend when presenting their own ideas.

As Evans shows, Warburton was initially a country parson who had been to neither university nor public school and had no immediate network of influential contacts who would disseminate his writings; *The Alliance* was his first major work, and though it would later be incorporated into sections of *The Divine Legation of Moses* (1737 and 1741),

---

23. Evans, *Warburton*, 44. The first quotation inside Evans's quote is from W. A. Shaw, "The Literature of Dissent (1660–1760)," in *The Age of Johnson*, vol. 10 of *The Cambridge History of English Literature* (Cambridge: Cambridge University Press, 1913), 375. Evans's source for the denunciation of Warburton's theory by Newman is from John Henry Newman, *Difficulties felt by Anglicans in Catholic Teaching*, 4th ed. (London: Burns, Oates, 1872), 166–71; the Gladstone quote is from William Ewart Gladstone, *The State in Its Relations with the Church* (London: John Murray, 1841), 1:18; the Warburton quotes are from William Warburton, *The Alliance between Church and State*, vol. 4 of *The Works of the Right Reverend William Warburton, Lord Bishop of Gloucester* (London: John Nichols, 1788), 77 and 240. See chapter 11 below for a detailed discussion of Gladstone's dissatisfaction with Warburton and the origin of that dissatisfaction in the works of Coleridge.

its publication raised him from a position of obscurity and made his reputation. In fact, not only did *The Alliance* make Warburton's reputation, but it also brought him a network of influential contacts from which to launch his career. Evans writes:

> Although it was anonymous, its authorship was generally known; and Warburton seems to have sent many presentation copies. One of these was sent to Sherlock, then Bishop of Salisbury, and another to Hare, the Bishop of Chichester. Both were very favourably received. Hare, an able and learned man, wrote to Warburton expressing his satisfaction with the book, hoping that "what was intended for the use of the public may prove also to be for your own," and promising that his endeavours would not be wanting for that object. He did not forget his promise. The book, Nichols tells us, "was much talked of at court"; and when Queen Caroline made it known that she wished to have about her a man of learning who could entertain her with reading and conversation, Hare recommended Warburton.[24]

So although *The Alliance* was Warburton's first book, it was in many ways by far his most influential—certainly within his lifetime. Its influence was also more lasting than that of *The Divine Legation of Moses*; well into the nineteenth century, writers such as Coleridge, Gladstone, and Newman were reacting to it—albeit now unfavorably. Indeed, *The Alliance* itself went through five separate editions, all published in London, in 1736, 1741, 1748, 1766, and, after a lapse of eighty-two years, 1848. This was in addition to four editions of his complete works (also published in London): the first of which appeared in twelve volumes in 1788, the second in 1811, the third, in thirteen volumes (containing some further literary and epistolary remains) also in 1811, and the last in 1841. The serial nature of the dates demonstrates the persistent influence of Warburton's works, for it suggests that each successive generation required a reprint. All told, at least 115 separate editions of various works of Warburton were printed—an achievement that few of his contemporaries could match.[25]

---

24. Evans, *Warburton*, 46–47.
25. Charles Etienne Pierre Wante and Frank Howard Warner, *National Union Catalog: Pre-1956 Imprints* (London: Mansell, 1979), 43:648.

As Colin Matthew makes clear, it was not only High Churchmen and the gathering forces of Toryism in 1820s and 1830s Oxford who felt Warburton to be a worthy adversary. The Whiggish Noetics also felt the influence of *The Alliance* strongly enough to disagree with it formally in print. Richard Whately, "the dominant mind amongst the Noetics in Oxford," launched a severe attack upon *The Alliance* in his anonymous *Letters on the Church* (1826).[26] This is how Matthew sums up Whately's attack on the contemporary establishment and on the Warburtonian heritage that suffused it:

> The presence of bishops in the House of Lords was a disaster; church property should only be protected in the same sense as any corporation's property was protected; the Church must regain its own voice through a revival of Convocation: "The connexion such as it is now subsists, between the State and the Church, which some, both statesmen and churchmen, from confused or partial and imperfect views of the subject, are so anxious to maintain, is not only in principle unjustifiable, but is, in every point, inexpedient for both parties." This applied to the state as well as the Church, because, by exclusively favouring a narrowly-defined Church of England, Roman Catholics, whose faith Whately and Arnold saw as the expression of the depravity of human nature and original sin in an unadulterated form, were encouraged to feel alienated and would be encouraged to permanent degradation. Hence the improvement towards grace which the Church of England represented was made less likely by the Roman Catholics' civic disaffection.[27]

It has been stated that Coleridge was part of a nineteenth-century tradition that attacked *The Alliance,* but it is important to remember that he came at the beginning of this tradition and that those who would attack Warburton's utilitarianism in the 1830s and 1840s, both Noetics and Tractarians, were in some measure plowing a field that Coleridge had already cleared and harrowed. Coleridge was not the first critic of Warburton, for, as B. W. Young has pointed out, there were many eighteenth-

---

26. Matthew, "Noetics," 203.
27. Matthew, "Noetics," 203.

century critics of Warburton as well, ranging from Arthur Ashley Sykes and Francis Blackburne to several Hutchinsonian divines, including Justus Bate. The list goes on to include more well-known figures such as William Law and Richard Brown (Fellow of Trinity College Oxford). The thrust of their attack, though, was not against Warburton's utilitarian theories of church and state but against his *biblical* scholarship. Samuel Wesley published an exhaustive commentary in Latin on the book of Job, arguing that Job should be interpreted as a work of true history; Richard Grey later used Wesley's work as an authority to take the same position but argued that Moses was the author of the book— thus opposing Warburton's interpretation. Richard Brown and Charles Peters attacked Warburton persistently, claiming that his hypothesis was inferior to Sherlock's. Peters went so far as to "censure" Warburton in *A Critical Dissertation on the Book of Job* (1751).[28] But all these writers were taking issue with Warburton's later work: primarily *The Divine Legation of Moses.* For example, Brown, using Wesley, specifically attacked Warburton's allegorical method of scriptural interpretation, while Law sought to show that the idea of the immortality of the soul predated the Mosaic religion.[29] It is important to note, however, that none of these eighteenth-century critics opposed Warburton's utilitarian stance on church and state. The theory presented in *The Alliance* was so congruent with Whig political assumptions that it remained unassailed until Coleridge chose to take up the older Hookerian stance against it. He probably did this in reaction to Warburton's respectful but lengthy and merciless attack upon Hooker's theory that ends book 2 of *The Alliance,* but he was encouraged to do so by the emergence of the forces of antiutilitarian Toryism that began to gather themselves together in the post-Napoleonic atmosphere of the 1820s.

Evans's description of Warburton's political and philosophical roots emphasizes the philosophical approach: "However unsound his method

---

28. B.W. Young, *Religion and Enlightenment in Eighteenth-Century England: Theological Debate from Locke to Burke* (Oxford: Clarendon Press, 1998), 193.

29. For an exhaustive and elegant discussion of eighteenth-century criticism of Warburton, see Young, *Religion and Enlightenment,* 175–205, especially 181–82 and 194–96.

of reasoning may now appear, it is typical of the legalist manner of controversy which was common in the first half of the eighteenth century, and its validity was unquestioned by his contemporaries. Warburton himself had no doubt that it was legitimate; he unhesitatingly admits that his theory is based on deduction and not on fact."[30] But this description does not give a full picture, nor does it place sufficient emphasis on the political roots of Warburton's method. The best discussion of Warburton's political heritage and pedigree comes from Norman Sykes in his benchmark work *Church and State in England in the XVIIIth Century* (1962). Sykes demonstrates that Warburton's work was a product of the political philosophy of his time and explains Warburton's intellectual links with the Whig politicians of his era:

> His starting-point in discussing the origin and purpose of civil society was the contemporary doctrine of a social compact, designed to provide "security to the temporal liberty and property of man." His adoption of this position had the dual advantage that his theory was based upon the current whig political creed, and that it delivered him from the objection that his own abstract scheme of the relations of religious and civil societies was a mere figment of his imagination. . . . Little difficulty attended his endeavour to demonstrate, upon the accepted whig principles, that civil magistrates had no concern with the religious opinions of their subject, since the end of civil society embraced, not the eternal salvation, but the temporal happiness of men.[31]

Sykes also accurately stresses that Warburton's emphasis on the church as a visible and corporate society of men, self-constituted and entirely separate from the state (seen as a separate, self-constituted corporate society), "delivered Warburton from the fruitless controversies into which Hoadly's sermon had drawn many writers."[32] Benjamin Hoadly had preached a sermon in 1717 on the text of John 18:36 ("My kingdom is not of this world"), in which he had argued that the Gospels provided

---

30. Evans, *Warburton*, 33–34.
31. Norman Sykes, *Church and State in England in the XVIIIth Century* (Hamden, CT: Archon Books, 1962), 318–19.
32. Sykes, *Church and State*, 320.

no basis or warrant for an independent church authority within the political scene; that in the kingdom of Christ, Christ himself was king and there could be no other authority; and that the church should be an invisible society rather than a regimented and hierarchical one. The laws of the Kingdom of God were fixed, and no one had the right to interpret them in a manner that bound others to follow that interpretation as law. This sermon had provoked several years of debate known as the Bangorian controversy (so named because Hoadly held the see of Bangor). The major outcome of this controversy had been Parliament's suppression of the Convocations of Canterbury and York, on the excuse that a group of Hoadlyan followers in the lower house of the Convocation of Canterbury had created a set of propositions from his works that were (correctly) held to be subversive by the government. Convocation would not meet again until 1852.[33] The point here is that Warburton was at pains to forge for himself an "ultra-Whiggish" position that would be immensely broad in both tolerance and appeal, acceptable both to High Church Whigs and to Whig politicians (the two groups that Sykes describes as active in the Test Act controversy of 1734). This intention was reflected in *The Alliance.* By making a fresh start on the subject of church and state, Warburton wished to avoid the entire Bangorian controversy altogether. Although he was careful to deny Hoadly's central premise that the church was an invisible and incorporate society, nevertheless he went to substantial lengths to write a work so broad that it would appeal even to moderate Hoadlyans. He therefore stressed in book 1 of *The Alliance* that the state had no power to make laws over the particulars of church practice since the "Magistrate" (Warburton's catch-all phrase for any state official) held no powers over men's opinions, which were relevant only to men's souls, whereas the Magistrate was concerned only with men's bodies.[34]

---

33. S. L. Ollard and Gordon Crosse, eds., *A Dictionary of English Church History* (London: Mowbray, 1912), 285–86.

34. Note that this carefully crafted position of Warburton's is very much abrogated by book 2 of *The Alliance,* which discusses the actual working of the allied relationship; here Warburton seems almost schizophrenic in that he presents a picture that clearly shows an Erastian relationship, even though he has gone through elaborate lengths of rhetoric and logic to protect the idea of an alliance from being Erastian in book 1.

This suggestion that Warburton made a fresh start runs counter to the interpretation of R. W. Greaves—who suggests that the theory of an alliance scheme was neither new nor original. Greaves argues that Warburton found it in Hickes's *The Constitution of the Catholick Church and the Nature and Consequence of Schism* and that Hickes in turn had found it in the Gallican theologian Du Pin. Warburton himself read French fluently and cited Bossuet's writings as a discussion that informed his work (even quoting from them in his footnotes). But Warburton was the first English clergyman to construct a complete systematic work proposing an alliance system as its theoretical basis.[35] Clearly, the theory of an alliance between two separate self-constituting societies, the church and the state, was deeply indebted to philosophers such as Locke and Hobbes; the shift in the philosophical landscape that took place in the decades preceding the drafting of *The Alliance* gave a philosophical platform from which Warburton was able to build such a cogent system and to write a work more exhaustive than any written in English before. Further, as Sykes aggressively emphasizes, Warburton considered the church-state alliance to be universal, and "The legal and unhistorical character of Warburton's universal convention between church and state was shared exactly by the famous original compact for the creation of civil society upon which contemporary whig political philosophy rested, as he pointed out with penetration and acumen."[36] In other words, Warburton was the quintessential Whig ecclesiologist.

Greaves argues that *The Alliance* actually helped to prolong the Bangorian controversy because it allowed the controversy to continue after the suspension of Convocation. He writes: "On the other hand, the very form of Warburton's argument helped to keep alive the very idea, hotly controverted in the early years of the Hanoverian règime *[sic]*, of there being any ecclesiastical authority at all, which was 'inherent' in the church as such, or necessary to its being, or not derived from the secular power. This is one reason why the *Old Whig, or Consistent Protestant*, denounced Warburton for priestcraft."[37] It is difficult to see how Warburton could be criticized for priestcraft, since in his writings

---

35. R. W. Greaves, "The Working of the Alliance: A Comment on Warburton," in *Essays in Modern English Church History in Memory of Norman Sykes*, ed. Gareth V. Bennett and John D. Walsh (London: Black, 1966), 164.

36. Sykes, *Church and State*, 322.

37. Greaves, "Working of the Alliance," 165.

the priest was clearly less powerful than the Magistrate, being responsible for the morality of society only. The church was merely meant to motivate society to follow its "imperfect obligations" (such as those of morality), whereas the state was capable of enforcing the "perfect obligations" of society itself through laws—which is to say by deterrence through punishment.[38] The priest in Warburton's scheme seems to have been an ethical advisor only and to have had no raw power. The only place where Warburton allowed the priest to appear powerful was in his long discussion of excommunication. Yet even here he made clear that the excommunicated person was solely driven out of the church and not banished from the state—because, Warburton claimed, to banish the excommunicated would be tantamount to the state treading on the powers of the church, and to excommunicate those banished by the state would be tantamount to the church encroaching on the powers of the state; he was in essence arguing against a form of double jeopardy.[39] The church, then, had the power to banish members of its own society from its ranks, but it had no power to banish them from the society constituted by the state. The central thrust of Greaves's article is formulaically demonstrating how the picture *The Alliance* presented, of the Church of England functioning as a part of the state, was not accurate in practice. And indeed he has found many instances that do not prove congruent with Warburton's theory. But Warburton himself made clear throughout the work that he was writing not about a specific alliance in England but about alliances between any state and any church generally. Greaves even suggests that Warburton adopted some Tory positions in his description of the Church's privileged position in England.[40] On the issue of Toryism Sykes has provided abundant evidence with which to contradict Greaves, who is surely wrong on this point. This is another fundamental difference between Coleridge and Warburton, for while Warburton was clearly discussing matters in England, he purported himself to be writing a purely theoretical work that could apply in any situation. Coleridge,

---

38. William Warburton, *The Alliance between Church and State,* vol. 7 of *The Works of the Right Reverend William Warburton, D.D. Lord Bishop of Gloucester,* ed. Richard Hurd (London: Printed by Luke Hansard & Sons, near Lincoln's Inn Fields, for T. Cadell and W. Davies, in The Strand, London, 1811), 29–30.

39. Warburton, *Alliance,* book 2, chs. 2–3.

40. See Greaves, "Working of the Alliance," 179–80.

on the other hand, specifically discussed only the Protestant Church of England as a part of the English constitution. Coleridge's pedigree and heritage, too, were far from apolitical; indeed, I seek to demonstrate that all Coleridge's later ecclesiological thought had political elements and that the pedigree of Coleridge's politics was "Tory" and not Whig. In fact it is Coleridge's attempt to revive Tory political philosophy in an age when Whiggism held the hegemony that makes his thought fresh and distinctive.

COLERIDGE AGAINST WARBURTON AND WHIG IDEOLOGY

The tradition of using the works of Richard Hooker to inform consti-tutional social debate was both broad and conservative. It stretched from at least the Nonjurors of the 1690s to the Oxford Movement and encompassed along the way Edmund Burke and the "old-fashioned High Churchmen" of the eighteenth century. Peter Nockles, for instance, writes: "The Orthodox theory had found its classic expression in Rich-ard Hooker's *Laws of Ecclesiastical Polity. . . . The underlying assump-tion was that the Church in a sense was the state and vice versa.* "[41] Later in the same chapter Nockles also states: "It was this Hookerian under-standing of a church-state theory in terms of an organic union . . . rather than of the pragmatic Warburtonian theory of an alliance which infused the churchmanship of Bishop Horsley."[42] As will become clear, this quo-tation from Nockles could serve as a precise and elegant description of Coleridge's views on the matter. The use of Richard Hooker in opposi-tion to Warburtonian theory best reveals Coleridge's political and High Church convictions.

Stephen Taylor has argued that, despite what has been thought by historians since the 1820s, the prevailing view of the relationship between church and state in England in the mid-eighteenth century was not War-burtonian.[43]

---

41. Peter Nockles, *The Oxford Movement in Context* (Oxford: Oxford University Press, 1994), 54.

42. Nockles, *Oxford Movement*, 63.

43. Stephen Taylor, "William Warburton and the Alliance of Church and State," *Journal of Ecclesiastical History* 43, no. 2 (1992): 271–86.

Most churchmen, however, differed from Warburton in their understanding of the basis of the relationship between Church and State. They were distrustful of the Erastian implications of Warburton's arguments and more importantly, they did not believe that the two societies were linked merely by a voluntary, "politic" alliance. On the contrary, they emphasized the unity of Church and State. Their ideas owed much to the tradition of Hooker and other Reformation writers, notably to the development of the Protestant concept of the godly prince. In his exposition of the royal supremacy in book viii of the *Ecclesiastical Polity* Hooker denied that there was a "perpetual separation and independency between the Church and the commonwealth."[44]

Even if Taylor is correct to say that the Warburtonian position was not held to be authoritative by most clergymen during the eighteenth century, Sykes and Evans have demonstrated that it *was* the politically correct view held at court and in Whig governing circles. As the Noetic and Tractarian reaction to it shows, those who differed from Warburton on the relationship of church and state still felt that he was a figure who needed to be refuted. His advocacy of a state church supported by a Test Act was certainly representative of clerical opinion. This in itself explains why later generations would come to see Warburton as an accepted paradigm.[45] Moreover Warburton himself presented *The Alliance* as representative of clerical opinion generally.

Taylor is certainly correct in pointing out that some clergy held different views from those of Warburton. He cites several instances of formal engagement with Warburtonian theory: notably Edward Bentham (Regis Professor of Divinity at Oxford, 1763–76), and William Frend (dean of Canterbury from 1760). But he also points out that Warburton's "was the only treatise devoted exclusively to the relationship between Church and State. Statements such as those quoted above were commonplace in the sermon literature of the period, but only a few churchmen made more than passing references to the subject."[46] The point is not to

44. Taylor, "William Warburton," 276.
45. Taylor, "William Warburton," 275 ff.
46. Taylor, "William Warburton," 278.

carp at an excellent article but to suggest that Taylor's conclusion that Warburton's theory of church and state relations as a "politic alliance" was not representative of opinion within the Church of England in the mid-eighteenth century is exaggerated.[47] For though Taylor himself does not cite any persons who agreed with Warburton during the eighteenth century, Sykes and Evans have provided more than enough evidence to demonstrate that there were many such persons. Taylor cites Sykes's chapter 7 in a discursive note to the final sentence of the article when writing about Warburton's *Alliance.* "In consequence its adoption by historians as the representative eighteenth-century text on the relationship of Church and State has created the impression that the contemporary theory subordinated the Church to the state to an extent that is not justified by a detailed study of contemporary writings." This is, however, extremely unfair to Sykes, who details very closely the contemporary concerns about Erastian implications of Warburtonian theory—and Sykes, like Taylor, had certainly made a detailed study of contemporary writings.

What Taylor has demonstrated is that there were dissenting views from Warburton's in Warburton's own time, that those dissenting views had links with Toryism, and that these men preferred the constitutional scheme of Hooker to that of Warburton. When Coleridge argued against utility and consulted Hooker on constitutional issues, he was consciously making himself a part of what might be called a subliminal, or implicit, anti-Warburtonian tradition; this tradition was probably not as self-consciously active as Taylor thinks, but it was a tradition that was at least identifiable to a later writer such as Coleridge. As a self-conscious tradition, anti-Warburtonianism began with Coleridge and proceeded in remarkably diverse directions, through both the Noetics and the Tractarians. This anti-Warburtonianism had much in common with early eighteenth-century Toryism, and to that extent, when Coleridge made himself a part of it, he was consciously linking himself to Toryism.

Such views were also central to the process whereby a genuine Tory party began to be re-formed in the later 1820s. In August 1833 Keble, writing to Newman, would raise the idea of separating the church and state in order to protect the former against utilitarian Erastianism—while Froude had held to such an extreme position all along.[48] But

---

47. Taylor, "William Warburton," 283.
48. Nockles, *Oxford Movement,* 83.

to Keble it could never be *more* than an idea; for him the separation of church and state as a reality was still anathema—which is why he, Froude, and Pusey would not follow Newman to Rome. For Keble:

> It was Hooker, albeit with the addition of his own gloss . . . who remained a sure guide on church-state matters. Keble would never have classed Hooker's theory as "conservative-Erastian," even if it required bolstering by Leslie's *Regale.* As late as 1839, when Keble's disaffection with existing church-state relations was total, he could assert that "[Hooker's] theory of Church and State is a development . . . of the Holy Catholic Church, i.e. of the continued presence and manifestation of Jesus Christ in the world, through the medium of that society which is called His mystical body." Yet Keble's Nonjuring source of inspiration for his later attitude to establishment was only marginally less acceptable to "Zs" such as Palmer and Hook than were the Hildebrandine idols of Hurrell Froude.[49]

The Oxford Movement was advocating positions that were clearly unacceptable to Whigs of their era, such as Palmer and Hook. These positions were consistent with ones Coleridge had taken some ten years earlier and were equally unacceptable to the Whigs of his period. When it came to church and state, Coleridge was a Tory.

While this identification will not surprise most historians, it is important to emphasize because it flies in the face of John Gascoigne's interpretation.[50] Gascoigne sees Coleridge as a Warburtonian: a misprision he arrives at through the fact that later thinkers who drew on Coleridge, most specifically Matthew Arnold, were Warburtonians. It is easy to see how Gascoigne might have arrived at this position: (1) Coleridge and Warburton both strongly emphasized the church's responsibility for education; (2) Matthew Arnold was influenced by Coleridge;[51] (3) in

---

49. Nockles, *Oxford Movement,* 84.

50. John Gascoigne, "The Unity of Church and State Challenged: Responses to Hooker from the Restoration to the Nineteenth-Century Age of Reform," *Journal of Religious History* 21, no. 1 (1997): 60–79.

51. As was demonstrated by Charles Richard Sanders in *Coleridge and the Broad Church Movement* (Durham: Duke University Press, 1942), which Gascoigne strangely does not cite, but which he gives every indication of having read and been influenced by.

Gascoigne's opinion, both Locke and Warburton *portrayed* Hooker as a defender of the social contract theory of government (which in the case of Warburton is absurd, as he goes to great lengths in book 2 to show exactly how different his position is from that of Hooker and how he, Warburton, is correct and Hooker wrong). The above concatenation of errors might lead one to the conclusion that Coleridge must have been Warburtonian, but as subsequent chapters will demonstrate, analysis of Coleridge's primary texts (which Gascoigne does not quote except for *On the Constitution of the Church and State*) does not support it.[52]

To sum up, as Nockles and Taylor have both demonstrated, Coleridge consciously made himself a part of a Tory tradition that included Burke, the old-fashioned High Churchmen, and later the Oxford Movement. To make himself a part of this tradition Coleridge used Hooker to argue against utilitarian, Whiggish theory of church and state. Coleridge was thus a bridge figure between the old-fashioned High Churchmen and the Tractarians; he was a part of the gathering forces of Toryism that would emerge as the Conservative party a generation later. This book will investigate how Coleridge came to hold these political views and the use he made of them. Coleridge's relevant published works, along with his unpublished *Opus Maximum* (hereafter *On the Divine Ideas*, its actual title) and his posthumous *Confessions of an Inquiring Spirit* (1840), will be investigated in chronological order so that a picture of his emerging opinions may be painted. Furthermore, because of the occasional and capricious nature of his thought, one must investigate each of his works in isolation, as a single "tree," before one can discern its place within the "wood" of his thought. It is an eclectic wood indeed, in which no tree seems to have grown up from seeds dropped by the tree next to it, that is, no work grows from the preceding work— yet another reason for examining each work individually. The overriding perspective that gives a coherent vista of the wood is Coleridge's reaction to the Whig philosophy and churchmanship of his period, for even in his radical youth he was reacting against this orthodoxy. This hermeneutic will be the thread that binds the chapters of this study together.

Chapters 2 and 3 discuss Coleridge's radical period. Chapter 2 discusses his relationship to Unitarianism in the context of his exposure to

---

52. Gascoigne, "Unity," 64.

it at Jesus College, Cambridge. Chapter 3 discusses his early theological writings, *Lectures on Revealed Religion* (1794), and shows his theology at that stage to have been a form of Christian socialism.

Part Two of this book, containing chapter 4, discusses the biographically opaque years of Coleridge's life between 1804 and 1809 and compares Warburton's and Coleridge's readings of Hooker. The section on Coleridge's reading is based upon a detailed discussion of his annotations to his own folio edition of Hooker's works, where three separate readings of the text are discriminated.

Part Three, encompassing chapters 5 through 10, takes up the discussion of Coleridge's mature project of Tory reaction. This begins with *The Friend* (1809) in chapter 5 and moves on through *The Statesman's Manual* (1816) in chapter 6. *Aids to Reflection* (1825) is discussed in chapter 7, and his unpublished *On the Divine Ideas* in chapter 8. The argument culminates with a detailed exegesis of *On the Constitution of the Church and State* (1829), set in counterpoint to an exegesis of *The Alliance* and book 8 of *The Laws of Ecclesiastical Polity* in chapter 9. Chapter 10 continues the argument for seeing Coleridge as part of a tradition that stretched onward after his time by examining his posthumous work *Confessions of an Inquiring Spirit* (1840).

Part Four contains chapter 11 alone, which is a synoptic evaluation of Coleridge's place in the history of Tory thought on church and state.

2

Coleridge's Religious Milieu

THIS CHAPTER HAS THREE SECTIONS: THE FIRST IS ON THE religious milieu of the 1790s and 1810s, the second is on Coleridge's religious experiences in his father's parish and at Jesus College, and the third is a discussion of *The Watchman*. It examines in detail Coleridge's boyhood, his years at Jesus College and those immediately after, and then describes his relationship with the Church of England up through 1816. The period preceding 1809 produced only two substantially relevant works: *The Lectures on Revealed Religion* (1795) and *The Watchman* (1796). *The Lectures* was Coleridge's first real attempt at writing a coherent and substantial theological text; its exegesis is the subject of chapter 3. Prior to its exegesis, though, there are important religious foundations of Coleridge's life to be illuminated: his father's churchmanship, his years at Jesus College, and the religious activity that was his engagement with British Unitarianism. *The Watchman*, which is more about politics than religion, is discussed first because, like the biography, it helps to place *The Lectures* in its political context. The second, biographical, section of this chapter sets the study of Coleridge's Unitarianism within the context of current ecclesiastical historiography; it seeks to explode the widely held opinion that Coleridge approached orthodox Christianity from afar and over time and demonstrates that, though these years encompass a period of radical (rather than reactionary) political allegiance, it is nevertheless an allegiance dissenting from Whig orthodoxy—which is where discussion of *The Watchman* becomes relevant. An important issue to keep in mind is that although Coleridge dissented from political orthodoxy in a liberal direction, his dissent from Church of England orthodoxy was in the opposite direction.

EVANGELICALS

The legacy of Tractarian hermeneutics has until very recently given us an inaccurate picture of the late eighteenth-century church: a picture that shows precisely what the Tractarians themselves attempted to address (an arid and atrophying institution in need of both restructuring and re-vitalization). This picture has been proved inaccurate. As Peter Hinchliff begins the 1995 Sion Lectures by emphasizing, no one in the eighteenth century would have thought of a High Church *party*—though there were certainly differentiated traditions within Anglicanism and they became involved in political debates.[1] Though the Blagdon controversy produced personal attacks on character and unwarranted venom in the weekly periodicals, there was not the factional party infighting that would occur when the Tractarians forced the issues of church and state. The church of the long eighteenth century was a remarkably tolerant community, and this era is probably the most stable period in the history of Anglicanism, but this is not to say that the eighteenth century was devoid of clerical controversy. The Evangelicals discussed in this chapter were communicating members of the Church of England and had no formal connection with post-Wesleyan Methodism, and they never brought up constitutional issues such as repealing the Test Act or Catholic emancipation. But in its own way Evangelicalism was as political as the Oxford Movement would be in the mid-nineteenth century.

As Peter Nockles has elegantly shown, there *was* a sacramentalist tradition extant during this period—and this tradition was by no means a rump.[2] Nockles prefers to call these eighteenth-century sacramentalists "orthodox," while Peter Hinchliff has called them the "old-fashioned

---

1. Peter Hinchliff, Sion College Lent Lectures, 1995, lecture 1, typescript given to me by Canon Hinchliff.

2. Nockles, *Oxford Movement*; see also Peter Nockles, "Our Brethren of the North: The Scottish Episcopal Church and the Oxford Movement," *Journal of Ecclesiastical History* 47, no. 4 (1996): 655–82, or (better than either of these later incarnations) Peter Nockles's "Continuity and Change in Anglican High Churchmanship in Britain, 1752–1850" (D. Phil. thesis, Oxford University, 1982).

High Churchmen" in order to differentiate them from the Tractarians. Hinchliff's term seems preferable for two reasons. First, Ford K. Brown's *Fathers of the Victorians,* which could be said to have cleared the land that Nockles later plowed, speaks of "orthodox" churchmen in the eighteenth century simply as standard members of the Church of England who were neither Evangelicals nor High Churchmen.[3] This seems a much more accurate use of the term *orthodox*—at least in the context of a Protestant state church. Second, Hinchliff's term *old-fashioned* emphasizes that the Tractarians were making a fundamental break from the intellectual tradition they grew out of—that they quite literally reinvented the High Church element of the Church of England. The term *old-fashioned High Churchmen* must not, however, be misinterpreted to suggest that these men were intellectually reactionary or necessarily committed to an old order. In fact, the opposite is true: they were forward-looking in biblical criticism and made advances in this field that were remarkably similar to those being made in Germany during the same period.

In the period in question neither biblical criticism nor the apostolic succession fostered political rivalry; rather, it was the rise to respectability of Evangelicalism and the discomfort most orthodox churchmen felt with it that constructed the political divide within the church (though for old-fashioned High Churchmen the word *distaste* might be more accurate than *discomfort*). Brown argued that the political successes of Evangelicalism were virtually entirely due to the work of William Wilberforce (1759–1853) and his associates. These "saints" (i.e., Evangelical MPs) helped to effect a great number of changes in British law, culminating in the destruction of the slave trade within their own political lifetimes. Allied to this group were several influential bishops (though never any archbishops), most notably Beilby Porteus of London. In these ways the Evangelicals undoubtedly changed the landscape of both British politics and the Church of England—though they did not do this without controversy.

The most publicized political uproar involving the Evangelicals was the Blagdon controversy, so called because it occurred in the parish of

---

3. Ford K. Brown, *Fathers of the Victorians: The Age of Wilberforce* (Cambridge: Cambridge University Press), 1961.

the same name, in the diocese of Bath and Wells, in the years 1800–1802.[4] It centered on the work of one pious laywoman, Hannah More, who, in addition to attempting to establish charity schools in the district, sought both to sponsor Evangelical preaching from local pulpits and to teach an Evangelical ideology in the schools that she established. The local clergy were not High Church, but they were orthodox and unsympathetic to the Evangelical cause, which was often associated with Methodism. The High Church elements in the area were outraged at More's precocity; Evangelicals rushed to defend her in print. Substantial controversy arose when the curate of Blagdon, Thomas Bere, demanded that More remove a Mr. Younge who was teaching an adult school in the parish and propagating what were perceived to be Methodist views and practices. More refused to remove him, and eventually thirteen dispositions were sent to the bishop of Bath and Wells, Charles Moss, charging Younge with ecclesiastical offenses via the absentee rector of Blagdon, Dr. Crossman. More countered this by sending a group of accusations against Bere to Bishop Moss without informing either Bere or Dr. Crossman. The bishop decided that Younge should be dismissed, and a further controversy subsequently ensued over his having had no opportunity either to face his accuser or to hear the evidence against him. This was eventually rectified on November 12, 1800, when a panel of neighboring clergy and gentlemen, all centrist orthodox men, had no trouble in convicting him after the evidence was heard. The Evangelical network then went to work behind closed doors. So when Bishop Moss, accompanied by his son (who was also his chancellor), visited London towards the end of the year, it is evident that substantial pressure was applied to them by high-ranking Evangelicals. Though the precise motivation for their visit remains unclear, it seems indisputable that while they were in London Porteus and Barrington exerted their substantial influence upon the Mosses—this is admittedly conjecture on Brown's part, but the actions of Crossman and Moss following this visit to London suggest nothing less. In January 1801 Bere received a strongly critical letter from Crossman demanding the tithes owed, and this was followed

4. This paragraph is essentially a précis of ch. 6 of F. Brown, *Fathers of the Victorians,* 187–233. Brown's intricate discussion of the Blagdon controversy is the authoritative one.

on the 16th by a second demanding his resignation on the grounds
that Bishop Moss was in possession of material proving Bere an anti-
Trinitarian. Bere refused to resign, Crossman removed him, and Moss
sided with Crossman. Bere then published a pamphlet containing the
entirety of his correspondence and pointing out that he too had never
met his accuser. The bishop (seemingly under the influence of the more
powerful Evangelical bishops, much more active political players than
Moss, and with his son's future in the church to consider) remained
unswayed. Bere then played a very shrewd move of his own. He too
went to London and took his pamphlet with him. Soon there was a war
of pamphlets, each salvo more damning then the last; perhaps the most
nasty was Shaw's burlesque *Life of Hannah More.* The periodical *The
Anti-Jacobin* waged a long and nasty campaign against the Evangelicals in general and More in particular, going so far as to sustain a serial
attack on Porteus over many issues. Bere was "reinstated" in September 1801, but Moss died in April 1802 and was succeeded by Dr. Richard Beadon, who was well disposed to More. The affair ended with the
protagonists in much the same positions as they had been at the beginning: Bere was still curate, More still had her schools, and the local community was still substantially orthodox. But what had been displayed
was an embryonic stage of political factionalism within the Church of
England.

The most recent discussion of the Blagdon controversy is by Anne
Stott, and though it adds little to the overall understanding of the controversy it does give a *slightly* more fleshed-out picture of More herself.[5] Stott rightly eschews recent feminist interpretations of More, which
tend to see the entire controversy as a gender issue, and argues that More
was a very clever networker who was even able to gain help from High
Churchmen when she needed it (for instance, by "spinning" a fact in
such a way that it raised the High Churchmen's own concerns about
matters such as due process under canon law).[6] This is a good point, and
it is well made.

---

5. Anne Stott, "Hannah More and the Blagdon Controversy, 1799–1802,"
Journal of Ecclesiastical History 51 (2000): 319–46.

6. For Stott's critique of feminist interpretations of More, see "Hannah
More," 319–20.

A second aim of Stott's article is to rein in Brown's conclusions by suggesting that "Brown's analysis is part of his controversial thesis in which the Evangelicals are portrayed as an almost Leninist vanguard movement, intent on a fundamental revolution in Church and Nation."[7] Here she is slightly unfair. While historians have long regarded as somewhat heavy-handed Brown's suggestion of a grand Evangelical plan, the phrase "Leninist vanguard movement" exaggerates and distorts his thesis. What one *can* take from Brown's evidence (introduced to support his conspiracy theory) is that Wilberforce organized political campaigns based upon a core number of reliable votes in Parliament and that these were reliable because the MPs concerned were Evangelicals. This sort of political organization and action is no different from that of any other faction in Parliament sharing a particular ideology; it is entirely similar to the way High Churchmen organized themselves and pressed issues important to their concerns. It is all very well for Stott to challenge Brown's "conspiracy" argument, but her own very convincing evidence as to More's immense networking capability undercuts her criticisms. This is demonstrably the case in one of her own footnotes. The relevant section of the note follows; it discusses More's and Wilberforce's attempt to effect the installation of an Evangelical Fellow in Lincoln College, Oxford. Though the bishop of Lincoln, Pretyman-Tomline (the Visitor of the College), had in a warm letter to More formally acquitted her and Wilberforce of "enthusiasm and irregularity," Stott draws the reader's attention to the following letter: "For More's distrust of Pretyman-Tomline see More to Wilberforce, 3 Aug. 1796 [NB: four years before the Blagdon controversy], MS Wilberforce (Duke). In seeking a Fellow for Lincoln College, Oxford, she wrote that she dared not apply to the bishop of Lincoln, as 'I know full well that he would recommend precisely such a man as wou'd mar our project.'"[8]

There is no question that More is speaking of the greater project of Evangelicalism in this passage, and if More was discussing a "project" of this nature in 1796, it only adds weight to Brown's argument that Evangelicals had from the 1780s onward been undertaking a program of disseminating Evangelical beliefs throughout the different layers of

---

7. Stott, "Hannah More," 319.
8. Stott, "Hannah More," 340, 113.

society. And in fact Stott's own conclusion (which is remarkably similar to Brown's concluding paragraphs on the Blagdon controversy) seems to step back slightly from her (valid) argument that Brown's thesis is contentious:

> Her agenda was indisputably conservative. She saw the majority of her pupils as destined for domestic service or agricultural labour and she taught them with these putative futures in mind. Her aim was paternalist and traditional, and she deplored what she saw as over-ambitious plans for the education of the poor. But at the same time she introduced them to the written culture, and in awakening their religious energies she enabled them to develop a greater sense of their spiritual and intellectual potential. Her aim was to create a spiritual elite in the midst of a social hierarchy, to bring about a new meritocracy while sustaining the existing political order.[9]

Compare this with Brown:

> They did more than bring some rudiments of the Evangelical religion where before there had not been even rudiments of the High Church religion. They brought in a little civilization, probably raised many of their destitute neighbours to some kind of good conduct, helped them to have a decency they had no way of having before. . . . Simply to show these colliery and farm labourers and their families that the gentry had concern about them must have done something to raise their social and moral tone. In addition, Mrs More was forced by the immutable nature of things to confer on these children and youths and a few of their parents an inestimable gift; in teaching them to read the Bible she had to teach them how to read.[10]

The conclusions are remarkably similar in tone. Both emphasize the class structure, the opening of a spirituality that had previously been un-available to the working classes of rural Somerset, and the inevitable ave-nue for self-betterment that the attainment of literacy provided. If any-thing, Stott seems to see the Blagdon affair as a more strongly integrated

9. Stott, "Hannah More," 339.
10. F. Brown, *Fathers of the Victorians,* 308.

part of an overall program—the creation of "a spiritual elite in the midst of the social hierarchy"—than Brown, who discusses it in a more isolated context.

Evangelical networking, as Stott has shown, was then both efficient and pervasive. It took place not only between acquaintances at the grassroots level but also at another level of organization—through that very English organization, the society. The Evangelicals created scores of societies and hundreds of auxiliary societies at both the local and national levels; the pervasiveness of societies and the membership that they commanded would eclipse even the medieval guilds in magnitude, and it was through the structure of these societies that the Evangelicals carried out what they viewed as their ultimate goal of being "missionaries in England"—the title of chapter 7 of *Fathers of the Victorians.* From the Proclamation Society and the Bettering Society, through the Philanthropic Society and the Marine Society for rescuing poor boys and training them to work at sea (both of which were taken over by Evangelicals rather than started by them), to those great bastions of Evangelicalism, the Church Missionary Society and the Bible Society, such organizations were omnipresent at the turn of the nineteenth century.[11] One of the most effective, or insidious (depending on the point of view), was the Stranger's Friend Society—which took on a new life beginning in 1801. Started by Methodists in 1785, it was taken over by Evangelical members of the Church of England in 1801 and put to the use of propagating the Evangelical agenda. Through the vehicle of visiting the poor, sick, and distressed, the newly reorganized society stated that the aim of its visitors was "to communicate religious instruction consistent with the New Testament, the liturgy and articles of the Church of England."[12] This was a classic Evangelical maneuver: to use an already existing society to put across their own views within the context of the state church. By 1817 the society had made over a hundred thousand visits. The project of direct visitation was carried out by lay persons, "amateur volunteers, chiefly the idle women of Evangelicalism," who made hundreds of visits annually.[13] Such visits were organized through the plethora of local societies, bearing a myriad different names.

---

11. F. Brown, *Fathers of the Victorians,* 225–36.
12. F. Brown, *Fathers of the Victorians,* 238.
13. F. Brown, *Fathers of the Victorians,* 240.

It is also noteworthy that, in addition to substantial political play-ers like Wilberforce and Porteus, the Evangelicals counted among their numbers a large number of gentry, aristocracy, and bankers—including the Hoares.[14] There was a great deal of centrally raised money in Evan-gelicalism, in addition to the rather abundant funds raised locally by charismatic preachers. This network of fundraising sources helped pro-pel the Bible Society to a substantially influential grassroots network used for disseminating the Evangelical ideology. The demonstrable suc-cess of using Bible distribution to propagate this ideology (which until this period had been attempted only in the Empire) had caused the ag-gressively High Church bishop Herbert Marsh to write an important tract commonly called "The Dangers of Distributing the Bible without the Prayerbook" in the early 1790s. (Marsh was famous at home for his list of more than 140 questions asked to candidates for ordination, which he referred to as his "cobwebs to catch Calvinists.") Distributing Bibles, most likely with an oral introduction to Evangelical principles and sug-gested passages for study, was in effect the moon that drew the Evangeli-cal tide that washed over England in the first quarter of the nineteenth century, and Brown argues that this tide had a substantial effect on the morals and practices of English society generally.

> What had happened in England to the religious and moral point of view so well represented by the Regent, the Dukes of Cumberland, Marquises of Hertford and Earls of Barrymore, the bucks, bloods, rips, rakes and faro queens, the gaming houses and the monks of Medmenham Abbey, the time-serving court-sycophant prelates and the episcopal despots who put down the Evangelicals in their dio-ceses, the swarms of fox-hunting three-bottle absentee parsons and their galloping curates, and sly leering clerical authors like Laurence Sterne? In the aspect of the Bible Society that was vital to the Evan-gelical Reformation, the creation of a serious moral and religious public in England, its failure abroad, if it was a failure, has no mean-ing. It is not because of restrictions of space or sympathy for the reader that there are no accounts in these pages of prodigious labours

---

14. For detailed lists of membership, see F. Brown, *Fathers of the Victorians*, 235, 236, 237, 242, 256, 279, 281.

in Borrioboola-gha and all other foreign parts. If every one of the 4,252,000 Bibles issued by 1825 had been printed in the language of the Esquimaux and piled up on the frozen tundra the Bible Society would still have been next to Abolition the most powerful agency of Evangelical reform. Sir James Stephen might have noticed a distinguished exception to his assertion that no nation seemed to have profited very much by the distribution of the Bible, namely the nation that was doing the distributing.[15]

It seems clear that the rise of Evangelical influence and the crystallization of this influence into a movement (*party* is not yet an appropriate term in this period) dominated the religious scene in Coleridge's early to middle life, though interestingly the questions of Wesleyan Methodism and Evangelicalism were never issues Coleridge wrote about. It was other avenues of dissent than post-Wesleyan Methodism, such as Quakerism and Unitarianism, that would captivate Coleridge's eclectic and capricious mind.

Brown's conspiracy argument is fairly universally acknowledged to be too heavy-handed, but the pendulum of interpretation seems to be currently swinging back in his direction. This may be part of a greater pendulum swing away from Namierite cynicism and back in the direction of Halévy—the acknowledgment that religious motivations were a very real part of both local history and the history of politics in the eighteenth century. Stott herself provides evidence that the vanguard of the Evangelical movement (More and Wilberforce) were involved in what they saw as a program. What is indisputable is Brown's evidence of controversy over Evangelicalism in the 1790s and 1810s. Whether or not there was a grand plan to propagate Evangelical beliefs, many persons of local and national influence and power *perceived* that such a plan was extant and fought to maintain the status quo. Often this fight took place within the pages of weekly penny papers—such as *The Anti-Jacobin* and its rivals—and this disseminated the arguments to the literate public at large. The question of Evangelical activity, whether that activity involved the distribution of Bibles or the installation of schoolteachers who appeared to have Methodist leanings, was aggressively debated in

---

15. F. Brown, *Fathers of the Victorians*, 260–61.

print, and this dialogue was nearly continuous during Coleridge's formative years—that is, from the time he went up to Cambridge until his departure for Malta. The question that should now be addressed is where his upbringing and collegiate life fell on the spectrum.

CONTEMPORARY UNITARIANISM IN THE 1790S

Coleridge's father was an old-fashioned High Churchman and a sacramentalist. This is clear for several reasons, all connected with Coleridge Sr.'s one published theological work, *Miscellaneous Dissertations Arising from the VIIth and VIIIth Chapters of the Book of Judges* (1768). The first clue comes from the list of subscribers who ordered the book—mainly West Country High Churchmen. The second clue is the biblical criticism practiced in the work, and the third is the wealth of reference to ritual practice made within it. Yet the most illuminating passage of the work regarding the ecclesiological stance in which Coleridge was raised is chapter 18, entitled "Levites no sacrificing priests in the Jewish church. Laymen not to be priests in the Christian church, according to a prophecy." Coleridge Sr. wrote:

> St. Peter in his 1 Ep. ii, 5, writes thus to all Christians in general *Ye also as lively stones are built up a spiritual house, a holy priesthood, to offer up spiritual sacrifices acceptable to God by Jesus Christ.* And in his 9th verse he stiles all Christians *a chosen generation, a royal priesthood.* But is it not a great and presumptuous mistake in these men, who affirm from these texts, that every Christian has equal right to the priestly office without a regular ordination? Christians are *priests,* as the Israelites were, *in holiness of life,* if they walk worthy of the vocation whereunto they are called; but not priests attending on the altar. Christians may offer up *spiritual sacrifices,* the sacrifice of a contrite spirit, the sacrifice of thanksgiving, and the incense of prayer and praise; but they must not presume to administer sacraments in the church. St John, Rev. i.6, tells us, that *Christ hath now made us kings and priests unto God;* i.e. kings and priests in a spiritual sense, in governing our passions conquering vice, and offering up the sacrifice of a good life. Christians must not pretend, from such a text, that they are all empowered to take on them

kingly power, and govern the civil affairs of state, because they are
stiled spiritually kings; no more must they presume to conduct the
ecclesiastical affairs of the church, because they are stiled spiritually
priests. . . .

It will not be looked upon as quite foreign to the present subject,
if we establish this distinction of the preaching priesthood of men
regularly ordained to administer the sacraments and of the spiritual
priesthood of all Christians in general, from a prophecy of Isaiah. . . .
And I will also take of them for priests, and of Levites, saith the Lord.
God promises *to take of them, excerpere quosdam ex illis,* as the original may be justly turned, to take out some from-among them; . . .
God therefore proposes to select some amongst them for priests, not
to make them all priests; since that would introduce a disorder sufficient to subvert his own worship.[16]

Note the substantial reiteration of the fact that the church is by nature
a sacramental institution and that only licitly ordained priests may properly consecrate those sacraments; departure from this position is held
to subvert the worship of God. Clearly this is a far cry from his son's
antiestablishment passages in *The Watchman.*[17] It also seems certain
that Coleridge Sr. would not have subscribed to the Warburtonian view
of ecclesiology because of his stress on the sacramental nature of the
priesthood in ancient Israel and on the fact that the Levites were a separate priestly class from the other tribes of Israel and therefore separate
from the secular government. There is, however, far from sufficient evidence to draw any firm conclusion on the subject of the Rev. John Coleridge and Warburtonianism.

Coleridge and his father were very close and their relationship was
extremely warm; nowhere in any writing, or table talk, or letter, does
Coleridge even criticize his father, let alone condemn his beliefs, and we
have a significant (though not vast) amount of material from the fairly
young Coleridge. It is also possible that Coleridge learned Hebrew from
his father; Coleridge Sr. was a fluent speaker of the language and achieved

---

16. John Coleridge, *Miscellaneous Dissertations, Arising from the XVIIth
and XVIIIth Chapters of the Book of Judges* (London, 1768), 179–83.
17. See below.

some notoriety for bursting into passages of it while preaching, saying that he felt moved to speak in that language closest to the tongue of the Holy Spirit.[18] Furthermore we know that Coleridge wrote sermons for his elder brother while at Jesus College, and perhaps even while a mature boy at Christ's Hospital—part of one of these survives, and it is completely orthodox. All of this is to say that Coleridge not only was surrounded by the established church during his boyhood but also *participated* in it.

This participation was equally evident within the walls of Jesus College. The fellowship was acutely aware both of Coleridge's intellectual potential and of his severe poverty; to do all they could to alleviate this, they awarded him not only the Rusat scholarship (along with distributing to him and the other recipients the excess dividends earned out of the endowment in most years—which they did not always do) but also the posts of chapel clerk and librarian, each of which carried a small stipend, and made him a Foundation Scholar. The position of chapel clerk required a participation in the compulsory chapel services rather than a mere attendance at them. In no letter, and again there are a fair number from the Jesus era, is there any complaint whatsoever of the obligations that the office of chapel clerk placed upon him—and most of the Jesus era letters complain about something; in fact *most* Coleridge letters complain of something. So it is clear that Coleridge was an active participant in the Church of England up to and during 1794. When he moved to a position of religious dissent, then, it was from a fairly solid and sacramental starting point: a conservative one. When he did move to a position of dissent, what he moved into was also a substantially conservative biblicist position.

It is impossible to say exactly what drew Coleridge to become interested in Unitarianism. William Frend's charisma clearly had something to do with it, and it is also likely that the novelty of the theological position drew his capricious young mind to it. General youthful intellectual rebellion against both parental beliefs and the status quo of society probably played a role as well.

Unitarianism as it existed in the 1790s had grown out of the ultra-Protestant heritage operative within Anglicanism; it did not fix itself

---

18. See below for further discussion of Coleridge's Hebrew.

upon ontological conceits but was rather a strictly biblically based interpretation of Christianity that saw the true emphasis of religion as the teachings and ethics of Jesus and dissented from what it felt was an undue stress placed upon adiaphora created through church tradition. This earlier strand certainly denied the divinity of Christ, but the emphasis of its worship and beliefs was entirely biblical. It must not be confused with the later rational and pantheistic tradition of Unitarianism that would grow out of the earlier tradition around the 1820s. The later strain was a liberal movement (actually influenced by the Romantic movement of which Coleridge was a part) and worked from a philosophical foundation rather than a biblical one.[19] David Young, in his excellent book *F. D. Maurice and Unitarianism*, describes the relationship of the two traditions of Unitarianism this way:

> Theologically, Unitarianism in the early decades of the nineteenth century was gradually dividing into two wings, the one conservative, with its roots in the Priestley-Belsham tradition, the other distinctly liberal and reflecting new ideas. Breakaway groups from the Old Connexion of the General Baptists and Methodism joined this more conservative branch. With strictly Bible-based views, denial of

---

19. Whenever I use the term *liberal* in this chapter, unless I state otherwise, I intend it to refer only to religious issues. Certainly Coleridge was an advocate of a liberal polity at this stage in his life, and I make no suggestion that his conservatism stretched to political issues at this point in his life. A liberal religion may be characterized as one that moves towards reason rather than revelation as its teleological pathway towards the truth of Christianity. This is especially true of the later eighteenth century and the rationalist theology that was extant within the dialogues of its time. We will see that Coleridge was in no way interested in discussing his ideas of Christianity from this hermeneutical perspective but rather would draw his foundations exclusively from the biblical corpus and then use reason as a secondary tool to expand them—a very traditional view of reason. While it is true that Coleridge would later give reason a heavier weight—as he would in *The Friend*, where it is seen as a vehicle for facilitating virtuous action and therefore as a pathway towards sanctification in this world—he was not at this position yet. Here he remains a fundamental biblical conservative—though modern enough to incorporate the basic elements of biblical criticism that the nascent group of English biblical critics (a group that included his father) had expounded a generation earlier.

the Trinity remained critically important for them. Leaders of this wing of the denomination included Aspland, Harris, Johnson Fox, and William Shepherd. Others who continued to keep the Priestleyan heritage alive were Lant Carpenter of Bristol and Charles Wellbeloved, minister of St Saviourgate Chapel in York and principal of Manchester College.[20]

If Coleridge can be said to have been introduced to Unitarian ideas, then this introduction must have come from Frend. There is enough positive evidence to conclude, rather than to assume, that Frend had an intellectual influence upon Coleridge—not least the fact that Frend borrowed books for Coleridge from the Jesus College library. And it is Frend's Unitarian writing, when coupled with the very few Unitarian statements Coleridge published, that provides the crucially convincing evidence placing Coleridge within Young's "conservative" biblical tradition.

One seminal tract, written in 1776, titled *An Address to the Inhabitants of Cambridge,* is an entreaty to the reader to worship the one true God extant in the scriptures. Frend argued that Christ himself had indicated the primacy of the Father and that the scriptures showed us that it was God the Father who had raised Jesus from the dead. He based his argument entirely on scripture; having quoted Mark 12:29, he argued:

> Throughout the whole of the Old Testament, Jehovah declares himself to be one, and that there is no other God beside him—the Children of Israel, while they obeyed him, worshipped him as the one and only true God; and when they mixed with the worship of Jehovah that of idols they were brought to their senses by severe punishments. When Christ preached to the Jews, Jehovah was the object of their worship; of him also Christ bears witness, namely that Jehovah is the only true God, that there is no one good but him, that he is his God and Father, that Jehovah his Father is greater than he.
>
> These few passages of Scripture are, I should think, sufficient to convince an unprejudiced mind, that they, who offer up prayers to Jesus Christ, to the Holy Ghost, or to the Trinity, are highly crimi-

---

20. Young, *Religion and Enlightenment,* 34.

nal: but since you have formed for yourselves, without any grounds from Scripture, such fanciful gods, let us consider each of them separately.[21]

The remainder of the tract was a formulaic examination of Christ, the Holy Ghost, and the Trinity; the first two were subjected to a scriptural refutation, and the Trinity was dismissed as a Latin word that was not found in the scriptures. The date of this tract, 1776, means that Frend had been advocating heretical positions for around twenty years before he was finally censured by the university. Frend was able to escape censure for so long because he was an ultra-Protestant, not an Arian.

Coleridge's own Unitarian writings—which comprised solely a small passage at the end of lecture 4 and the entirety of lecture 5 of *The Lectures on Revealed Religion* (1795)—also followed a *sola scriptura* principle. He began his anti-Trinitarian argument by undermining the doctrine of the Trinity at the end of lecture 4. He did this by continually referring to Jesus as a *man* who had embodied all that was good and charitable in Man and then following a rational line of argument, demonstrating (and this is key) that the scriptures were entirely consistent with the rational conclusions at which he had arrived.[22] For instance, he wrote: "Thus though I had never seen the Old or New Testament, I should become a Christian, if only I sought for truth with a simple Heart. But if we can demonstrate the authenticity of the Scriptures their genuineness will be found to imply the Truth of the Facts which they contain."[23] His discussion of the ethics of Jesus presented them as an immediate and eternal law of Jubilee—Jubilee having been discussed in lecture 3. The methodology of the *Lectures* was deeply scriptural:

---

21. William Frend, *An Address to the Inhabitants of Cambridge and Its Neighbourhood, Exhorting Them to Turn from the False Worship of Three Persons to the Worship of the One True God* (St. Ives: Printed by T. Bloom and sold by all the booksellers in Cambridge, W. Davis, Ely and the Printer, 1788).

22. I use the word *Man* when I need to refer theologically to both the particular individual and the universality of created persons. When I am speaking only of created persons I use *humanity*.

23. Samuel Taylor Coleridge, *Lectures, 1795: On Politics and Religion,* ed. Lewis Patton and Peter Mann, vol. 1 of *The Collected Works of Samuel Taylor Coleridge,* Bollingen Series 75 (Princeton: Princeton University Press, 1971), 177.

Coleridge presented a scriptural position first and then backed it up with philosophical arguments. Always scripture was primary and reason in concord with that revelation; it was never the other way round. It sufficed for Coleridge to summarize his own argument with the following statement: "From the Gnostics the Christians had learnt the trick of personifying abstract Qualities and from Plato they learned their Trinity in Unity."[24]

Basil Willey has described the Jesus College of the 1790s as being a place that gave rise to left-wing ideas, and in the case of Frend and Malthus this is probably true.[25] Willey is a highly respectable authority, and he is correct to observe that John Coleridge was the "prime mover and influence" in Coleridge's life, but about Jesus College generally he is simply wrong. A more accurate description of the fellowship comes from the current fellow archivist of Jesus College: "They were a pretty boring lot really."[26] Yet this also is not entirely true. Two minds to emerge from Jesus other than Coleridge during this period were William Frend and Thomas Robert Malthus, each of whom made a significant contribution to English thought. Malthus was not a fellow of the college during Coleridge's tenure—though the borrowing logs from the Jesus College library that cover this period demonstrate that Malthus was using the library during years Coleridge was in Cambridge. It might be better to say that with the exception of Frend, the *tutorial* fellows were a pretty boring lot. They consisted primarily of two men (Thomas Newton and George Plampin), with a third fellow (Caustobardi) doing some occasional teaching. Frend has already been discussed and was far from being a liberal; Malthus's reputation needs no comment; Newton, Plampin, and Caustobardi are so insignificant that no comment on their politics or religious conceits is possible. In other words, the received wisdom on Jesus College, as expressed by Willey, is an equal misprision to the received wisdom on Unitarianism.

The syllabus at Jesus during this period was extremely orthodox; it consisted of classics; mathematics for those who were interested (though

---

24. Coleridge, *Lectures,* 208–9.

25. Basil Willey, "Coleridge and Religion," in *Writers and Their Background: S. T. Coleridge,* ed. R. L. Brett, 221–43 (London: Bell, 1971).

26. Mr. Mills, fellow and archivist of Jesus College, Cambridge, pers. comm., June 14, 1995.

this was not a requirement); more history than one might expect; a significant amount of natural philosophy; maps and globes, along with many explorers' accounts; and the philosophy of Hume and Locke. Theology was strong but consisted almost entirely of classic Anglican theologians. John Jortin's sermons were virtually compulsory (most likely because he was a former fellow of the college), and a few patristic readings were common. That Jortin was taught is interesting for two reasons. First, he had been Warburton's assistant at Lincoln's Inn from 1747 to 1750 (making him very much a centrist establishment figure); second, Warburton had fiercely attacked his *On the State of the Dead, as Described by Homer and Virgil* (1755), in which he discussed the antiquarian aspects of the doctrine of an afterlife. Jortin's five-volume *Ecclesiastical History* (1751–52) was a standard work of the day, and overall he should be considered a solid orthodox Anglican—his work was far from fomenting radicalism, and Coleridge did mention Jortin in later life, quoting him without citing the reference.

If surprises are to be found in the Jesus syllabus, they are, first, the amount of history that was taught and the fact that the same students would be assigned Hume's, Macaulay's, McPherson's, and Rapin's histories of England (which means that the subject of historiography was taught), and, second, the fact that for those pursuing theological interests learning biblical Hebrew was compulsory. The *Biblica Hebraica* was one of the most widely borrowed books from the Jesus library (possibly no copies of the work were available for sale in the Cambridge bookstalls). The fact that Coleridge himself never had the book out of the library suggests that he might have learned Hebrew from his father. It is clear that he was undertaking theological study, so his not borrowing the *Biblica Hebraica* is odd, since every other student undertaking theological studies in this period borrowed it; but, of course, once Coleridge became librarian it is impossible to track his reading, as he simply ceased to use the borrowing logs. He did read Hebrew, for his annotation of Psalm 87 reads, "I would fain understand this Psalm; but first I must collate it word by word with the original Hebrew."[27]

---

27. These annotations are taken from Samuel Taylor Coleridge, *Complete Works,* ed. W. G. T. Shedd (New York: Harper and Brothers, 1853), 7 vols. They do not yet appear in the Bollingen *Collected Works* volumes that contain the *Marginalia.* This annotation appears at 5:27.

Jesus College during the 1780s and 1790s, then, was anything but in a ferment of left-wing ideas. It was a solid centrist educational establishment in which supervision actually took place and disputations were likely to have been given before degrees were awarded. The education at Jesus College, though it may well have introduced Coleridge to biblical Unitarianism, did not introduce him to the radical political ideology that he would become famous for a few years later. The borrowing logs from the Jesus College Library give a fairly accurate idea of what the syllabus was, though they cannot present a full picture because they cannot show what undergraduates were purchasing on their own.

To recap: Coleridge grew up in the sacramentalist atmosphere of his father; he participated in a fairly centrist tradition at Jesus, while at the same time he came into contact with a very conservative scriptural Unitarianism advocated by William Frend—a Unitarianism that was so scriptural that Frend could survive within the university for twenty years while advocating it. Finally, Coleridge in turn advocated this scriptural Unitarianism in his *Lectures on Revealed Religion* in the year following his departure from the college.

A great deal has been said and written on Coleridge's relationship with the Unitarian Church in the Bristol area, but extremely little evidence has been produced to prove any activity within this community. There are documented accounts of Coleridge twice preaching to a Unitarian congregation that was considering employing him as a pastor, and there are hearsay accounts that the congregation was deeply impressed with him. There are two extant sermons from notebooks in the period of the *Lectures* that summarize sections of lectures 2 and 4, and we have both Coleridge's assertion that he preached at the Unitarian Church in Bristol when beginning his subscription recruitment tour for the *Watchman* and independent confirmation of this sermon. There is also direct evidence that Coleridge dropped the idea of Unitarian pastorship like a hot stone when the Wedgwood annuity was granted him. In fact, he left before delivering the third of three sermons that he was to have delivered in order for the parish to assess him.

Coleridge asserted in a letter that he "preached often" on the *Watchman* tour—by which he hoped to gain subscribers—yet there is no independent evidence that any of these supposed sermons were delivered. This is odd considering that there is independent confirmation for all the other sermons he mentions, and even odder considering that this evidence often comes from the congregation commenting upon how memorable the sermons were. Critics have tended to take Coleridge at his word on this issue, but this is probably an error. Coleridge was one of the great liars of all time, and his penchant for self-aggrandizement is well known. Since there is independent confirmation of all the sermons that Coleridge ever preached in Unitarian congregations, it seems most likely that he was simply lying about preaching to gain subscribers— and the lack of subscribers that the tour was able to produce supports this interpretation. Coleridge was a moving and powerful speaker, but laziness was one of his defining characteristics, and though he certainly did complete the subscription tour (there is confirmation of his travel) he was probably too exhausted by the journey to force himself to make the effort to busk for subscriptions. In other words, Coleridge's relationship with the organized Unitarian church was at arm's length at best. All of this is to say that, though there is residual commitment to a scriptural Unitarianism in *The Watchman,* the theological sections of the journal are primarily concerned with the Christian socialism that Coleridge believed the scriptures advocated, and Coleridge did little Unitarian preaching on the subscription tour suggesting that Unitarianism was not the primary focus of his religious thought during the post-Germany and ante-Malta period.

In fact, the young Coleridge was always a religious conservative. He moved from a conservative sacramentalist upbringing to an ultra-conservative Protestantism that eschewed even the Trinity as adiaphora contrary to scripture. Though he flirted briefly with Roman Catholicism for one Eastertide (while in Rome in 1805), in the years following his Unitarian period he maintained an arm's-length relationship with the establishment before identifying himself as part of a reactionary High Church group—during the serial publication of *The Friend.*[28] Two things stand out. First, Coleridge never left the Christian community—and hence could not have progressed towards Christianity during the period 1796–1816. What he did do was reconsider his belief in what constituted the true form of Christianity, and he did it twice, first adopting a radically scriptural Unitarianism and then returning to Church of England orthodoxy. Religiously, Samuel Taylor Coleridge was *never* a

---

28. This issue is discussed in detail in chapter 5 below.

liberal, and he was certainly never a pantheist; his religious activity during the 1790s and through his time in Malta is well documented, and there is no evidence that he ever even flirted with radical religion in the form of pantheism—the fact that his excursus from orthodoxy followed the path of hypermonotheism makes this indisputable.

It is difficult to track accurately the realignment of Coleridge's belief with the doctrines of the Church of England. Some detail is possible, but it is far from constituting a complete picture. Coleridge mentioned to Robert Southey in a letter of August 9, 1802, that he had attended morning church the day before at Gretta Hall,[29] yet he wrote to John Prior Estlin on December 7 of the same year that "the Quakers and Unitarians are the only Christians, altogether pure from Idolatry."[30] This is confusing, as there was no Unitarian church in walking distance from Gretta Hall. So it seems that, in this period (if the letter is to be believed), while Coleridge was still committed to the biblical Unitarianism of his youth, he was willing to attend establishment churches— possibly with the Wordsworths. It was of course in Malta—at precisely 1:30 p.m. Malta time on February 12, 1805—that Coleridge came to the conclusion "No Christ, No God. . . . No Trinity, No God. . . . Unitarianism in all its forms is Idolatry." In May of the next year while in Rome he spent Holy Week at St. Peter's but found the Roman faith still alien to him. So his realignment with Anglicanism really came on his return to England in 1806, de facto, and there is evidence that Coleridge had at least had contact with the established church for several years prior to that. Within two weeks of his return to England he was writing extended letters to his brother-in-law (his wife's brother, not Southey) concerning the nature of the Christian faith. Yet indisputable positive evidence of Coleridge's alignment with *High Church* elements of Anglican orthodoxy comes only in an allusion to the Lancaster-Bell debate that he made in the *Lay Sermons.*

The Lancaster-Bell debate is one of the most laughable controversies during the Regency period. Briefly, two schoolmasters—Joseph Lancaster, a Quaker from Manchester, and Dr. Bell, a missionary in Madras—

---

29. Samuel Taylor Coleridge, *Collected Letters of Samuel Taylor Coleridge,* ed. Earl Leslie Griggs (Oxford: Clarendon Press, 1956–71), 2:846–47.
30. Coleridge, *Collected Letters,* 2:892–93.

each independently invented an identical system of student tuition in which older students taught younger students lessons that they themselves had already mastered. By this system each schoolmaster was able to cope with class sizes of upwards of one hundred students. Each system progressed and received patronage: the king became Lancaster's patron, and Lancaster in turn constructed a set of reading lessons that used patriotic phrases as their set texts. Bell, being a missionary priest, constructed his set texts out of the Prayer Book, Bible, and creeds. Each progressed independently without incident until one of Bell's schoolmasters discovered a charity school using Lancaster's system and accused Lancaster of stealing Bell's system. Intellectual war then broke out between the two factions; the establishment comes out as looking far less charitable and actually quite venomous. The fact that a Quaker could be teaching religion to the children of poor Church of England parents became the point of battle. Into this intellectual battle marched Herbert Marsh and several priests of his acquaintance, such as Rev. N. J. Hollingsworth, who savaged Lancaster as a plagiarist and thief. Also into the battle marched Robert Southey, who wrote by far the longest compilation of the issues involved—a monograph of some two hundred pages—in which he came down firmly on the side of the establishment.[31] In the *Lay Sermons* Coleridge refers to Southey's book as the most thorough and fair treatment of the subject. In fact Southey's historical objectivity is laughable. Simply put, when Coleridge sided with Southey and Marsh he sided with a radically High Church element of Anglican orthodoxy that was attacking Quaker beliefs—beliefs that in 1802 he had called the only elements of Christianity other than Unitarianism completely free from idolatry.

And so the circle is complete, but not until 1816 can an indisputable positive realignment between Coleridge and the High Church environment in which he grew up be demonstrated. (*The Friend* of 1809 shows a positive realignment with the church establishment.) Throughout the period of the preceding ten years, 1806–16, he had been a nominal Anglican but not necessarily a High Churchman. The participation in the

---

31. Robert Southey, *The Origin, Nature, and Object of the New System of Education* (London: John Murray, 32, Fleet-Street; Edinburgh: W. Blackwood; Dublin: J. Cumming, 1812).

Lancaster-Bell debate, however, is solid proof of his loyalties. Only High Churchmen attacked Lancaster. Here we see Coleridge's reactionary dissent from Whig orthodoxy definitively extend to the religious sphere.

COLERIDGE AND *THE WATCHMAN*

Dissent from Whig orthodoxy did not take place only in the religious sphere of Coleridge's early life; separate from his temporary rejection of the Trinity, and his utopian idealism of the Pantisocratic scheme with its abolition of property, was the radicalism of *The Watchman.* There is no question that the political positions advocated in *The Watchman* are radical—almost to the point of verging on Jacobinism. One need look no further than Coleridge's act of publishing George Washington's letter accepting the Colours of France, which contains the line "But above all, the events of the French Revolution have produced the deepest solicitude, as well as the highest admiration."[32] This letter was published without comment, suggesting that Coleridge found much in it with which he agreed. It is difficult to find a more potent example of radical dissent published during the 1790s. As such the political elements of the work constitute active dissent from Whig orthodoxy, but this radicalism was also in many ways unique.

The Watchman is a hodgepodge of material collected from other newspapers, from friends of Coleridge who wrote in to him, and from his own works, both prose and poetry. Take, for example, his discussion of and argument against the slave trade in issue 4, March 25, 1796.[33] It stems from moral outrage, as all arguments against the slave trade did, but he is curiously neglectful of Wilberforce's commitment to this issue. He mentions Wilberforce by name only once in the ten pages, and there only as the author of the bill "to abolish the slave trade," and not at all in his discussion of the parliamentary debate of the bill later in the issue, titled "Proceedings in the British Legislature" (which appeared as part

---

32. Samuel Taylor Coleridge, *The Watchman,* ed. Lewis Patton, vol. 2 of *The Collected Works of Samuel Taylor Coleridge,* Bollingen Series 75 (Princeton: Princeton University Press, 1970), 42.

33. Coleridge, *Watchman,* 130–40.

of the regular section "Domestic Intelligence" that was part of every issue).[34] The figure who does emerge as a heroic character in this second discussion is Fox:

> Mr. Fox replied,—That as even the opposers of the present Bill allowed the inhumanity and injustice of the trade, the only difference that could remain was the policy or impolicy of this particular mode of abolishing it. On this part of the subject the Right Hon. Gentleman [Pitt] had endeavoured to prove, that we could not abolish the Slave-Trade without the consent of the colonies; in other words, that the Slave-Trade could never be abolished. But he himself had proposed two regulations to take place without their consent—and if these were practicable, the abolition was practicable. If it were possible to prevent any but negroes under twenty from being imported, it was possible to prevent any at all. If it were possible to prevent an intercourse between our own islands, it was possible to prevent an intercourse between those islands and foreign colonies.—The Right Honourable Gentleman had complained that the planter had been represented as men utterly destitute of humanity, &c. Now on this subject the House has heard evidence, and they found, what every man of sense expected to find, that where there is slavery there is cruelty. *Good God! While the House is hesitating, the West-India planters are tearing children from their mothers, and husbands from their wives, and hurrying them in chains and torment to slavery in a strange land.* Four years ago the House ordered this Trade to be abolished in February 1796; that period had now elapsed, and the House were only called on to carry into effect its own resolution, and to keep its promise with the Public.[35]

Coleridge was certainly putting his own spin on the proceedings of the House. He also put his own spin on the refutation of the argument that slaves were happier on the plantations then they had been in their own indigenous cultures. He described the indigenous life of the tribes who were enslaved: "The peaceful Inhabitants of a fertile soil, they cultivate their fields in common, and reap the crop as the common property of all.

---

34. Coleridge, *Watchman,* 135, 155–58.
35. Coleridge, *Watchman,* 157.

Each Family, like the Peasants in some parts of Europe, spins, weaves, sews, hunts, fishes, and makes baskets, fishing-tackle, and the implements of agriculture: and this variety of employment gives an acuteness of intellect to the Negro which the Mechanic whom the division of labor [*sic*] condemns to one simple operation is precluded from attaining."[36] This description has a Pantisocratic ring to it; the common land and common labor provide an environment that fertilizes the intellect. What emerges from this discussion of the slave trade, and from *The Watchman* as a whole, is that Coleridge was definitively against Pitt and implicitly pro-Fox. For example, the following poem from issue 3 indicates Coleridge's loathing for the Pitt administration:

Supposition—A New Song
Tune—Shelah Negari

Ye Friends give attention awhile to my lay,
'Tis what you can't meet with (at least ev'ry day),
'Tis all Supposition, of this and of that,
For the Devil himself cannot tell what I am at.
Some Wiseacres doubtless to puzzle their brains,
May try to find out, Sir—"my Ways and Means."
Tho, my Budget is ope till I give 'em the cue,
They'll ne'er find me out—I'll be d—d if they do.
Fol de ral, &c.

II
Supposition's my motto—then let me *suppose*
A parcel of Asses, who're led by the nose;
Suppose then again that their Masters are such,
They'd load the poor devils a little too much;
Suppose from the top of the head to the toe,
They're burthen'd so heavy they cannot well go:
Yet forc'd to jog on, Sir, their *strength* to evince,
Now Supposing all this—don't you think they might wince?
Fol de ral, &c.

---

36. Coleridge, *Watchman*, 134–35.

III
Suppose then again, for the sake of the joke,
(As Asses of old, we are told once have spoke:)
These Asses complain'd of this heart-rending grief,
And beg'd their Taskmasters to give some relief.
"Oh no!" says their Leaders, "find fault to our face?
But now, my dear Creatures, we'll alter the case.
Mum Chance you shall live—not a Word shall you say,
For we'll MUZZLE you so, that you never shall bray."
Fol de ral, &c.

IV
Some Asses I'm told—but *suppose* it a hum,
Rejoic'd when they found that the "Order was Mum!"
And said they would go if their Leaders thought fit,
Blindfold down the gulph—of the bottomless Pitt.
The muzzles were made, and it then came to pass,
They stop'd up the mouth of John Bull's simple Ass,
Who then sunk, alas! Is a woeful condition;
But remember, my friends—This is all *Supposition!*
Fol de ral, &c.

MUSEUM, Birmingham, March 3 [1796][37]

The political picture that emerges from the editorship of *The Watchman* is of a man who was committed to radical politics: a man who saw the French Revolution as progress and as a laudable enterprise, a man who hated Pitt and lampooned him in song and by making his policies—especially the continuance of the slave trade—look immoral. He consistently presented Pitt's adversaries within the House of Commons as looking eloquent while presenting Pitt as a bumbling orator whose

---

37. Coleridge, *Watchman*, 110–11. The editor suggests that the "Museum, Birmingham" identifies James Bisset as the author of this verse, but I am not convinced. The poetics of the verses and the editing are too Coleridgean not to suggest that Coleridge had at least so heavy an influence he should be considered a coauthor.

policies were rife with logical contradictions. But the picture is also of a radical without ties to any group of affiliates; Coleridge's radicalism stemmed from his Christian beliefs, as did the politics of Wilberforce's group of Saints (who were very far from radical), but Coleridge also retained an idealized picture of a possible society where property was held in common and work of the hands stimulated the activity of the mind. It was a Pantisocratic radicalism that Coleridge sought to pursue. Pantisocracy receives its fullest explication in *The Lectures on Revealed Religion,* and it is time to examine this text in detail.

3

A Theology of Pantisocracy

In the book of Pantisocracy I hope to have comprised all that is good in Godwin—of whom and of whose book I will write more fully in my next letter. (I think not so highly of him as you do—and I have read him with the greatest attention—)

Samuel Taylor Coleridge to Robert Southey,

October 21, 1794[1]

COLERIDGE'S MYTHICAL *BOOK OF PANTISOCRACY* FOUND

This chapter discusses the constructive theological work of Coleridge from the 1790s; it includes all extant theological material, including correspondence, through the year 1795. That material is *The Lectures on Revealed Religion* (six delivered in April/May of 1795) and two sermons on faith, from a notebook, dated 1794 (which are actually a thumbnail sketch for the *Lectures*). Extant but not considered

---

1. Coleridge, *Selected Letters*, 1:114–15.

here are several theological fragments from the era of the *Lectures*—indeed, originally collected by Hartley Coleridge as fragments from the lectures themselves—which are left out of the discussion because they add nothing to ideas presented more cogently and extensively within the *Lectures*. Also considered is the text of a sermon given as a fundraising enterprise for a Unitarian charity school in Bristol that Coleridge was invited to deliver late in 1794 (the sermon was an annual event); though it adds no new thought or discussion to the material presented in the *Lectures*, the very fact that it adds no new material will be remarked upon.

As has already been stated, Coleridge's theology of the 1790s was a theology of Pantisocracy. The principles of his Pantisocratic scheme shaped the form of the *Lectures,* and the *Lectures'* biblical citations sought to demonstrate the grounding of those principles in scripture. That is, although the lectures were written during what has been loosely called Coleridge's "Unitarian period," Pantisocracy rather than Unitarianism was foremost in his mind. True, there were Unitarian elements, and some of the sources that Coleridge seems to have drawn the most heavily upon were written by Unitarian theologians, but it is the question of a primary motivation and influence that is important, and the *driving* thesis within the *Lectures* was the Pantisocratic ideal, not the Unitarian theological position.

This is clear because the main focus of the *Lectures* was the creation of a utopian society through the implementation of Christian principles. Within the text Coleridge preached a "social gospel" based on the Old Testament laws of Jubilee; he did not embark upon an elaborate discussion of the Trinity, though there are anti-Trinitarian passages, one of which has been quoted in the last chapter. If the title *Lectures on Revealed Religion* is taken at its word, it indicates that Coleridge (in 1795) believed that the primary focus of the Christian revelation was its social teachings and not the Trinitarian question. Furthermore, several letters written late in 1794 and early 1795 indicate that the lectures were written as "the book of Pantisocracy" that Coleridge mentioned in the letter that serves as epigraph to this chapter, whether or not they were titled as such when delivered; it is my suggestion that Coleridge wrote the text as "the book of Pantisocracy" and then decided to deliver it under a different title as a means of obtaining income. These letters will be discussed directly after the text of the lectures themselves.

The Theology of *The Lectures on Revealed Religion*

Central to both the Pantisocratic project and the *Lectures* is the abolition of property. This is the primary link between the two projects; a corollary link is that within Coleridge's project the faculty of reason was the avenue by which he arrived at this identical conclusion in both schemes (which I premise here to be one scheme). The first two lectures set the metaphysical/ontological basis for revelation and then discuss the social context in which it occurred (ancient Israel); the third moves on to the specific revelation of Jesus as the Christ—which is where the subject of the abolition of property comes up specifically. Lecture 4 deals with the proof of the Christian revelation from non-Christian (pagan) sources and from "internal" arguments, all of which show the beauty and truth of Christianity from its own precepts. Lecture 5 is a short, and very select, history of doctrine and what Coleridge sees as its perversions, and lecture 6 discusses the special relevance of Christianity in the Hanoverian age. Though the subjects of the ethics of property and inequality appear continually from their introduction through the discussion in lecture 3, and though they are the real crux of the work's theology, the ontological base on which Coleridge built his presentation of the Christian revelation, and its precursors in Judaism, is also important (especially Israel under the Davidic monarch). So, to do justice to Coleridge's own rhetoric and argument, I will discuss lectures 1 and 2 before moving to the "substantive" argument in lecture 3.

Lecture 1 begins with a discussion of reason and religion in the form of an allegorical journey through the valley of life and an encounter with the Goddess of Religion in her temple. Led by figures in black robes "marshaling" the populace of the valley, Coleridge is directed to enter the temple of the great Goddess. When he enters the innermost hall, he sees many inscriptions upon the wall, but although he can make out particular words individually he can make no sense of the inscriptions as a whole. They are "incomprehensible and Contradictory." "Read and believe said my guide—These are Mysteries," writes Coleridge—setting out a hermeneutical position that will be used throughout the *Lectures*.[2]

---

2. Coleridge, *Lectures, 1795*, 90. Subsequent page citations to this work will be given parenthetically in the text.

Going out of the temple, Coleridge encounters a female allegorical figure named Religion, who gives him a spyglass that allows the viewer to see far beyond the hills encircling the valley of life by aiding natural sight without altering it (91)—indicating that religion, or revelation, builds upon reason without altering or contradicting the former. Coleridge presents revelation as a sort of "high-powered" reason (a "hyper-reason," if we wish to suggest an influence of the Greek fathers) that allows Man to see far beyond his normal existence using exactly the same faculty by which he operates normally. Coleridge then moves this ontological discussion of reason into a discussion of natural religion and introduces an "argument from design" for the existence of God: "In all nations and in all ages these causes have operated and the belief of an intelligent first Cause has been only not universal *[sic]*. In all nations and in all ages however great selfwilledness joining with great coldness of Affections has produced in a few the principles of atheism" (96). His central point throughout the first lecture is that the divine forces that act in the world are incomprehensible to us when examined (remember the hermeneutical principle "Believe and you will understand" [90]) in the context of atheism.[3] In other words, only through the gift of revelation—"hyper-reason"—can we make sense of the world around us. Coleridge writes: "Our nature is adapted for the observation of Effects only and from the Effects we deduce the Existence and attributes of Causes but their immediate Essence is in all other cases as well as Deity hidden from us" (97). He then uses the forces of gravity and magnetism as examples of this principle: we can observe the effects but cannot (i.e., could not at that time) show a specific locus of the cause. From metaphysical objections Coleridge moves to ethical objections to the existence of a deity (and for the purposes of the *Lectures* these are the more important ones).

Next comes Coleridge's treatment of the problem of evil, an extremely important supporting buttress of the "social Christianity" that the *Lectures* describe, since it shows evil to be constituted purely by moral evil and hence to be solely the work of Man rather than that of Satan, or of natural forces. This is in essence a fusion of the Augustinian position and Kant's dictum that moral evil is radical evil (and hence far

---

3. Though the paradigm is clearly drawn from Anselm, I do not see Coleridge as being particularly Anselmian throughout the *Lectures.*

worse than natural evil): "By Deity we mean a creative or at least an or-
ganizing Intelligence. This Deity is either indifferent or Malignant or
benevolent or a mixture of both. An indifferent Deity is a contradiction
in terms or rather a word for no Deity. He that Created must have created with some view or other. A malignant Deity the experience of all our
senses shews to be an absurdity—he must be therefore either benevolent or a mixture of the two principles" (104–5).

If Deity is a mixture of the two principles, then either benignity
or malignancy must dominate and overpower the weaker: Deity in that
scheme must be either malignant or benign. A malignant Deity has already been disproved by "the evidence of all our senses," so therefore
Deity is benign. Deity having been proved benign, Coleridge dismisses
the word *evil* in favor of the word *pain*. The direct causing of pain
(moral evil) is the greatest possible evil—as pain is then an intended effect rather than an accidental effect. In all other cases (i.e., those that the
Divine may have authored), pain is an accidental effect: "So we shall find
through all Nature that Pain is intended as a stimulus to Man in order
that he may remove moral Evil" (106). The existence, or rather the possibility, of pain was necessary in the divine plan because it is impossible to conceive of happiness that does not grow out of "progressive-
ness"; true virtue can come only from knowledge of the consequences,
so pain is necessary for both true virtue and true happiness to exist. The
problem of evil as an argument against the existence of a deity is thus
eliminated.

At the conclusion of lecture 1 Coleridge treats the question of
miracles. It is simplest to quote him:

Nothing is more common or constant then the effect of Gravity
in making all Bodies upon the surface of the Earth tend towards
its centre—yet the rare and extraordinary Influences of Magnetism
or Electricity can suspend this Tendency. Now before Magnetism
and Electricity were discovered and verified by a variety of concurrent facts, there would have been as much reason to disallow the evidence of their particular effects attested by Eyewitnesses, as there is
now to disallow the particular Miracles recorded in Scripture. The
miracles may have been and I doubt not were worked according to
the Laws of Nature—although not by those Laws with which we are
as yet acquainted. For the belief of any historical fact we can require

three things only. That the testimony be numerous & manifestly disinterested—that the Agent be sufficiently powerful and the final Cause sufficiently great. These three Requisites the Scripture Miracles will be found to possess by him who previously believes the existence of a God & his Attributes. (112–13)

So at the end of the lecture Coleridge has turned full circle to his opening hermeneutical dictum "Believe and you will understand." His closing caveat for the lecture is that "they who would build the house and begin at the Top, they who should regard the Stream only and neglect the Capacity of the Vessel, would be charged with gross Folly—yet not more justly than they who measure divine Revelation by their ideas of God's Perfections and not by the minds that were destined to receive it" (114–15). The minds that were to receive the divine revelation were those of Israel: "a safe Receptacle of the necessary precursive Evidences of Christianity" (116). The point is that the Bible must be read in its historical context.

Lecture 2 is primarily concerned with demonstrating that the ancient state of Israel (as a *democratic* federal state of twelve tribes), through the special revelation of the law of Jubilee, functioned as a proper seedbed for Christ's specific abolition of property among his disciples. There is apparently great similarity with Moses Lowman's *Dissertation on the Civil Government of the Hebrews* (1740)—which Coleridge seems to have read, and from which he seems to have adopted the basic idea of taking the contemporary social contract theory of government and "Christianizing" it by suggesting that it had roots in the ancient state of Israel (Lowman also remarked upon the law of Jubilee).[4] But to see lecture 2 as plagiarizing Lowman—the suggestion of Lewis Patton and Peter Mann in both the introduction to volume 1 of the Bollingen edition of *The Collected Works of Samuel Taylor Coleridge* and virtually all of the notes to lecture 2—is mistaken (123–45). (These authors also suggest that War-

---

4. Lowman (1680–1752) was a Nonconformist who was trained at Leyden and Utrecht (under De Vries and Witsius). In 1710 he began ministering to the Presbyterian community in Clapham and remained with that congregation until his death. So his theological perspective was not dissimilar to either Frend's or Coleridge's (in 1794)—though not identical.

burton was an influence on lecture 2, but this is absurd. Though Coleridge was clearly influenced by Lowman, his system is too radical to have had any constructive influence from either *The Alliance* or *The Divine Legation of Moses*. As has been argued in chapter 1, Warburton was an ultraestablishment figure, whereas Coleridge's lectures advocate an antiestablishment, radical position; to suggest that Warburton's *Alliance* or *Divine Legation of Moses* had a constructive influence on a work that advocated the abolition of property displays an unfamiliarity with Warburton's own position.) In reality, Coleridge took over Lowman's emphasis upon the law of Jubilee and, having made it his own, used it in his own unique way to give a biblical ground to the Pantisocratic ideal.[5]

The law of Jubilee played a fundamental role in Coleridge's Pantisocratic theology because it reequalized the inequality of property every seven and every fifty years: every seven by requiring the forgiveness of all debts within the state of Israel (thus making usury both unprofitable and difficult), and every fifty by requiring each member of each of the twelve tribes to return to, and take possession of, the fifty acres of land allotted to him and his descendents by the Covenant. Thus, argued Coleridge, the son was not punished for the foolishness of the father: if the father lost the land that he owned, the son would retain it again at the next Jubilee year, which was virtually certain to be within that son's lifetime. "Hence such a spirit of Fraternity might be gradually produced by the expectation, as almost to supersede the actual execution of the law" (127).

The purpose of the special revelation to Israel was to make exploitation through inequality of wealth or property so impracticable that it would simply not be attempted. "All vices arise immediately or remotely from political inequality" (134), and the original state of Israel was constructed in such a way that inequality was inconceivable until the state of Israel ceased to be ruled by the "Judges" and chose to be governed

---

5. Coleridge's use of Lowman in the *Lectures* was similar to his use of Leighton in the *later* aphorisms of *Aids to Reflection*: the quotation of snippets as a basis from which he expanded ideas and made them his own. No one has ever accused Coleridge of plagiarizing Leighton—though Coleridge did credit Leighton in *Aids to Reflection*.

by a king. At this point, Coleridge observed, the possibility of political inequality was born: "Such if candidly examined will be found the fair Interpretation of this famous Passage [1 Sam. 8:11–18] which I have dwelt upon as it is one strong proof among very many others, that the Dispensations of God have always warned Man against the least Diminution of civil Freedom" (134). Coleridge presented Israel as an idyllic (utopian) democratic society that had existed before modern contract theory and had had a form of social government so pure that Moses ("familiar with all Aegyptian forms of government" [135]) would not have encountered it at all—hence its origin had to be divine rather than worldly. Dubious tricks of logic aside, it is important to note the heavy stress Coleridge placed upon the equality accomplished by the law of Jubilee and the society it created.

The support of the priestly tribe of Levites by tithes from the other twelve tribes in the original state of Israel was often invoked to argue for tithing as a means of maintaining the modern clergy; therefore Coleridge considered this question as well (a subject treated in some depth by his father in *Miscellaneous Dissertations on the Book of Judges*). Because there was only enough land for twelve tribes to have fifty acres for each and every man, the thirteenth tribe of Israel, the Levites, agreed to act as a priestly tribe that held no land in return for a 10 percent tithe paid from each of the twelve. For their part, in exchange for the Levites' preserving and cultivating knowledge of the Covenant, the other twelve preserved and cultivated the land of the Covenant—in this division of responsibility the Levites guarded against idolatry on behalf of all Israel, protecting the ephemeral Covenant, while the other twelve tribes protected the physical product of the Covenant. Coleridge's point in relation to property was that, though there was not enough land, Israel had found a solution that allowed the thirteenth tribe an equal share without placing them (the Levites) above the other tribes. Each tribe looked after an equal portion of the Covenant, whether land or worship. But to Coleridge the eighteenth-century Church of England placed its clergy above the community in a nonreciprocal way different from that of the Levite tribe, for contemporary Christianity was in no danger of falling into idolatry. Further, Christ had superseded the arrangements described in the Old Testament by abolishing property among his disciples to destroy inequality and had appointed all Christians priests in the same way that he said, "Ye are all kings," which was the same as saying there was no priest and no king among Christians. Therefore, Coleridge believed, Church of England priests should support themselves with the work of their hands, as all other Christians did—a very Pantisocratic ideal indeed.

In lecture 3 Coleridge moves from God (lecture 1) and Israel (lecture 2) to Christ, and here he is more concerned with the indisputability of the Christ event than with the ramifications of the special revelation of Christ itself (though Coleridge does dismiss that revelation here). Accordingly, the lecture begins with a discussion of the Hebrew prophets in general and then, interestingly, moves on to a discussion drawn from the Hebrew commentaries on the Old Testament (which of course do not hold that Jesus was the Messiah), designed to prove the truth of the prophecy extant within the Old Testament.[6] Unfortunately, Coleridge also employs unconvincing arguments, such as the "projected times" given in specific prophecies, which he manages to calculate so that they coincide with the date of the birth of Christ. He also cites the idea, almost a cliché in that period, that the debauchery within the state of Israel at the time of Christ's birth displayed the fitness of history (so to speak) for the reception of the Messiah. This last point he reinforces with Gentile philosophy—expanding the point to include debauchery in the Gentile world by emphasizing the prevalence of a hedonism that placed great importance on immediate satisfaction through physical pleasures. "The Wine is beautiful to him when it sparkles in the cup— and the Woman when she moves lasciviously in the Dance, but the Rose that bends on its stalk, the clouds that imbibe the setting Sun— these are not beautiful" (158). That Christ's teachings should emerge from such a context shows, for Coleridge, the miraculousness of his revelation all the more.

> That in the most corrupt Times of the Jewish State there should arise the Son of a Carpenter who in his own conduct presented a perfect example of all human excellence and exhibited a system of morality, not only superior to the ethics of any single Philosopher of antiquity but to the concentrated Wisdom of every Philosopher of every age and nation, and this unspotted by one single error, untinged

---

6. This is further evidence that Coleridge could read Hebrew.

with one prejudice of that most prejudiced people among whom he
was educated is a fact that carries with it an irresistible force of conviction and is of itself in the most philosophical sense of the word a
Miracle. (160)

Coleridge disputes any potential charges of forgery leveled at the au-
thorship of the New Testament on the grounds that in forgery "charac-
terizing traits imagine and execute a character always perfect yet always
inimitable" (162); Jesus was knowable and is imitable because he was a
son and knew a mother. This is certainly not a new point, but neither is
it particularly Nonconformist. He writes: "Jesus knew our Nature—
and that expands like the circles of a Lake—the love of our Friends,
parents and neighbours leads us to the love of our Country to the Love
of all Mankind" (163). This passage is important because it shows the
implicit thrust of the doctrine of Christ that Coleridge will advocate in
the remainder of the *Lectures*: a communitarian Christology. The love
of Christ leads us to the love of our neighbor and of our "Country"—
which I should note is a remarkably orthodox, Church of England conclusion for a Nonconformist to arrive at. The fact that Coleridge brought
out the relationship between England and ancient Israel at all shows that
the roots of this theology are far more orthodox than he might have
believed—whether or not he criticized corrupt clergy. He ends the lecture by summarizing the thrust of his theology of Pantisocracy: "He
[Jesus] demanded from his Disciples a total annihilation of all the merely
selfish Passions—and enforced an ardent benevolence and the preserva-
tion of perfect Equality among themselves—he tempted by no hopes of
Wealth or Honor but expressly forbade them to be higher or lower each
than the other" (165). Though Coleridge does not say this explicitly, he
suggests that Christ's revelation should be viewed as a personal, eternal, and universal law of Jubilee, for it is open to all humanity, whereas
the law of Israel was open only to those of a Jewish maternal line. Jesus
brought the law of Jubilee into an ontological position that the entire
world is both bound by and benefits from; this is the beauty and perfection of his imitable, general revelation. It is also the irresistible force
of this revelation that is itself a miracle in the most philosophical (ethical) sense of the word.

Lecture 4 is primarily concerned with discussing the external truth
of Christianity, giving historiographical arguments taken from Tacitus

and Pliny. These sections are fairly irrelevant to the argument of this chapter. The sections that *are* relevant are internal arguments for the cogency of Christianity: specifically a summary of what constitutes the Christian faith, spoken through the voice of a shipwrecked Christian sailor who must explain the tenets of Christianity to a disinterested nonbeliever without the aid of a Bible. Here is one of the most interesting statements from this dialogue: "This same Jesus, who taught these precepts, told us likewise *from God himself* [emphasis mine], that after Death they who observed his precepts here would be happy for ever here after—and that they who were wicked in this world would suffer for it in the next!" (174–75). Obviously, the notable point is the passage I italicized, which distinguishes Jesus from God the Father—and hence falls into the pattern of Socinian heresy of which Coleridge would later accuse himself. It is perhaps more interesting, though, that this particularly Unitarian passage is spoken in the voice of an average layman in the Christian community (a voice very different and much more simple and direct than the narrative of the *Lectures*). Coleridge is tipping the Unitarian hand to suggest that it is the natural belief of the layman to separate Jesus from God the Father—which is exactly what the biblical Unitarians of the 1790s did.

The Bollingen editors, however, interpret this passage very differently. They present the meek Christianity of the shipwrecked sailor as markedly different from the combatively expressed Christian egalitarianism and radical social equality expressed elsewhere in the *Lectures* and suggest that "the social and religious views of the sailor's are closer to the orthodox quietism of, say, Paley's *Reasons for Contentment*" (175 n. 1). This cannot be strictly correct, because Paley did not separate Jesus from Christ. The editors' interpretation may stem from Coleridge's argument for the *internal authority* of the Gospels (i.e., the impossibility of forgery and the cogent beauty of the imitable ethic of the abolition of property), which seems to have been influenced by Paley's *Horae Paulinae*. But this influence was simply an employment of Paley's almost proto-redaction criticism, which argued that the internal contradictions within each synoptic Gospel, and more so the intra-Gospel contradictions, were in fact proof of honest witnesses—suggesting that forgers would have created a more cogent and correlated parallel Gospel set.

In retrospect, lecture 4 seems to suffer from an identity crisis; it was intended to provide both internal and external proof of the Christian revelation itself, but it actually presents a unique version of Christian revelation in the process. So, though lecture 5 is structurally designed to be a prescriptive presentation of Christian doctrine and its perversions, much of the original presentation of Coleridge's interpretation of Christianity has already taken place in lecture 4.

Lecture 5 begins with a summary of Christianity: "That there is one God infinitely wise, powerful and good, and that a future state of Retribution is made certain by the Resurrection of Jesus who is the messiah— are all the *doctrines* of the Gospel. That Christians must behave towards the majority with loving Kindness and submission preserving among themselves a perfect Equality is a Synopsis of its Precepts" (195, emphasis in original). From this rather socio-ethical summary presentation of Christianity Coleridge moves on immediately to discuss the aptness of Jesus's command, "Go preach to the poor." He argues that the poor are the best wax extant to take the stamp of the new revelation in the same way that Israel was the most fit culture to receive the revelation of the Covenant. They have the greatest chance of believing and understanding it because they have no possessions on which to anchor a belief in the old ethical system.

Coleridge moves on immediately, and without a proper transition, to distinguish this revelation from the early Gnostic heresy, on the grounds that the Gnostics distinguished a preexistent Christ from Jesus and suggested that Christ attached himself to Jesus. In this interpretation it is to the Christ essence that Jesus cries, "My God, my God, why have you forsaken me" from the cross. Coleridge singles out Gnosticism as producing all the "Mysteries, Impostures, and Persecutions" (199) that have disgraced the Christian community in its history. He believes that the prologue to John is a counter to the Gnostic idea that the world was created as a mistake; the "Word" (which Coleridge preferred to call "intelligence") is not an emanation from God but God himself and is also Creation: "These passages were written to condemn the doctrine of the superangelic nature of Jesus. St. John here asserting that the same intelligential Energy which operated in Jesus had been in the World before his existence, teaching the Law to Moses and foreknowledge to the Prophets" (200). Coleridge cites Gnostic dualism as a reason for the maltreatment of the human body by Gnostics—and as the basis for a debauchery that led to the groundless charges against Christianity cited by Tacitus. What is significant here is that Coleridge's attack focuses on the mysterious metaphysics of Gnostic dualism and its perversion of Christianity into a radical sort of "metaphysical rebirth" through the action of a strong redeemer. This is a fairly traditional line of criticism. What is new is the ethical flanking maneuver that he adds to the classical ontological frontal attacks on dualism and exclusivity. For Coleridge, Gnosticism is evil because it excludes the majority of persons from the ethical equality created by Christ through the abolition of property. Its dualism gives rise to aggressive debauchery in this world and creates a mysterious metaphysics that runs counter to human reason rather than working in tandem with it (hence in Gnosticism revelation is not hyper-reason).

Coleridge rejects Gnosticism on a further ground; he states that it gave rise to what is in his mind the great Christian misunderstanding: a doctrine of the Atonement through redemption, which he sees as a confusion of metaphor and reality. To understand the Atonement truly, as discussed in scripture, says Coleridge, we must examine the meaning and use of language as it discusses sacrifices and victims: "To awaken Gratitude, to confirm Purity, to evidence sincerity the pious Jew for himself offers a part of his property, the first fruits of his Flock—to effect the same ends in others Christ offered himself, i.e. he evidenced his sincerity by voluntarily submitting to a cruel death, in order that he might confirm the Faith or awaken the Gratitude of Men. Such is the moral sense of Atonement in Scriptures" (203). For Coleridge, the Atonement functions through the teaching and example of Christ delivering a universal and eternal law of Jubilee (a Pantisocratic Atonement), rather than through a substitutionary (or satisfactionist) mechanism.[7] The Atonement, like the rest of Christianity in the *Lectures,* is an ethical teaching rather than a "metaphysical" change in the human condition effected by a specific redemptive act of Christ that atones for the sins of Man. "He who foresees and permits what he might have prevented predestines" (204–5); and the concept of a God both loving and just forbids the predestination of Christ to the cross because it was not just for Christ to suffer on the behalf of humanity. Justice is "the best means of producing

---

7. It is not entirely clear which interpretation of the Atonement Coleridge is attributing to orthodox Christianity, though he attacks both the Christus Victor and Juridical paradigms.

the greatest Happiness" (205), and the suffering of the innocent for the guilty is not just. Instead, the ethical revelation of Christ will produce a society of equals who regarded God as their only sovereign—this will accomplish Coleridge's definition of justice. So, clearly, Coleridge sees the idea of redemption to be the second great perversion of the doctrine of Jesus in the history of Christianity. In closing this subject Coleridge notes that an actual and full redemption (through satisfaction) would abrogate the need on the part of humanity for repentance and good works—the creation of equality—which he sees as central to the ethic of Jesus.

The final subject in lecture 5 is the Trinity. Coleridge's objections to the doctrine follow a *sola scriptura* principle: he feels that the Trinity is analogous to a piece of flint that will create broth when boiled with salt—if turnips and beef are added. It is extraneous. "From the Gnostic the Christians had learnt the trick of personifying abstract Qualities, and from Plato they learned their Trinity in Unity" (208). The real principle of the attack is that each Christian finds all he needs in the ethic of Jesus, as presented in the Gospels, and that the Trinity only confuses the matter through the imposition of alien Gentile philosophy (the flint) into a Hebraic broth. The Christian is given the beef, turnips, and salt in the Gospels; he is then handed the flint of Trinity and told that it is the central ingredient to the soup of religion. To Coleridge the beauty of the Gospels is "that he who may run may read" (209). He asserts that the Trinity was created by the orthodox elements of the church because he who can do for himself will not pay another to do for him (again, attacking a professional clergy supported by the laity). The Trinity requires an educated clergy to interpret it, but scripture (according to Coleridge) does not. The Trinity is seen as perpetuated by a property-ridden church. The simplicity of the ethic of Jesus, equality and the abolition of property, is raped by the doctrine of the Trinity. Lecture 5 also contains a mention of Warburton (211). In it Coleridge is critical of Warburton, calling him an "Arch-heretic" because of his support of the establishment and its professional clergy. It is, therefore, clear that Coleridge was both aware of Warburton's position and critical of it from a very early point.

Hence, having defined the doctrines of his Pantisocratic theology (in lectures 3 and 4) and having described the history of its perversions by heretics and the church (in lecture 5), in lecture 6 Coleridge concerns himself with the special relevance of this Pantisocratic theology of his own day, drawn purely from biblical ethics rather than any patrological sources. The lecture begins with the "fable of the maddening rain" (a fable Coleridge will use again several times in his later writings). In this fable, a Golden Age ends with a rainstorm that symbolizes the destruction of an ethic of equality and the acquiescence to a corrupting and maddening regime of greed. Only one man, who has sheltered himself from the rain, still remembers and longs for the Golden Age, and the others view him as mad. In the end, when he can no longer endure holding out against the majority, he leaps into a ditch full of rainwater and, on being immersed, becomes mad and wicked like the rest—indeed, so mad and wicked that the rest of them make him their priest and governor. What is most important in the fable, as it is employed in the lectures, is that the allegorical prophet figure (and the quintessential figure of the prophet is always one who calls for a return to the Covenant and yet is ignored by his own people) is attacked for using the words "our fields," a phrase that is "no longer understood" by the people. The allegory clearly suggests a turn away from the covenant of common ownership through the law of Jubilee in ancient Israel and the abolition of property preached by Jesus (who is the eternal and *personal* jubilee extended to humanity generally, rather than just to the people of the Covenant). The fact that the prophet goes mad when ignored, becomes more filled with vice than all the others, and is then immediately elected to the post of "Priest and Governor" is a fairly obvious assault on the constitutional Church of England and its established relationship with the state. Coleridge's fable ends: "Such, I believe, has been the Fate of more than one Reformer—many a veteran Impostor began his career with high efforts of zealous Patriotism, till finding his exertions fruitless and himself calumniated, from despair he has sunk into acquiescence, and from hopeless Conformity into active Guilt. Where the causes of evil exist, Good cannot be—In the moral world there is a constant Alternation of Cause and Effect—and Vice and Inequality mutually produce each other" (216).

The assurance of an afterlife, Coleridge holds, diminishes the importance of the present: Jesus's assurance of a life after death where justice will prevail is the panacea for inequality. Christ alone is the great equalizer on earth, not democratic governments. (This is a point that we will soon see reiterated in a letter to his brother, the Rev. George Coleridge.) Like the pious Jew of ancient Israel, the Christian should owe his allegiance directly to God and not to the state (or any person) as well, for government (as a part of the fallen world) is never truly equal to all—a theme already seen in Coleridge's virulent attack in lecture 2 on Israel's decision to make Samuel king.

> To appreciate justly the value of this Panacea, we should behold the dreadful effects of the disease which it removes. Inequality originated in the institution of landed Property—In the early ages of the World the right of landed Property must have been none or transient—a man was the proprietor of the Land only while his Flocks were feeding on it. The weapons necessary for hunting and the Utensils for domestic accommodation, introduced the separate arts of manufactures and the necessity of Barter, but the Occupations of the Manufacturer ill accorded with the wandering life of the Shepherd—towns and Cities were soon built. . . . Thus the jarring Interests of Individuals rendered Governments necessary and governments have operated like quack medicines; they have produced new diseases, and only checked the old ones—and the evils which they check, they perpetuate. (218–19)

Throughout history, Coleridge argues, governments have perpetuated inequality. This is most especially true in the form of taxes, for the common person receives no return for his contribution; the lack of any state system of education allows the "lower orders" to be kept as ignorant beasts so that they may be worked as brute beasts.

Lecture 6, then, explicitly sets forth Pantisocratic tenets as being grounded in ancient Israel and delivered through the mouth of Christ. Any residual doubts about the relationship between Coleridge's theology and the Pantisocratic community are dispelled by the pastoral, agrarian slant of the lecture's conclusion. With the decline of agrarian culture, he holds, began the rise of inequality: if all labor were shared equally between all men, "it is evident that none of us would work more than two hours a day of necessity, and that all of us might be learned from the advantage of opportunities" (223). (Note the actual Pantisocratic diary plan for each day: two hours of work, and the remainder to cultivate the mind with study.) All society needs to give up to achieve this, he argues, are the unnatural luxuries that a society whose economic basis has become manufacturing rather than agriculture has caused us to desire—and that the rural farmer does without happily. The pastoral life is religious to Coleridge, for in it the work is shared equally: "but in the Cities God is everywhere removed from our Sight and Man obtruded upon us—not Man the work of God, but the debased offspring of Luxury and Want" (224). The city propagates inequality.

> But if we understand by Riches comparative wealth the meaning is clear and conveys a sublime Truth. That as long as anyone possesses more than another, Luxury, Envy, Rapine, Government & Priesthood will be the necessary consequence, and prevent the Kingdom of God—that is the progressiveness of the moral World. . . .
>
> Emperor and King are but the lord lieutenants of conquered Souls—secondaries and vicegerents who govern not with their own right but with power delegated to them by our Avarice and appetites! Let us exert over our own hearts a virtuous despotism, and lead our own Passions in triumph, and then we shall want neither Monarch nor General. If we would have no Nero without, we must place a Caesar within us, and that Caesar must be Religion! (227, 228–29)

Christ has abrogated riches, and we are to understand riches as comparative wealth; truly to follow Christ, we must give up comparative wealth entirely. To avoid the "Nero without" (meaning inequality) we must place the "Caesar of Religion" within: that Caesar is the abandonment of riches.

The lectures present a Pantisocratic theology, grounded in reason and revelation, correlated with the revelation of the Old Testament, shown to be both internally and externally verifiable, and shown to be the pure form of the Christian revelation, untainted by the "perverted" doctrines of redemption or the Trinity. Finally, this pure form of the revelation is shown to be of special importance and relevance to the emerging industrial age. From lecture 2 onwards there has been a strong stress on a communitarian principle of equality through equal ownership and a revulsion against the forces that erode equality and perpetuate a hierarchy of wealth, such as luxury, envy, and government.

FURTHER SUPPORTING EVIDENCE

Other relevant contemporary primary sources further support the suggestion that the *Lectures* is the book of Pantisocracy, and these begin with a sermon on faith (written in the Gouch notebook in the second half of 1794). As mentioned at the outset of the chapter, this is a sort of abbreviated version of several of Coleridge's key points in the *Lectures*: the relationship between faith and reason; the credibility of the scriptural account of miracles on the grounds that they are as believable as any other account of an imperfectly understood occurrence, such as magnetism; the suitability of the Old Testament revelation to the minds of those who received it; and finally (and perhaps most importantly) the correlation between the motivation of faith and the motivation of law. The following quotation (it is a notebook entry and so appears somewhat choppy) is important not only because it contains the communitarian motives of the *Lectures* or because it anticipates by a good number of years the "Essay on Faith" (which would appear in the reissued edition of *The Friend* [1818]) in its conception of faith as "Fidelity," but also because, unlike the remainder of the sermon, it contains some ideas not found in the *Lectures*: "Rom. 14; 20–23.—the *motive* contradistinguished from mere action: Gal 3. 24—the revelation of and specified duties prior to the Revelations of *Motives*—(memory itself an act of faith, in many cases.)—<The whole, or sum total of the applications of the word, Faith, reducible to Fidelity—as Loyalty to God, Fidelity to our fellow-Creatures—hence the most grievous of Injuries not to be believed—resented as a Wrong, which seems to imply an original compact, or promise between each Spirit & all Spirits in their depth of Being below, & radicative of, all Consciousness.> 1794."[8] The notebook entry shows, first, that in 1794 Coleridge was already considering many of the theological ideas he would later expound in the *Lectures*. Thus the *Lectures* are not simply a string of plagiarized passages from Lowman and other authors collected in the Bristol library. Second, it shows that the *Lectures* were composed with a specific purpose in mind. This purpose did not include an extensive discussion of faith as fidelity to fellow creatures, God, or ourselves (though this point, only touched on in the notebook entry, would become an important theological point in Coleridge's later thought). The purpose was, I believe, to be the "book of Pantisocracy": a sort of charter for the project—and extant letters of this period, such as that quoted in the epigraph to this chapter, support this idea.

---

8. Coleridge, *The Notebooks of Samuel Taylor Coleridge* (London: Routledge and Kegan Paul, 1957–2002), vol. 1, bk. 1, 8.

Several letters—in the Griggs edition, numbers 65, 66, 68, 69, 83, and 87, all written between October 21, 1794, and August 1795, are relevant to the Pantisocratic interpretation of *Lectures*. Whenever Coleridge discusses the intended Pantisocratic community in his letters of this period, its description is identical to that of the community Coleridge suggested would be produced if the ethic of Jesus were followed as presented in the *Lectures*. Furthermore, Pantisocracy is spoken of in a religious sort of language and with identical phrases—clarion calls of Coleridge's ethic of Jesus. "He who does not leave his mother and family to follow has no place in the kingdom" is applied to Pantisocracy in several letters in reference to the reservations of prospective Pantisocrats' families and friends. Letter 65, written to Robert Southey on October 21, 1794, states that "the leading Idea of Pantisocracy is to make men necessarily virtuous by removing all Motives to Evil—all possible Temptations." Even more significant is a passage quoted from in the epigraph to this chapter:

> All necessary knowledge in the Branch of Ethics is comprised in the Word Justice—that the Good of the whole is the Good of each Individual. Of course it is each Individual's *duty* to be Just, *because* it is his *Interest*. To perceive this and to assent to it as an abstract proposition—is easy—but it requires the most wakeful attentions of the most reflective minds in all moments to bring it into practice—It is not enough, that we have once swallowed it—The Heart should have fed upon the truth, as Insects on a Leaf till it be tinged with the colour, and shew it's food in every the minutest fiber *[sic]*. In the book of Pantisocracy I hope to have comprised all that is good in Godwin—of whom and of whose book I will write more in my next letter.[9]

Not only is the desired end of Pantisocracy correlative with the intended end of the ethic of Jesus as Coleridge presents it in the *Lectures*, but Coleridge specifically mentions composing the book of Pantisocracy and including what is good from Godwin's social theory. (The influence of Godwin upon the *Lectures* may well be considerable and is discussed

---

9. Coleridge to Robert Southey, October 21, 1794, in Coleridge, *Collected Letters*, 1:115.

in detail in the introduction to the Bollingen edition.) Both Pantisocracy and Coleridge's interpretation of revealed religion alleviate evil by
removing the motivation to evil and destroying all temptation through
the employment of ethical reasoning and the abrogation of property;
they are one scheme.

Letters 66 and 68 express Coleridge's concern that the women
(wives) who would accompany the men in the Pantisocratic scheme
might teach the children, not a Pantisocratic Christianity, based on reason working in tandem with revelation, but a Christianity based upon
traditional "corruptions," which, Coleridge felt, had destroyed the true
ethic of Jesus concerning the abolition of property and inequality.
Thus in November 1794 he wrote Southey, "That Mrs. Fricker! We shall
have her teaching the infants *Christianity*,—I mean that mongrel whelp
that goes under its name—teaching them by stealth in some ague fit of
Superstition!"

Letter 69, to George Coleridge, is important in this context because of the following quotation:

> I have been asked what is the best conceivable mode of meliorat-
> ing Society—My answer has been uniformly this—"Slavery is an
> Abomination to every feeling of the Head and the Heart—Did Jesus
> teach the *Abolition* of it ? NO! He taught those principles of which
> the necessary *effect* was—to abolish all Slavery. He prepared the
> *mind* for the reception before he poured the Blessing—.["] You ask
> me, what the friend of universal Equality *should* do—I answer—
> ["]Talk not of Politics—*Preach the Gospel!*"—Yea! my Brother! I
> have at all time in all places exerted my powers in the defense of
> the Holy One of Nazareth against the Learning of the Historian, the
> *Libertinism* of the wit, and (his worst Enemy!) the Mystery of the
> Bigot![10]

This passage again casts Pantisocracy in a religious light. Furthermore,
it is a mirror image of the argument up to this point: this letter presents
Pantisocracy as the pure form of the ethic of Jesus, whereas up to that
point the argument had centered on showing Coleridge's ethic of Jesus

---

10. Coleridge, *Collected Letters*, 1:126.

as a form of the Pantisocratic ideal. The language is the same, but importantly, the subject and object of influence have been reversed.

Letter 83, to George Dyer, is important because it contains a passage on the subject of evil in the city that is virtually identical to one in the *Lectures* (lecture 5) and uses the same analogy of seeing God in the natural world like an image in a convex mirror. Furthermore, Coleridge directly links the amelioration of this evil with the establishment of a Pantisocracy in England.[11] It is perhaps the strongest piece of external evidence that the ideas of Pantisocracy and the lectures were congruent, that the lectures are in fact the "book of Pantisocracy" of which Coleridge spoke in letter 65—presented in a form that would earn some money.

Finally, letter 87 is important because it contains the most explicit employment of religious language to describe the Pantisocratic scheme. In this long letter Coleridge attempts (successfully in the end) to prevent Southey from becoming a clergyman of the Church of England (out of the fear that ordination would lead to Southey's abandoning the Pantisocracy scheme—something that eventually happened anyway).

> Our prospects are not bright—but to the eye of reason as bright as when we first formed our Plan—nor is there any opposite Inducement offered, of which you were not then apprized, or had cause to expect. Domestic Happiness is the greatest of things sublunary—and of things celestial it is perhaps impossible for unassisted Man to believe any thing greater—: but it is not strange that those things, which in a pure form of Society will constitute our first blessings, should in it's present morbid state, be our most perilous Temptations—!— "He that doth not love Mother & Wife less than me, is not worthy of me!"[12]

This is a fairly clear indication that Coleridge links the Pantisocratic scheme with the Kingdom of God. The Kingdom of God is the traditional orthodox Christian nomenclature for the utopian community that it is every Christian's duty to strive to establish here on earth—though

---

11. Coleridge, *Collected Letters,* 1:154–55.
12. Coleridge, *Collected Letters,* 1:158.

the orthodox interpretation sees the Kingdom as an unreachable telos that humanity is always in pilgrimage towards but at which it never arrives (Augustine's City of the Earth toiling both ever closer to and always a horizon away from the City of God).

In conclusion: the lectures present a theology that is remarkably close to the ideals of Pantisocracy; in fact, the extant letters from the era in which the lectures were written strongly indicate that they were composed as a charter for the Pantisocratic scheme upon Christian principles. This gives sufficient evidence to conclude that Pantisocracy itself is a much more Christian enterprise than it has been given credit for. Pantisocracy was a utopian Christian community of the purest form; it would not be far from the mark to call it a predecessor to Christian socialism. Its tenets sprang solely from the interpretation of the scriptures, and the temptations of inequality were abolished through reason. Like the ancient Israelite living under the law of Jubilee, the member of the Pantisocratic community acknowledged only the sovereignty of God over him—and not that of any other man. For Coleridge, Jesus had brought to the earth an eternal, universal, and personal law of Jubilee in the form of his ethical teachings.

Part Two

The "Landing-Place"

THE FIRST THREE CHAPTERS OF THIS BOOK SOUGHT TO DEPICT
the intellectual activity of the young Coleridge as cogent if somewhat
disjointed.[1] The radical philosophy that he sought to propagate was coherent, though he had difficulty in expressing it in a form that was either consumable by others or able to provide him with sufficient income
to support his family. The annuity of 150 pounds, provided by the Wedgwood family two years after the publication of *The Watchman* ended,
helped a great deal to relieve these financial pressures, and there is general
agreement that the granting of the annuity prompted him to abandon his
attempts to find a placement as a Unitarian pastor—which was what it
was designed to do (the Wedgwood family wanted him to be free to pursue intellectual activity without the burden that a church office would
have created). Clearly, the propagation of his philosophy was more important to him than the propagation of the Unitarian religious message.

The period between *The Watchman* and Coleridge's next periodical, *The Friend* (1809), though significant for Coleridge's biographer, is
not a focus of this book because any developments that took place in
Coleridge's religious and social thought during this time are, frustrat-
ingly, virtually undocumented. Undoubtedly these were formative years
for Coleridge. After ending the serial run of *The Watchman* he dedicated himself completely to poetry and freelance journalism, and during the later 1790s he produced all of his great poems. These years also
include his trip to Germany—which of course introduced the tradition
of German Idealism into his philosophical outlook—and the beginning
of his friendship with Wordsworth. But although these events affected

---

1. When he republished *The Friend* in 1818, Coleridge inserted three sections, each of which he termed a "Landing-Place, or Essays Interposed for
Amusement, Retrospect and Preparation." *The Friend,* 1:vii–ix. The "landing-
place" in this book is for retrospect and preparation.

Coleridge's overall intellectual position, they did not shape his theories on the relationship of church and state in England.

The first few years of the nineteenth century, which include his trip to Malta, are hard to evaluate because the evidence is lacking. This is frustrating, since it was in Malta that he abandoned his commitment to Unitarian beliefs, but there are very few primary sources from the period other than Coleridge's own journals—which are a very unreliable source, especially during his second trip to the Continent.

Coleridge moved to Nether Stowey in December 1796, and in 1797 he produced nothing but poetry. In 1798 the financial crisis in which he found himself ended with the Wedgwood annuity, and in October he embarked on his year in Germany. At the end of November 1799 he returned to London to write for the *Morning Post.* In April of the next year he left London and went first to the Lake District, then to Stowey, and in July he moved his family to the Lakes. In November 1801 he returned to London to continue writing for the *Morning Post,* and in March 1802 his marriage began to break up for good. He wrote on and off for the *Morning Post* over the next two years and traveled fairly widely among his circle of friends. On April 9, 1804, he left for Malta, where he hoped, by working in the civil service, to earn a more substantial living than journalism and poetry could provide. He did not return to England until August 17, 1806.[2]

No material survives from the time he left for Malta to the time he returned to England. Coleridge claimed that the chests containing his work of those years were stolen—an unlikely story, considering that his notebooks survive. It is more likely that Coleridge simply did not produce any substantial material during this period: his opium addiction was at its height, and the dosage was not yet under the careful control of Dr. Gillman. This must have made it very difficult to produce any coherent work of substantial length. The years 1807 and 1808 were spent in an almost "mendicant" series of visits to friends; November of 1806 had seen the final split between Coleridge and his wife, and though he spent June of the next year with the family in Nether Stowey, domestic life was

---

2. Valerie Purton, *A Coleridge Chronology* (London: Macmillan, 1993). This excellent resource provides a day-by-day account of Coleridge's activities without editorial comment.

over for him. Much of 1807–8 was spent in London, where he delivered a set of lectures on "poetry and the principles of taste" in the first half of 1808. On the first of September he moved to Grasmere to be near to the Wordsworths, and in November the first prospectus for *The Friend* was printed. The periodical was first published in June of the following year.

It is a great shame that so little material survives from the years 1804–8 (the notebooks from the period are not substantially informative in a cogent or even quantifiable way), because by the time *The Friend* emerged in 1809, the author's ideological views were substantially different from those displayed in *The Watchman*. In short, Coleridge had become a reactionary. The second number of *The Friend* contains both Coleridge's first discussion of Hooker and a display of his disgust with Warburton. Sadly the philosophical road that he traveled to arrive at this position is unmapped.

This chapter might be considered as a "Landing-Place" within the book's argument. Because the remainder of this book discusses Coleridge's mature project of a theological polity and seeks to demonstrate a consistent reaction to Warburton's contract theory and a consistent influence from Hooker, two separate preliminary discussions are necessary: one to demonstrate Coleridge's careful and constructive reading of Hooker, and one to describe Warburton's reaction to Hooker within the text of *The Alliance*. The two authors are considered in chronological order.

4

Warburton's and Coleridge's Readings of Hooker in Counterpoint

WARBURTON

Warburton's delineation of the church and state as two separate corporate bodies that enter into contract with each other brought him into direct conflict with the Hookerian position that the two entities of church and state actually constituted one organically unified society, given that each person in the nation was a member of both. If Hooker's position is assumed, no church-state alliance is possible, since a contract requires that the two parties to it be separate societies making a "*free convention*" with each other.[1] In the fifth and final chapter of book 2 of *The Alliance*, Warburton therefore sets out to refute this position—by attacking Hooker.

Warburton first attempts to demonstrate that it is logically impossible for a person to contract with himself. He holds that two things are necessary for a contract: (1) the concurrence of two wills and (2) a mutual obligation on the two persons to fulfill the contract. He concludes that in one man having one will there is no foundation for a compact (209). This is not particularly deft logic, nor is his next step: to show that the two societies of church and state have two separate wills by

---

1. Warburton, *Alliance*, 208, emphasis in original. Subsequent page citations to this work will be given parenthetically in the text.

discussing them as a "body" politic and a "body" ecclesiastic, then concluding that a body must have a will. Having created this artificial corporate will, he suggests that the same number of persons may erect more than one society, each of which has its distinct corporate will, *ad nauseam.*

> It follows that the self-same number of individuals, which have formed and erected of themselves, one society or factitious body, endowed with a distinct personality and will, may erect, of themselves, as many such societies as they please. Because the body, personality, and will, of such societies being all factitious, the storehouse, from whence they come, is as inexhaustible as the wants of mankind. Whereas, were the will and personality of the individuals, the will and personality of the society composed by them, then, on the contrary, the self-same number of individuals could not erect above one society: Because their personality and will being already bestowed upon one society, they had them not to give again, in order to animate any other.
>
> Here then we have two societies, made up of one and the same number of individuals, with each its distinct personality and will; each different from the personality and will of the other, and from the personality and will of the individuals. (211)

Warburton goes on to suppose that societies are created for different ends and that these ends motivate the will of each society. Finally he suggests that only under a democratic form of government could any objection to his theory arise because in a monarchical dictatorship the will of "at least one" of the societies (the state) lies not in the whole body but only in a part of the society (the dictator). The conclusion he draws from this discussion is, of course, his premise: that there are two distinct societies of church and state and that because they *are* two distinct societies the administration of them can, logically, never be in the "same hands at once" (213). None of this is particularly agile philosophy, and the reader is left with a picture of the same administrators with an infinite number of different hats for an infinite number of different societies. In essence, Warburton has claimed to defeat the argument that there is only one society, which comprises both the corporate body politic and corporate body ecclesiastic, by ignoring it.

Clearly Warburton's attempt to defeat this argument through logic is an attempt at a philosophical preface to the remainder of the chapter: an assault on Hooker—whose theories Warburton was clearly aware were the substantial danger to his alliance theory. "But, to crown the whole, let me observe, that nothing so clearly evinces the importance and necessity of this THEORY for justifying the right which the state hath to interfere in church matters, as the mistakes into which the excellent HOOKER was betrayed, on his missing of that capital idea of an ALLIANCE, when he came to defend *the right of civil princes to ecclesiastical dominion,* in the eighth book of his immortal work, intitled *[sic],* OF THE LAWS OF ECCLESIASTICAL POLITY" (213). Here there is an abrupt break in the flow of the argument. Warburton moves directly from discussing the corporate will of a society on philosophical terms to this almost bizarre broadside at Hooker. Furthermore, it is statements such as "the right which the state hath to interfere in church matters" that draw charges of Erastianism to Warburton. Though he goes to substantial length in the first two books of *The Alliance* to demonstrate that constitutionally the church is the more powerful of the two and thus he could fairly be said to have avoided the Erastian trap, he consistently sees the state as administering day-to-day operations of the church (86–134). The remainder of the chapter, some eight pages, is a *refutatio* of Hooker; the two sections do not fit, and it appears as if they were written separately and "glued" together with the quoted paragraph. Warburton's attack on Hooker is violent and even goes as far as to suggest that Hooker "introduced persecution for opinions" into English society (221–22).

It is clear that Warburton made a fairly detailed study of book 8 of the *Laws.* He was aware that there was a question of textual corruption in book 8, and he quoted from it eight times in the discussion and at substantial length (though these quotations were all drawn from pages 407 to 411 of a 1723 edition of Hooker). He saw the core of book 8 as an attempt to defend

the civil magistrate, in the administration of ecclesiastical supremacy, against the PURITANS of the time, who denied the spiritual legality of such a supremacy, and supported their opposition on this capital argument—*The church and commonwealth being societies or corporations totally distinct and independent of one another by nature, there is a separation perpetual and personal between the church and commonwealth.* This argument HOOKER attempts to overthrow. The position of his adversary is loosely worded. But the contest, at the time, subsisting between the *Puritans* and the *Church of England*, shews the meaning to be this. That "that INDEPENDENCY which a *religious* society had by nature, it could never give up to the *civil.*" (214)

Unsurprisingly, Warburton believed that all disagreements could have been solved had it been demonstrated that the church had entered into an alliance with the state through a free compact of its corporate will and that therefore no violation of that separation necessary to the Puritan divines would have been necessary: "I have shewn, how the church became enabled to exercise civil power without *tyranny;* and the state, to exercise ecclesiastical power without *usurpation*" (215). This argument certainly rang true to mid-eighteenth-century theologians, but it is doubtful whether it would have held much currency for John Knox or Walter Travers, or other Puritan writers of the sixteenth or seventeenth centuries—a fact of which Warburton seemed blissfully unaware.

The substantial core of his criticism of Hooker in *The Alliance* is, of course, that Hooker sees church and state as one society:

He too hastily conceded to his adversaries, that those things which were separated by *nature,* and more especially by divine *institution,* and so, INDEPENDENT of one another, must always continue independent. An absurd assertion! Which the Reader will see confuted at large in the *Postscript,* against the reasoning of Lord Bolingbroke, who lately revived this Puritan principle. Instead therefore, of exposing the error of the *conclusion,* HOOKER addresses himself (as we said) to confute the PREMISSES; and to shew, that *church and state were not two societies totally distinct and independent by nature,* but rather *one and the same society;* . . . (215)

It is interesting to see how absorbed in his own arguments Warburton actually is; he seems unable to comprehend the very idea that the persons who compose the Church of England and the civil society of England (being the same) are one society. He cites no other sources to support his disagreement with Hooker and argues that Hooker's premise is wrong because it does not take into account philosophical terms Warburton himself coined nearly 150 years later. "Now all this strange reasoning [Hooker's] ariseth, as the reader sees, from not distinguishing between a *natural* and an *artificial* PERSONAGE; which latter every society, community, or corporation, necessarily creates; as hath been just now shewn at large in this very chapter; so that when this distinction is applied, the absurdity becomes apparent" (216–17). Warburton sees the basis of Hooker's "error" arising from denying the premise of the Puritan argument, rather than its conclusions, and this is ironic because Warburton's own critique of Hooker proceeds along this same line. He simply, and repetitiously, denies the premise that church and state are one society; nowhere does he take Hooker on in Hooker's terms—but merely repeats his own premises over and over again.

Warburton also denies any legitimacy to drawing biblical support for the state church from the ancient Israelite model. Of course he has to do this because it is the biblical ground for Hooker's argument that the church and state are one corporate body; it is also Coleridge's biblical ground for this assertion and the biblical ground for most Anglican theologians who discuss the concept of a state church. He sees the employment of the biblical model as an argument "*ad homines*" because the Puritans were "accustomed to support their dissent from the established discipline of the church, on peculiarities in the Mosaic economy, ill understood, and worse applied" (217). Again Warburton has failed to understand Hooker's central premise. Hooker's employment of the biblical model was meant to provide a solid and lasting divine imprimatur for the entire concept of a state church, and not merely to defeat the Puritan arguments on their own ground. Warburton, in fact, sees Hooker's employment of the biblical model as dangerous and Erastian. He sees the argument as having been constructed to refute the Puritan principle that the church and state were separated by nature and that this separation was perpetual: "To combat this Principle, which makes the *state a slave to the church*, HOOKER ran to the opposite extreme, which makes the *church a slave to the state*" (218). Charging Hooker with Erastianism is, again, an ironic position for Warburton to have taken in view of the number of times he himself would be subjected to the same charge.

It is fairly clear that Warburton deeply misunderstood Hooker on all levels, especially the latter's employment of biblical support for the

idea of a state church. He draws two conclusions about Hooker's doctrine of church and state. The first is that the church became a slave to
the state because, "if it be the first duty of the civil magistrate to see to
the good condition of *things spiritual, the chiefest of which is religion,*
he must, on being invested with his office . . . be endowed with power
to put and to keep *spiritual things in this condition*" (209).[2] This conclusion he bases largely on Hooker's statement that Christian kings had authority and power over all matters in their kingdom, including matters of
religion. The second conclusion that Warburton draws is truly bizarre:

> These principles support and authorize *persecution for opinions:*
> for if, when the magistrate decrees in religious matters, whether of
> doctrine or discipline, men will not submit, the absolute power here
> given him justifies him in using force, for *he beareth not the sword
> in vain.* And to confess the truth, these principles, recommended by
> so great an authority, soon becoming the principles in fashion; the
> practice soon followed: the magistrate became a *persecutor;* and so
> continued; till *civil necessity,* arising from a state revolution, not the
> *religious choice* of a better theory, put a final stop to this opprobrium
> of humanity. (221)

There is no doubt that Hooker's theology had a tremendous influence
on English society and history, but to suggest that it was Hooker's influence and constructive arguments that gave rise to the tradition of the
state enforcing religious practice, and violently repressing those who
disagreed or refused to accept the dicta of the Crown, ignores fifty years
of Tudor history before Elizabeth. That Hooker's theology gave the state
religious authority is true, but that it created a climate of repression for
ideas and violent suppression of dissent cannot be correct. Further, while
it might be true that Hooker gave his imprimatur to both the anti-
Puritan position and the state's legal authority to suppress divergent
factions, to suggest that this led to the climate that eventually gave rise
to the English Civil War is going vastly too far. To suggest, as Warburton
does in the final sentence to book 2 of *The Alliance,* that "HOOKER'S

---

2. Emphasis in original. See also 86–234, especially 211, 213, 214–18, 220,
and 221–22.

[principle] introduced PERSECUTION FOR OPINIONS" (222) is equally absurd, since persecution for opinions long preceded Hooker. Even if it be true that Hooker gave such a governmental program tacit approval—and Warburton does not provide a quotation from Hooker that definitively demonstrated this—he could not possibly have "introduced persecution for opinions."

The venom in Warburton's critique of Hooker was probably due to both his misunderstanding of him and his awareness that for the idea of an alliance to be possible the church and state *must* be viewed as separate societies, something Hooker had very forcibly denied. To propagate his own view Warburton needed to abrogate Hooker's position, and he chose to do so by accusing him of both promoting Erastianism and fomenting persecution. He dismissed Hooker with immense aggression—especially considering that Hooker's theories were very much the accepted doctrine of the era[3]—and it was this degree of aggression that Coleridge, ironically, found deeply offensive.

It may be significant that the last section of book 2 did not exist in the first several editions of *The Alliance* but was added to the 1766 edition in response to a formal attack on Warburton by Henry Bolingbroke, who criticized him along Hookerian lines. Warburton must have recognized two things: first, that his attempt to sidestep Hooker's theory through some fairly complex "broken field running" had failed, and second, that Hooker's reputation was so substantial that homage must be paid to him during the destruction—in other words, that he would have to attempt to use Hooker's own words against him.[4] The postscript to the 1766 edition (here taken from a copy of the edition published in 1788) includes the following section of a larger attack on Bolingbroke, Hooker, and Locke:

> In the mean time, we see to what little purpose this great philosopher and statesman had read his HOOKER; of whom he confesses something is to be learnt. Now, HOOKER would have shewn him,

---

3. See chapter 11 below.

4. For a discussion of Bolingbroke's criticism of Warburton and Warburton's response to it, see Diarmaid MacCulloch, "Richard Hooker's Reputation," *English Historical Review* 117 (2002): 773–812.

that divine authority does not reduce all its laws to one and the same species—"Positive laws (says this truly great man) are either permanent or else changeable. . . ." [Here Warburton quotes book 1, i, section 15 at length.] So much for this country parson. And how poorly does his lordship figure before him with his assertion, that divine law makes every thing, which relates to the church, equally unalterable? Yet this noble haranguer, thus ignorant of the very first elements of law, can dictate with the authority of an oracle, and be received with the reverence due to one, concerning civil liberty, church usurpations, a patriot king, and the balance of power. But master Hooker will tell you how easily all this may be done by any one, without knowing more than their neighbours. (300–304)

Warburton had to make it appear that Bolingbroke had misunderstood Hooker (which he had not) and then to attack Hooker's substantive intellectual premises while appearing to do him homage. It is a thin veil, and it is transparent. One of the two, Hooker or Warburton, may be correct, but not both of them.

Part of what drove Warburton to create the alliance position was to put to bed forever the issues of Jacobitism that had led to the fiasco of the Sacheverell trial; if Warburton could create a system where the governments of both England and Scotland chose to ally with the prominent church (the Kirk north of the border, the Church of England south of it), then the fact that the Crowns were united presented no conundrum— that is, the idea of a single monarch as head of both churches, which constituted two separate religious societies, presented no problem.[5] He was in fact trying to solve a problem he perceived in the Tory position of seeing the two societies as one organic unity because the Kirk was a separate religious society from the Church of England. Coleridge, despite the existence of the Church of Scotland and the Act of Union, chose to resurrect the Tory position and used Hooker to do so; Gladstone sided with Coleridge. Coleridge and Gladstone may have been able to do this only because of the stability of the united crowns after Anne and throughout the Hanoverian period—another hundred years of history had given them the opportunity to see England and Scotland

---

5. See chapter 11 below.

as one society (especially following the second Act of Union in January 1801), but choose to do it they did; their mutual foundation was Hooker.

COLERIDGE

Coleridge's copy of Hooker resides in the British Library. It is Ashley collection number 5175: a folio edition of the complete works of Hooker printed in 1682, edited by John Gauden, the former bishop of Exeter. It contains the entirety of *The Laws of Ecclesiastical Polity*, Walton's *Life of Hooker*, *Travers' Supplication to the Council*, *Hooker's Response to Travers' Address*, *A Discourse of Justification and Works*, *The Sermon on Pride*, *A Remedy against Sorrow and Fear*, *A Sermon of the Certainty and Perpetuity of Faith in the Elect*, and the *Sermon on St. Jude*. The folio was rebound when it came into the collection of the British Library, and as such the boards are missing—thus there is no bookplate inscription, which would have been very helpful. There are, however, two cover leaves from the original binding left within the new boards, and one of these holds a short annotation in Coleridge's hand that points to a passage discussing fasting on pages 328 and 329 of the folio. The annotation both praises Hooker's discussion and states that it is important.[6] Given these facts—and a conversation with British Library staff who are familiar with the work of the binder—it is unlikely that the

---

6. See below for a detailed discussion of the date at which Coleridge is likely to have acquired the folio. It should be noted, however, that the only place where Coleridge ever discusses the question of fasting is in *The Watchman*; this annotation is also in the A cut of ink (again, see below for explanation), which suggests that he was reading Hooker as a constructive influence at a very early stage in his career. Furthermore, this comment of Hooker's is decidedly not important to the overall argument of this section of the *Laws*—which strongly suggests that it was written during the period of *The Watchman*. This is because the capricious nature of Coleridge's early thought led him to see the theological landscape through a pair of hermeneutically tinted spectacles that showed the issue at hand to be the most important issue in Christianity, whatever it was. Fasting was important to Coleridge, and thus in his eyes to Hooker, only during *The Watchman* period and earlier.

loss of any holographic material has taken place. It is, however, still necessary to rely upon the annotations themselves to date the folio.

Within the entirety of the folio there are three separate sets of identifiable annotations in three different cuts of ink and using three different nibs; I identify them as cut C, cut B, and cut A. Cut C is internally dated as August and September 1826; this date appears throughout the annotations, and the ink cut is always identical when it is written. Cut B is dated by note XXXVII; this note, an annotation to *Hooker's Response to Travers' Address*, is a two-part note in two separate cuts of ink. In the second part it remarks (in the C cut of ink) that "a year or more" after the first part of the annotation (which is in the B cut of ink) Coleridge has changed his mind. This shows two things: first, the difference between the C and the B cuts of ink, which are very similar and differentiated only by the B cut's having less strong black pigments in the heavy areas of the letters and stronger browns throughout the text; second, the approximate date of the B reading, which the note makes clear is sometime around January 1825. The chronology of Coleridge's own work also indicates that he was preparing *Aids to Reflection* on or about January 1825, and this is important; the reading of books 1 through 5 and 8 of *The Laws of Ecclesiastical Polity* is certainly a major undertaking and must therefore have some identifiable motivation to prompt it. The preparation of *Aids to Reflection* is the only major project afoot within the time frame given by the C section of XXXVII and as such provides a motivation for the reading and annotation. Indeed one of the aphorisms in the second half of the *Aids* is drawn from Hooker and receives commentary.

The A cut notes have no internal date. They are written with a much thicker cut of ink, with a broader nib and a larger hand that is less polished and fine than that of the C and B cuts. Furthermore, they occur only in the "short pieces" of the collected works and nowhere within the context of the *Laws*. There is ample evidence for concluding that they were written during the Cambridge period. First and most importantly, the paleography of the A annotations matches the paleography of Coleridge's prizewinning essay in the archives of Jesus College and does not match the paleography of any of the later manuscripts—though it is unquestionably the same hand. The second opportunity for dating them as from the Cambridge period is the text of a note in response to Gauden's dedication of the work to Charles II, on the opening page of the volume; the note responds to Gauden's phrase "Although I know how little leisure *Great Kings* have to read large books, or indeed any, save only *God's* (the study, belief, and obedience of which, is precisely commanded, even to Kings, <u>Deut</u> 17; 18–19)." The text of Coleridge's annotation follows in its entirety: " ?<u>Little</u> Kings I presume are better off! O how hateful yet alas! How common is adulation in the mouth of a Protestant Bishop—Whether even Dogs, from whom the method is derived perpetrate with their tail! Read the first paragraph so worthy of of *[sic]* a Christian Minister—Then what follows of 'Prudent care, unparalleled bounty, Transcendent Merit,' &c &c and reflect on the even generally <u>suspected</u> papistry and Known <u>notorious</u> profaneness and profligacy of the heartless Brotheller, Charles II!!"[7]

Note the heavy anti-Catholicism displayed by the slight against "papistry," the phrase "so worthy of a Christian Minister," and the sneer against "a Protestant Bishop"; this paragraph was clearly written before Coleridge's theological "encounter on the road to Damascus" in 1805 and his abandonment of Unitarianism. Now, also note the antimonarchist slant of the entire note. It is an attack not merely on Charles II but rather on the relationship between the monarchy and the church as a whole—again, this is in line with the young Coleridge's Nonconformist position and radical political ideology. This is not the voice of the older Coleridge of *On the Constitution of the Church and State,* nor is it even the mature Coleridge of *The Friend* of 1809, nor even is it the (if nothing else) more considered radical voice of the Coleridge in the period of *The Watchman.* It is the voice of the very young, very radical Coleridge. The pure fury of the stance against the monarchy suggests the Pantisocracy era. When this is taken in concert with the fact that the hand is much less polished than that of the older man and the fact that the nib is so much broader (and even more importantly dispenses so much more ink), it suggests a well-trimmed quill pen (the other annotations are written with an iron nib). All this suggests a very young man. In short, I believe that this note was written during the Cambridge years. And again, the A annotations are appended only to the short works in the volume. The fact that only the short pieces within the volume are annotated in the A cut also suggests the situation of a rather less-than-diligent student producing an essay out of reading only the short pieces of the volume.

---

7. Ashley folio, dedication of volume.

There is further support for the Cambridge suggestion from the fact that the folio itself would have been a fairly rare and reasonably expensive volume, so that Coleridge probably could not have bought his own copy. As the librarian of Jesus College, however, he would have had access to the copy in the college library. The two contemporary accession catalogs in the Jesus Old Library show that a folio of the same date disappeared from the library during this period. One catalog was entirely made before Coleridge arrived in Cambridge, the other was made after he left.[8] Coleridge, however, as the college junior librarian, was in a perfect position to remove it without its loss being recorded. This is something it would have been in his character to do.

Still further support for the Cambridge hypothesis is found in Coleridge's mentions of Hooker in three letters written some twenty years before the earliest possible date for the B annotations. In a letter to Robert Southey written in July 1803, he outlines a grand scheme for a *Bibliotheca Britannica,* or a history of British literature, to take the form of seven volumes. He mentions Hooker as a candidate for inclusion in the fifth volume—the one designed to outline the metaphysics and theology of Christianity other than the Roman Catholic religion—in the company of Richard Baxter, John Biddle, and George Fox.[9] It is on one hand a list of ultra-Protestant theologians: Biddle was a Unitarian (consistent with Coleridge's radical political philosophy during this period), Baxter left the Church of England as a matter of conscience,[10] Fox was a Quaker. But when Hooker, who defined Anglicanism, is included in the list, it is a list of *very different* Protestant theologians: in other words, a cross section of English Protestant thought. Though this evidence is circumstantial and threadbare if standing on its own, as part of the larger concatenation of evidence it is highly supportive.

It seems probable that Coleridge made another superficial and very quick perusal of book 1 of the *Laws* in 1809, since Hooker is quoted in

---

8. The two borrowing logs have no catalog call numbers. They can, however, be requested in the Jesus College Old Library by their description.

9. This is most likely George Fox the "Quaker." Coleridge was infatuated with the Quaker religion during this period—if only sporadically. There is a serious mention of Quakerism in several letters of this period, specifically letters 473 and 634.

10. See chapter 11 below on Chalmers's discussion of Baxter.

the text of *The Friend*,[11] and the page where the passage appears is annotated.[12] It is indisputable that Coleridge was thumbing through the folio looking for ideas to fill his periodical in 1809 and he annotated the quoted passage later when he went back to undertake serious reading of the text in its entirety, as the following excerpt from the annotation demonstrates: "See the Essays on method, in the Friend. Hooker's words literally and grammatically interpreted seem to assert the antecedence of the thing to its kind i.e. essential characters; and to its force together with its form and measure of working, i.e. to its specific and distinctive characters; in short, the words assert the pre-existence of the thing to all its constituent powers, qualities, and properties." Further persuasive evidence of an 1809 reading is found in a response to a letter Coleridge received from Robert Lloyd (a subscriber to the journal). Coleridge did not publish Lloyd's letter, but the response was published in *The Friend* number 11 (October 26, 1809) and dated October 23, 1809.[13] In this letter Coleridge answered the quite reasonable and well-guided charge that *The Friend* was written in such purple and inbred prose that it was completely incomprehensible to any reader but Samuel Taylor Coleridge. It is worth quoting a fairly long section of Coleridge's answer:

> An Author's pen like Children's legs, improves by exercise. That part of the blame which rests in myself, I am exerting my best faculties to remove. A man long accustomed to silent and solitary meditation, in proportion as he increases the power of thinking in long and connected trains, is apt to lose or lessen the talent of communicating his thoughts with grace and perspicuity. Doubtless too, I have in some measure injured my style, in respect to its' [*sic*] facility and popularity, from having almost confined my reading, of late years, to the Works of the Ancients and those of the elder Writers in the modern languages. We insensibly imitate what we habitually admire; and

---

11. Samuel Taylor Coleridge, *The Friend*, 2 vols., ed. Barbara E. Rooke, vol. 4 of *The Collected Works of Samuel Taylor Coleridge*, Bollingen Series 75 (Princeton: Princeton University Press, 1969), 2:122 (also 1:186); Hooker, *Laws*, bk. 1, ch. 1, para. 2.

12. The annotation is number XIII, a B cut annotation.

13. Coleridge, *Collected Letters*, 3:255–59.

an aversion to the epigrammatic unconnected periods of the fash-
ionable *Anglo-gallican* Taste has too often made me willing to for-
get, that the stately march and difficult evolutions, which character-
ize the eloquence of Hooker, Bacon, Milton, and Jeremy Taylor, are,
notwithstanding their intrinsic excellence, still less suited to a periodical Essay. This fault I am now endeavouring to correct; though I
can never so far sacrifice my judgment to the desire of being immediately popular, as to cast my sentences in the French moulds, or affect a style which an ancient critic would have deemed purposely invented for persons troubled with the asthma to read, and for those
to comprehend who labour under the more pitiable asthma of a
short-witted intellect.[14]

This passage implies that Coleridge had been reading Hooker during
the immediately previous years. It is also significant that it is mentioned
in the context of the college Classics syllabus (i.e., as a part of a broad
taught course in the liberal arts, including theology and history). This
is a context into which an encounter with the shorter works through
the Jesus Classics syllabus, then shored up by the briefest of perusals of
book 1, would fit neatly.

The third letter in which Hooker is mentioned was written to Coleridge's friend Henry Crabb Robinson, a lawyer, on December 3, 1817.[15]
The letter concerns the possibility of bringing a charge of libel against
the publisher of *Blackwood's Magazine,* which had printed a seriously
critical review of the *Biographia Literaria.* Here Coleridge merely mentions that "as Hooker observes what is wanting in the writer is made up
for in the predisposition of the readers." The reference is fleeting, but it
does show that Hooker was on Coleridge's mind during this period and
suggests that Hooker was a pervasive and lasting influence.

Conclusions may be drawn about the date of the A annotations
based upon this further historical evidence. Any conclusion must be
qualified by the recognition that, simply because a given letter mentions
a name, it does not necessarily indicate that the writer has actually read
the author he is mentioning. It is therefore possible that Coleridge had

---

14. Coleridge, *Friend,* 2:150.
15. Coleridge, *Collected Letters,* 4:785.

not read Hooker by the time he was name-dropping in the letters, but the evidence strongly opposes this interpretation. The safest conclusion is probably a middle ground: that Coleridge's knowledge of Hooker was more than mere name-dropping and less than an informed familiarity with the entirety of the complete works. It seems likely that he had read only those sections of the complete works annotated with the A cut before 1809. These are the prefatory material, the life of Hooker, Walton's appendix to the life, and the shorter pieces already named at the back of the volume. This would be a sufficient quantity of prose to familiarize Coleridge with Hooker's style and some of his basic theological precepts—in fact, it might well have been an assignment for an essay on Hooker in the context of the Jesus Classics course.

The overall conclusion is that Coleridge read the shorter pieces of the complete works, the A cut, while up at Cambridge, and that this is where he obtained the folio. He did a slightly more detailed perusal of book 1 in 1809 when writing *The Friend* in serial, but still only a superficial reading of part of book 1. He undertook a fairly detailed reading of *The Laws of Ecclesiastical Polity* while writing *Aids to Reflection* in the early months of 1825—these are the B annotations. Finally, Coleridge reread *The Laws* during August and September of 1826 while he was drafting *On the Constitution of the Church and State*—these are the C annotations. The informed influence of Hooker would then demonstrably occur in any work written after 1825 and in an inchoate form after 1809. What is indisputably clear, however, is that Coleridge read Hooker in a meticulous and detailed fashion twice during the 1820s and that he had dabbled with Hooker somewhat less extensively before that time. Hooker's name and thought were prevalent throughout the theological landscape of Coleridge's mind after 1805. At several extremely important points—*On the Constitution of the Church and State, Aids to Reflection,* and *Confessions of an Inquiring Spirit*—they came forcefully into the foreground.[16]

---

16. Coleridge's *Confessions of an Inquiring Spirit* begins with an epigraph taken from Hooker (interestingly, from material covered by the A annotations).

Part Three

Coleridge's Mature Project

5

───────❧❧❧───────

The Friend

The Project Outlined

THE FOLLOWING QUOTATION IS FROM THE JUNE 8 ISSUE OF
The Friend of 1809:

A second Species of this unamiable quality, which has been often
distinguished by the name of *Warburtonian* arrogance, betrays itself,
not as in the former, by proud or petulant omission of proof or argument, but by the habit of ascribing weakness of intellect or want
of taste and sensibility, or hardness of heart, or corruption of moral
principle, to all who deny the truth of the doctrine, or the sufficiency
of evidence, or the fairness of the reasoning adduced in its' support.
This is indeed not essentially different from the first, but assumes a
separate character from its' accompaniments: for though both the
doctrine and its proofs may have been legitimately supplied by the
understanding, yet the bitterness of personal crimination will resolve
itself into naked assertion, and we are authorized by experience, and
entitled on the principle of self-defence and by the law of fair retali-
ation in attributing it to a vicious temper arrogant from angry passions, or irritable from arrogance. This learned arrogance admits of
many gradations, and is palliated or aggravated, accordingly as the
Point in dispute has been more or less controverted, as the reasoning
bears a greater or smaller proportion to the virulence of the personal
detraction, and as the Persons or Parties, who are the Objects of it,
are more or less respected, more or less worthy of respect.[1]

---

1. Coleridge, *Friend,* 2:33–34.

Coleridge supplies a note of his own to this passage:

> Had the Author of the Divine Legation of Moses more skilfully ap-
> propriated his coarse eloquence of Abuse, his customary assurances
> of the Ideotcy *[sic]*, both in head and heart, of all his opponents; if
> he had employed those vigorous arguments of his own vehement
> Humor in the defence of Truths, acknowledged and reverenced by
> learned men in general, or had confined them to the names of Chubb,
> Woolston, and other precursors of Mr. Thomas Payne, we should
> perhaps still characterize his mode of controversy by its' *[sic]* rude vi-
> olence; but not so often have heard his name used even by those who
> never read his writings, as a proverbial expression of learned Arro-
> gance. But when a novel and doubtful Hypothesis of his own forma-
> tion was the Citadel to be defended, and his mephetic hand-granados
> were thrown with the fury of lawless despotism at the fair reputa-
> tions of a Sykes and a Lardner, we not only confirm the verdict of his
> independent contemporaries, but cease to wonder, that arrogance
> should render men an object of contempt in many, and of aversion in
> all instances, when it was capable of hurrying a Christian Teacher of
> equal Talents and Learning into a slanderous vulgarity, which escapes
> our disgust only when we see the writer's own reputation the sole
> victim. But throughout his great work, and the pamphlets in which
> he supported it, he always seems to write, as if he had deemed it a
> duty of decorum to publish his fancies on the Mosaic Law as the Law
> itself was delivered "in thunders and lightnings" and had applied to
> his own Book instead of the sacred mount the menace—*There shall
> not a hand touch it but he shall surely be stoned or shot through.*[2]

The Friend is both a turning point and a work of some substantial
significance in the corpus of Coleridge generally and especially for the argument of this book. It resembles a shrouded précis of his mature project, since nearly all the later works center on a theme or political position
first expounded in *The Friend. The Friend* is the first work in which
Coleridge quotes Hooker, and the work where his dislike of Warburton becomes most explicit.

---

2. Coleridge, *Friend,* 2:34.

If the period between the delivery of the *Lectures on Revealed Religion* and the return from Malta was surprisingly unimportant for this study, the decade following (1806–16) is important on account of the composition of *The Friend*. It is as if Coleridge, after his repudiation of Unitarianism, had simply returned to the classical education that served him so well at Cambridge and had begun drawing upon it to construct his new philosophical project—starting over from the same point as though the ten intervening years, and his work during them, had not existed (except for the training in German Idealism that he had acquired while abroad). Evidence of the conservative, establishment (as opposed to radical or dissenting) nature of his project may be found, for instance, in the second preface to the 1809 edition (which occurs in issue 2).

> From all my readers I solicit a gracious attention to the following explanations: first, on the congruity of this number with the general Plan and object of "the Friend"; and secondly, on the charge of arrogance, which may be adduced against the Author for the freedom, with which in this number and in others that will follow on other subjects he presumes to dissent from men of established reputation, or even to doubt of the justice with which the public Laurel-crown, as symbolical of the *first* Class of Genius and Intellect, has been awarded to sundry writers since the Revolution, and permitted to wither around the brows of our elder Benefactors, from Hooker to Sir P. Sidney, and from Sir P. Sidney to Jeremy Taylor and Stillingfleet.[3]

An even more Anglocentric conservatism is evinced in this passage in issue 4 of *The Friend*:

> The Cranmers, Hampdens, and Sidneys; the Counselors of our Elizabeth, and the Friends of our other great deliverer the third William,— is it in vain, that *these* have been our Countrymen? Are we not the Heirs of their good deeds? And what are noble Deeds but noble Truths realized? As Protestants, as Englishmen, as the Inheritors of so ample an estate of Might and Right, an estate so strongly fenced,

---

3. Coleridge, *Friend*, 2:26.

so richly planted, by the sinewy arms and dauntless hearts of our Forefathers, we of all others have good cause to trust in the Truth, yea, to follow its pillar of fire through the Darkness and the Desert, even though its Light should but suffice to make us certain of its own presence. IF there be elsewhere men jealous of the Light, who prophecy *[sic]* an excess of Evil over Good from its' *[sic]* manifestation, we are entitled to ask them, on what experience they ground their Bodings? Our own Country bears no traces, our own history contains no records, to justify them. From the Great areas of national illumination we date the commencement of our main national Advantages.[4]

So it is clear that Coleridge had altered his ideology substantially from that displayed by his attacks on British society in *The Watchman*. This new emphasis upon the grace and bounty of the English intellectual heritage was precisely what would cause him to emphasize the Anglican theological heritage (and Hooker specifically) in the later works; and it is within the context of the later published works of magnitude that Hooker's influence is traceable.

THE SERIAL EDITION OF 1809 AND TORYISM

This chapter will examine the text of the serial edition of *The Friend* printed in 1809 and 1810. The earlier text is especially relevant here because of this project's chronological approach and because of the dramatic and fundamental reorientation that Coleridge effects within its pages. The differences between the serial and the composite version of the work (the 1812 edition) are, with few exceptions, cosmetic—though the latter adds three interludes that Coleridge calls "Landing-Places," one of which includes the "Essay on Faith." There is only one commentary of value written solely on *The Friend*, Deirdre Coleman's *Coleridge and "The Friend" (1809–1810)*, and she also views the serially published version as the important one. It is also of note that Gladstone chose to read the serial rather than the revised version in 1829.[5]

---

4. Coleridge, *Friend*, 2:55–56.
5. See chapter 11 below.

The Friend is the first of Coleridge's works that can be placed within the canon of his mature religious thought. It is the first to reveal Hooker as a constructive influence and the first in his career as an apologist for the religious establishment (and the secular establishment). Each of these facets will be focused on, and the points at which his political pronouncements and positions link him with the political grouping that would in time (ca. 1820) come to be called the Tory party will be highlighted. Chief among these his detailed discussion of the Napoleonic campaigns and his public criticism of Canning's choice of utilitarian philosophical grounds to defend the British seizure of the Danish fleet to keep the ships from falling into French hands; Coleridge argued that although the decision to seize the fleet was right and conscionable the action had to be defended on moral grounds rather than utilitarian ones.

The central importance of *The Friend* is that it contains everything that would encapsulate Coleridge's later career; in fact, it can be seen as a microcosm of his adult work and contains proleptic versions of all his later works on social issues. His next publications were his Lay Sermons and then a revised and slightly expanded one-volume edition of *The Friend* itself (in order to present it in a more marketable form). This second edition should not be seen as an attempt to draw something up from nothing—that is, to reshape a failure—but rather as an attempt to disseminate his lifetime project in a more accessible form. This view of *The Friend* of 1809 as the *starting point* of his life's project is reinforced precisely because Coleridge's next publications *were* the two Lay Sermons—addressed to the gentry and the middle classes (though he characteristically failed to produce a third addressed to the general populace). They contain an early version of his theories on the Christian in English society that is later presented more fully in *On the Constitution of the Church and State*. All this demonstrates conclusively that by the time of *The Friend* (i.e., by 1809) Coleridge had embarked on a project that he saw as his future: delineating the roles of religion and politics in society. In other words, these two subjects are the focus of the *Lay Sermons, The Friend* in its reissued form, *On the Constitution of the Church and State*, and *Confessions of an Inquiring Spirit*. The role of religion and politics in society could also be said to be the subject of *Aids to Reflection*, which was written as a manual for young clergy.

The Friend is a microcosm of Coleridge's later work because it presents, though in a rough form, Coleridge's thoughts on both Christianity and the Christian's role in society: both in its discussion of the Christian in society and in its discussion of politics, for the two are inextricably braided together in Coleridge's mind. Further, *The Friend* demonstrates not only the project of his mature years but also the political position from which he would approach it.

By 1809 Coleridge had become a traditionalist Tory. Though it had become clear from letters to his brother that he had repudiated Unitarianism some four years earlier, and that he was toying with a return to Anglicanism, it was not yet evident that he had returned to an orthodox, establishment, position. But this becomes demonstrably obvious in *The Friend*.

Coleridge's support of the establishment church position in *The Friend* was not voiced as straightforwardly as one might find in *On the Constitution of the Church and State*. In *The Friend* it was more subtle, taking the form of a political position rather than an ecclesiastical one. This does not diminish his commitment to the Church of England or the importance of this commitment in his work. In the serial edition of *The Friend* Coleridge began to place himself within the group that would eventually be called "Tory," and it was through this nascent conservatism that his links with Anglicanism and the Anglican establishment were first manifested. Coleman has noted *The Friend*'s interlacing of the political and the religious in the very title of her concluding chapter, "The Gordian Knot," but what she has missed is that this is the Gordian knot not only of *The Friend* but of Coleridge's entire adult project.

Christian polity *is* the Gordian knot of Coleridgeana, and *The Friend* is the first work to make this clear. It was hinted at in the *Lectures on Revealed Religion,* but Coleridge subsequently repudiated the Pantisocratic theology of those lectures, and now in its place was an Anglican polity influenced by Hooker. The important point to note is that when Coleridge joined the Establishment, when he "came out" as a social critic within the Tory school of thought, he repudiated neither his tremendous confidence in humanity (as displayed prevalently in the early works) nor the great confidence in human nature that was one of the nineteenth century's general characteristics. He participated in this confidence not through a confidence in Man *sui generis* but in humanity as Christians— *created* persons—which is to say that his confidence in Man had become irrevocably tied to his *confidence in the truth of Christianity.* Gone was the early confidence in humanity born of the French Revolution (that through reason humanity could progress beyond history). Here was a confidence in Man as part of God's creation. The confidence came through the individual person's ability to enact a Christian program that would allow progress within the world towards the state of the Kingdom of God.[6] This was a conservative confidence based upon the presupposition that the government was bipolar: Canterbury and Westminster.

Coleman has recognized the bipolar nature of Coleridge's view of government, but she chooses to treat the subject in a chapter titled "Some Unresolved Conflicts."

> Nationalism suffuses *The Friend,* at the level of private morality the dictates of conscience give way to the higher dictates of Public duty, an illiberal aspect of Coleridge's nationalism can be seen in his sneering at the Quakers' pacifism. Their refusal to adapt religious principles to the exigencies of political life, and their tendency to regard the inner Light as the sole authority in all matters, disturbed Coleridge's Kantian belief in a necessary distinction between the realms of Morality (Ethics) and Politics (Ius). At the level of international morality, Coleridge suggests that the strict requirements of virtue must sometimes be overruled by the broader requirements of justice or right. Although he is at pains to point out that nations and individuals are bound by the same spirit of morality, he none the less holds that the circumstances of political action give rise to wholly different duties from those attaching to private life.[7]

What Coleman fails to see throughout her treatment of this bipolar project is that for Coleridge the two poles reach unity through the dialectic. The conflicts are not unresolved; rather, they are brought to a synthesis. What she calls Coleridge's "sneering" at Quaker pacifism is rather his

---

6. Coleridge's idea of progression is certainly very different from late nineteenth- and twentieth-century American ideas of progression towards the Kingdom of God in that it maintains a heavy emphasis on the doctrine of original sin and does not see progression through secular society as possible; instead, this progression takes place within the established state church. The ability to progress in fact depends on a polity that assures the church a place in government; society can progress only if the church is part of its governing body. Progression in a secular state such as America is not supposed to be possible under this paradigm.

7. Deirdre Coleman, *Coleridge and "The Friend" (1809–1810)* (Oxford: Clarendon Press, 1988), 11.

aversion to the individual Quaker's refusal to take up the sword in a virtuous conflict and fight for the life of his fellow Christian. He takes care
to discuss this by using a contemporary moral paradigm about a gentleman on a shooting party with a Quaker companion. In this paradigm the
Quaker has not discharged his gun while his companion has; the pair
then encounter a notorious highwayman who has previously made clear
his intention to dispatch the companion (who was at the time unarmed)
were they ever to meet again. The paradigm set, the question was then
posed as to whether the threatened man would be guilty of an immoral
assault were he forcibly to remove his Quaker companion's weapon in
order to defend himself. Coleridge comes down unequivocally on the
side of self-defense.

This paradigm is telling because, though it operates on the micro
scale (individual rather than group action) of moral theology, it shows
Coleridge's determination to allow the lawfulness of a preemptive strike
in national self-defense on the macro scale (group rather than individual
action). He is setting up the intellectual model of applying morality to the
state as if it were an "individual." This is most likely where Gladstone
began to see Coleridge as a constructive influence for his own thought
on the subject of viewing the state's actions as those of an individual
(when he read *The Friend* in 1829).[8] This discussion also anticipates
Coleridge's appropriation of Augustinian just-war theory in his later
discussion of Nelson's seizure of the Danish fleet.

Coleridge also uses Augustinian criteria when he discusses the
"spirit and the letter" of international law—an Augustinian appropriation that Coleman, surprisingly, entirely fails to notice or identify.[9] The
omission is all the more surprising in that Coleman has already noticed
and remarked upon the fact that Coleridge's conservatism was not the
doctrinaire court Whiggism of his age.

---

8. See chapter 11 below.
9. Coleridge's concept of the distinction between the spirit and the letter
of law is, of course, Pauline in its original formation. But it is doubtful that Coleridge was drawing directly from Paul for two reasons. First, it is extremely doubtful that he was reinventing this particular theological wheel—Augustine having
written widely on the subject in both *On Christian Doctrine* and *On the Spirit
and the Letter*. Second, Coleridge was not in the habit of quoting directly from
the Bible in any of his works, but he was in the habit of quoting or paraphras-
ing other thinkers at length.

. . . It is clear from Coleridge's letters that he intended to swim with the party in power and not in the "muddy yet shallow stream" of the Whigs (*CL* iii. 195). Like the *Quarterly Review* whose first issue appeared in February 1809, *The Friend* formed part of a Tory reaction against those who questioned the need to continue the war, a doubt aired in what Southey described as the "base and cowardly politics" of the *Edinburgh Review* (Warter, ii.107). Coleridge shared Southey's contempt for the doubters, and in an article written soon after the last number of *The Friend,* attacked the very stance of independence and impartiality which he had officially adopted for his own journal. The Whigs and Edinburgh Reviewers who stationed themselves on an "Isthmus" of neutrality and moderation, far removed from the strife, were contemptible for looking down upon "the agitation of the vessel of state, and the conflict of hostile factions" with "a sort of tranquil delight arising from a consciousness of security" (*EOT* ii. 102–3).[10]

Coleman's identification of Coleridge as a Tory is surprising for both its absolute boldness and its inaccuracy: the word *Tory* would not come back into use as a normative concept until about 1820. The year 1809 saw two prime ministers: the Duke of Portland (a thoroughgoing Whig) and Spencer Perceval (a professed Evangelical). Coleman is correct, though, to see his conservatism as shockingly different from the current Whig orthodoxy of 1809; it was a much more classical conservatism than that which even the Foxite Whigs were displaying in this period.

Coleridge's was a retro-Tory conservatism different in spirit from that of those whose names would become associated with neo-Toryism in the 1820s. This is evident from his attack on Canning in *The Friend.* Although the two men often reached the same political conclusions, as in the case of the seizure of the Danish fleet, Coleridge was critical of Canning's motives. Coleridge approved of the seizure but attacked Canning's defense (which he thought did not go far enough), making the seizure an issue of just-war theory and thus putting England in the position of absolute right—which he faulted Canning for not doing. In other words, Coleridge was a traditionalist "Queen Anne" Tory rather than a "Whiggish" or "New Liberal Tory" like Canning. Coleridge was a Tory of the

---

10. Coleman, *Coleridge,* 11.

"old school" who believed in divine right and in a national church that would support the right of the state to defend itself and to conquer in the name of its sovereign monarch when the cause was just—especially when faced with a secular adversary, such as the new Republic of France and the French Empire under Napoleon.

The real issue here is that when the Tory party "reformed" as an organized political party it had moved substantially towards what could be called the contemporary political center. The new Tories operated in a political climate that was entirely suffused with the ideology of Court Whiggism, and though their emergence as a party demonstrated that Whiggism was on the wane and there was a need for a new conservative opposition, the new Tories were still intellectual heirs to this Whig ideology: they had been raised in its climate and it was a naturally integrated part of their thought architecture. This is why Canning and his contemporary Tory intellectuals have been termed new "Liberal Tories." Though they self-consciously defined themselves as Tories, they still felt the need to be avant-garde in their polity and philosophy; hence Canning saw nothing wrong with using utilitarian philosophical foundations to argue a Tory position.[11] In fact it was Coleridge's High Toryism that was truly avant-garde because it entirely rejected the intellectual presuppositions of Court Whiggism and sought to rebuild Tory ideology on classical, early English Tory foundations that had existed prior to the advent of Court Whig ideology.

What differentiated Coleridge's Toryism from the Toryism being recreated through men like Canning and the other (new liberal) Tories was the extent of its dependence upon the establishment, with its "one-sided reciprocity" of church and state.[12] Coleridge looked to the church and to Hooker's divine right theory to give an imprimatur to the actions of the navy. When Coleridge attacked Canning for the methodology behind the latter's defense of naval action, this was not "inexcusable

{

---

11. See, for example, Boyd Hilton, *Corn, Cash, Commerce: The Economic Policies of the Tory Governments, 1815–1830* (Oxford: Oxford University Press, 1977), 304 ff.

12. See Peter B. Hinchliff, *The One-Sided Reciprocity: A Study in the Modification of the Establishment* (London: Darton, Longman and Todd, 1966), chs. 1 and 2.

sophistry," as Coleman charges.[13] It was in fact as far from sophistry as possible, because it discussed the very core of the motivation for a state's international actions. For Coleridge, the state had to have the imprimatur of the church in order to act. This suggests that in Coleridge's polity the reciprocity was less one-sided than it might seem, for though the state might appoint the governors of the church it would then be bound by the moral codes of action that they were willing to approve. For Canning, the state merely needed the utilitarian motivation of necessity to act; the state could transgress in order that a greater good might come. This ideology was anathema to Coleridge, who wished to impose the criterion of virtue upon the actions of the state. Coleridge's discussion of the seizure of the Danish fleet and its Augustinian basis will be examined later in this chapter, but first it is necessary to examine Coleridge's employment of Hooker's *Polity* in more detail. This requires an analysis of Coleridge's treatment of Hooker, and then of Coleman's discussion of that treatment—which will be shown to be superficial.

HOOKER'S INFLUENCE AND DEIRDRE COLEMAN'S COMMENTARY

The first major instance in *The Friend* where Hooker's influence is directly traceable occurs in the epigraph to issue 9 (October 12, 1809), which immediately precedes essay 6, "On the Grounds of Government as Laid Exclusively in the Pure Reason; Or a Statement and Critique of the Third System of Political Philosophy, Viz. the Theory of Rousseau and the French Economists." The epigraph itself is the second paragraph (in its entirety) of Hooker's *Laws of Ecclesiastical Polity*, book 1, chapter 1, and though this particular paragraph is not itself annotated in the Ashley folio, one further down the opposing page is annotated. The extremely laudatory annotations to Hooker's shorter works in the Ashley folio, when examined in the context of the strong interest in the English intellectual tradition that Coleridge expressed in *The Friend*, give ample cause to suggest that while researching *The Friend* he went back to Hooker and began reading the *Laws* at, logically, book 1, chapter 1. Hooker's emphasis here on the theological anthropology of reason

---

13. Coleman, *Coleridge*, 188.

is completely consistent with Coleridge's plan of discussing reason throughout *The Friend*—and more specifically consistent with the specific discussion of reason as the grounds of government. All of this provides ample evidence both to posit Hooker as an influence on *The Friend* of 1809 and to perform a Hookerian reading of whichever passages of the text are consistent with such a reading—specifically Coleridge's delineation of a unique concept of reason, drawn from a melding of German Idealism with a fundamentally Hookerian concept of reason. Hooker is the foundation of Coleridge's conception of reason; German Idealism merely helped build the superstructure.

Coleridge had probably operated with a Hookerian concept of reason in the back of his mind since his time at Cambridge, where he might have gleaned such an idea from lectures and supervisions, though it cannot be proved that he read Hooker's specific passages on reason during the first half of the 1790s. It is more than likely that Coleridge purposefully read Hooker's extended discussion of reason in book 1 of the *Laws* in 1809, and it is clear from the text of *The Friend* that he was deeply influenced by Hooker's discussion of reason. His invoking of that discussion within the context of *The Friend* comes as early as issue 4, where Coleridge, employing Hooker's hermeneutics, wrote:

> For every Depository of the supreme Power must presume itself rightful: and as the source of law, not legally to be endangered. A form of Government may indeed, in reality, be most pernicious to the governed, and the highest moral honor may await the patriot who risks his life in order by its subversion to introduce a better and juster Constitution, but it would be absurd to blame the Law, by which his life is declared forfeit. It were to expect, that by an envisioned contradiction, the Law should allow itself not to be law, by allowing the State of which it is a part, not to be a State. For as Hooker has well observed, the Law of men's actions is one if they be respected only as men; and another when they are considered as parts of the body politic.[14]

Though this particular interpretation of Hooker is not grounded with a citation, its origin is book 1, chapter 16, paragraph 8 of the *Laws*. The

---

14. Coleridge, *Friend*, 2:57.

Hookerian influence can further be traced to issue 5 by Coleridge's use of the idea that through the communication of knowledge we may find a way of facilitating virtue in others. In revising *The Friend* in 1816 he wrote the "Essay on Faith" (situated in the first "Landing-Place"), one of the very few substantive and important revisions; in it he was to define faith as "fidelity to oneself"—or fidelity to God through the symbol of God extant within the *Imago Dei*. To Coleridge knowledge was the vehicle through which fidelity operated, and the essay presents the answer to the question of what constitutes true piety.

> Virtue would not be Virtue, could it be *given* by one fellow-creature to another. To *make use* of all the means and appliances in our power to the actual attainment of Rectitude, is the abstract of the Duty which we owe to ourselves: to *supply* those means as far as we can, comprizes our Duty to others. The question then is, what are these means? Can they be any other than the communication of Knowledge, and the removal of those Evils and Impediments which prevent its' [sic] reception: it may not be in our power to combine both, but it is in the power of every man to contribute to the former, who is sufficiently informed to feel that it is his Duty. If it be said, that we should endeavour not so much to remove Ignorance, as to make the Ignorant religious, Religion herself, through her sacred Oracles, answers for me, that all effective Faith presupposes Knowledge and individual Conviction. If the mere acquiescence in Truth, uncomprehended and unfathomed, were sufficient, few indeed would be the vicious and the miserable, in this country at least, where speculative Infidelity is, Heaven be praised, confined to a small number.[15]

This interpretation is congruent with Hooker's position in book 1, chapter 5 of the *Laws*, where Hooker describes a teleology of virtue (which he calls "goodness") that operates from Man's desire to emulate the goodness of the Divine; this emulation is effected by proceeding in the knowledge of the truth (knowledge facilitates virtue). Hooker writes:

> But the desire of those perfections which grow externally is more apparent; especially of such as are not expressly desired unless they be

---

15. Coleridge, *Friend*, 2:70.

first knowne, or such as are not for any other cause, than for knowledge it selfe desired. Concerning perfections in this kind, that by proceeding in the knowledge of truth and by growing in the exercise of vertue, man amongst the creatures of this inferiour world, aspireth to the greatest conformity with God, this is not only knowne unto us, whom he himself hath so instructed, but even they do acknowledge, who amongst men are not judged the neerest unto him.[16]

Coleridge argues that by coming to a fuller knowledge of the created universe through any branch of investigation—literature, science, philosophy, politics (all of which he, of course, viewed as artificial distinctions)—one may, by transmitting this knowledge to others, facilitate a deeper understanding of the creation on their part, and with that deeper understanding they will become naturally more virtuous persons because they will see the natural sense of the divine plan. Knowledge will bring enlightenment, and enlightenment will bring moral progress—not a new idea on Coleridge's part, but Coleridge makes it much more theological by employing the concept of virtue.

As in Hooker's system, reason is an organic component of Coleridge's doctrine of Man, not a mere faculty of the human mind. "Perhaps, the great majority of men are now fully conscious, that they are born with the god-like *[sic]* faculty of Reason, and that it is the business of Life to develop and apply it? The Jacob's ladder of Truth, let down from Heaven, with all its' *[sic]* numerous Rounds, is now the common Highway, on which we are content to toil upward to the Objects of our Desires? We are ashamed of expecting the end without the means?"[17] Reason is Man's through the doctrine of the *Imago Dei*; in order to arrive at the top of the "Jacob's ladder of truth" rather than at the end of the "common High-way," Man lives by faith. Principles of action became purer through reason applied through the filter of Christianity. All of this is not far away from Hooker's assertion in book 1, chapter 3, paragraph 1 of the *Laws* that "the law of *reason* that which bindeth creatures rea-

---

16. Richard Hooker, *The Folger Library Edition of the Works of Richard Hooker*, 7 vols., ed. W. Speed Hill (Cambridge, MA: Harvard University Press, 1977), 1:73–74.

17. Coleridge, *Friend*, 2:51.

sonable in this world, and with which by reason they may most plainly perceive themselves bound; that which bindeth them, and is not knowen but by speciall revelation from God, *Divine* law; *humane* law that which out of the law either of reason or of God, men probablie gathering to be expedient, they make it a law."[18] Here Hooker is discussing natural law generally. In its universal context it applies to states as bodies politic: a collection of persons under the rule of God. Coleridge and Hooker constantly discuss human action and human virtue on both the micro scale of personal action and the macro scale of corporate action as a body politic.

The legalistic language of Coleridge's discussion of the state and the individual within the context of *The Friend* can in and of itself be taken as an influence of Hooker. For instance, in issue 7 Coleridge describes naval discipline as "the awful power of LAW, acting on natures pre-configured to its influences."[19] Here the word *awful* is used to mean "awe inspiring"; Coleridge's point is that the awe men hold for the concept of law is the source of the respect for discipline on ship rather than the deterrent fear of the pain of corporal punishment. This is surely Hooker's influence, as it is virtually a restatement of Hooker's systematic idea that the positive law of humanity is created in concert with a preconfigured natural law and divine law; awe is inspired by God, not human beings. A further link in this chain of thought is forged in issue 12. Though the link is subtle, it displays at least a consciousness of Hooker's heritage as well as (arguably) a direct influence: "To what then do we owe our strength and our immunity [to Napoleon]? The sovereignty of Law; the incorruptness of its administration; the number and political importance of our religious sects which in an incalculable degree have added to the dignity of the Establishment; the purity of, or at least the decorum of private Morals and the independence, activity and weight of public Opinion? These and similar advantages are doubtless the *materials* of the Fortress. . . ."[20] The reverence for the sovereignty of law is a direct result of Coleridge's assertion that positive law, gleaned and administered through reason, is itself drawn from both divine law (the

18. Hooker, *Folger Library Edition,* 1:63.
19. Coleridge, *Friend,* 2:100.
20. Coleridge, *Friend,* 2:162.

established relationship of church and state) and the laws of nature—
an assertion constructed under Hooker's direct influence. So the picture
of Coleridge's beliefs that emerges in the first dozen numbers of *The
Friend* of 1809 (and it is within these numbers that the great bulk of the
ground of his philosophical discussion takes place) is really a fairly Anglican position: a Protestantism with a classically English aversion to
Continental philosophy, and an emphasis upon a relationship of church
and state that is supported through divine law—with supporting quotations from the Old Testament specifically designed to draw links between the Hebrew state and the Anglican state. Coleridge will go on to
argue that the cement is the national debt and the system of credit. But
what is important here is not the cement (for he is speaking in purely
economic terms here) but the discussion of British law and established
Protestantism extant within the question of debt.

All this is witnessed by a passage expressing his admiration for
Erasmus and Luther (whom he calls "Two Purifiers of Revealed Religion now neglected as obsolete"), immediately followed by a stringent
attack on Rousseau and Voltaire (whom he contrasted with the purifiers of revealed religion as "the two modern conspirators against its
authority who are still the Alpha and the Omega of Continental Ge-
nius"). Coleridge is especially critical of Rousseau's confidence in what
he calls "unaided" reason: "Rousseau . . . in the inauspicious Spirit of his
Age and Birth-Place, had slipped the Cable of his Faith, and steered by
the Compass of unaided reason, ignorant of the hidden Currents that
were bearing him out of his course, and too proud to consult the faithful Charts prized and held sacred by his Forefathers."[21] And all this
comes at the end of essay 5 (contained in issue 8), which immediately
precedes the above-mentioned essay 6: "On the Grounds of Government as Laid Exclusively in the Pure Reason; Or a Statement and Critique of the Third System of Political Philosophy viz. the Theory of
Rousseau and the French Economists." Coleridge is using the Hookerian Anglican position to critique Continental philosophy by combin-
ing its discussion of reason with the language of German idealism and
the latter's *implementation* of its own ideas on reason within its own
system. For Coleridge to build an ethics of pure reason within the text

---

21. Coleridge, *Friend*, 2:113 ff.

of *The Friend,* using the Anglican view of reason, was a far different project from Kant's building of an ethics of "reason alone" using the German conception of reason. Even though Coleridge borrowed the contemporary philosophical language of Kant in building the superstructure of his system, the foundation upon which he erected it was Hooker.

The central problem with Coleman's approach to Hooker is that she seeks to understand *The Laws of Ecclesiastical Polity* as a piece of literature and not as a work of pure theology. She seems to view *The Laws* as a primarily political text, without a theological dimension. Consequently, in her interpretation of Hooker's influence on *The Friend,* she quotes from book 5 only in a political context and ignores the importance of book 8 of the *Laws.* It would seem that her dismissal of any influence is based solely on the fact that Coleridge did not annotate book 8 of the Ashley folio (providing she has read it)—but then he did not annotate beyond book 5 in the Ashley folio, and it is impossible to conclude that he did not read the later books of *The Laws* from this. There is also no way to conclude that he had not read someone else's copy of book 8.

It bears repeating, then, that Hooker's *Laws of Ecclesiastical Polity* is theological in its focus. The concept of the secular had not yet arisen when it was written, and in the sixteenth century all fields of study were still viewed as "*sub ratione Dei*" (as St. Thomas had phrased it earlier). Discrete fields of the academy did not exist, and as such it was natural to address multiple concerns within the corpus of a broad theological treatise. Hence to apply modern categories of interpretation to the text is misguided, and when this practice is followed to its logical conclusion it gives rise to interpretations that are simply wrong. But even this is not the central point. The central problem with Coleman's view of Hooker's focus is not that it applies discrete modern categories to a text that would not have comprehended them when it was written but that she applies these modern categories to *Coleridge's interpretation* of that text. While it is possible to impose modern categories upon a text when it is being used in a modern discussion, it is not possible to impose modern categories upon an intermediate discussion of that text when that intermediate discussion is the subject of debate. It might be debatable whether *The Laws of Ecclesiastical Polity* is best seen as a theological or political text today, but it was not debatable in 1809; in the Georgian period *The Laws* was seen as a theological text—indeed, in 1809 the move away from viewing everything as *sub ratione Dei* was only just beginning, and of course Coleridge was actively fighting against this movement in the text of *The Friend*. The crucial points are whether Hooker believed that laws had their ultimate authority from God or humanity, and whether Coleridge believed that Hooker understood law to derive ultimately from God or humanity. Coleman has the backing of most modern political theorists when she interprets Hooker in terms of the consent of humanity, but she is not correct in imposing it upon Coleridge. She writes:

> A number of other features of Hooker's work can be traced in *The Friend*. For example, Coleridge employs Hooker's notion of consent to sanction the authority of inherent inhuman law. If there be any difference, Coleridge writes, "between a Government and a band of Robbers, an act of consent must be supposed on the part of the People governed" (*TF* ii.103). In Book I of his treatise, Hooker had made it clear that laws derive their ultimate validity from the consent of the people who are to be governed by them: "Lawes they are not therefore which publique approbation hath not made so" (*Lawes*, I. 10.8). Although this notion of consent looks like an eminently liberal idea, it in fact forms the keystone of Hooker's conservatism and of his defence of the established Church. Since a law is the deed of the whole body politic, of which all men are members, every man has a duty to observe that law; thus, the Puritans were duty-bound to conform to the laws of the established Church as laid down by those who had lived before them.[22]

The link she seeks to draw is made by quoting Coleridge from page 103 of *The Friend*; it does not hold. In the paragraph previous to the one she quotes from, Coleridge discusses the idea of a political contract in much more detail:

> . . . It assuredly cannot be denied, that an original (in reality an ever originating) Contract is a very natural and significant mode of ex-

---

22. Coleman, *Coleridge,* 115.

pressing the reciprocal duties of Subject and Sovereign, when we consider the utility of a real and formal State Contract, the Bill of Rights for instance, as a sort of *Est Demonstratum* in politics; and the contempt lavished on this notion, though sufficiently compatible with the Tenets of a Hume, may well surprise us in the Writings of a Protestant Clergyman, who surely owed some respect to a mode of thinking which God himself had authorized by his own example, in the establishment of the Jewish Constitution. In this instance there was no necessity for *deducing* the will of God from the tendency of the laws to the general Happiness: his will was expressly declared.[23]

Coleridge is both grounding this idea in his beloved ante-Davidic Hebrew state and using the model of ancient Israel to contradict Hume's godless philosophy by showing that the idea's roots are theological. Nowhere is Hooker's name mentioned. Here, in its entirety, is the paragraph from which Coleman actually quotes:

With this explanation, the assertion of an original (still better, of a *perpetual*) Contract is rescued from all rational objection; and however speciously it may be urged, that History can scarcely produce a single example of a State dating its primary Establishment from a free and mutual Covenant, the answer is ready: <u>if there be any difference between a Government and a band of Robbers, an act of consent must be supposed on the part of the People governed.</u> Le plus Fort n'est jamais assez fort pour etre *toujours* le maitre, s'il ne transforme sa force en droit et l'obeissance en devoir. ROUSSEAU.— *viribus* parantur provinciae, *jure* retinentur. Igitur *breve* id gaudium, quippe Germani victi magis, quam domiti. FLOR. IV 12 [Coleridge's italics; my underlining][24]

---

23. Coleridge, *Friend*, 2:103.

24. Coleridge, *Friend*, 2:103. The underlined passage is the section quoted by Coleman. The author whom Coleridge cites as FLOR is L. Annaeus (?) Florus, who wrote an epitome of Roman history. His date (even his name) is uncertain. He probably wrote under Hadrian. His work was much used as a school text in the medieval period and was quoted by many authors. This quotation comes from book 2, chapter 30, sections 29–30 (Loeb ed., 338):

In the two paragraphs discussing contract theory Coleridge attributes the idea in its modern form variously to Hume and Rousseau and to Florus. The point is that he is attempting to show that the idea was biblical and not modern. Coleridge's contract theory always derived from the biblical covenant; that is one of his trademarks. His mention of several other philosophers makes clear that if he had drawn the idea from Hooker he would have mentioned Hooker here as he mentions him elsewhere in the text of *The Friend.* Coleman is simply wrong to conclude that the idea was drawn from Hooker's statement in book 1, "Laws they are not therefore which public approbation hath not made so."[25] Coleridge's specific attribution of contract theory to the biblical corpus demonstrates that he did not view the idea as discrete from being *sub ratione Dei.*

Coleman's extensive discussion of Coleridge's politics as a discrete subject, and her criticism of Coleridge's attack on Canning's motives as "inexcusable sophistry," suggest that she has ignored the wider importance to Coleridge of divine right theory as a whole.[26] Again what is important is not the contemporary interpretation of Hooker but the interpretation Coleridge used in 1809. Coleridge's implementation of classical Augustinian just-war theory and his implementation of Augustine's conception of the spirit and the letter suggest that he was working with a very classical theory of state action, and such a classical model would certainly include an element of divine right. Coleridge's system certainly puts a nineteenth-century spin on divine right in which the Christian state acts morally as a corporate body, through its govern-

---

sed difficilius est provincias obtinere quam facere;
viribus parantur, iure retinentur. igitur breve id gaudium.
quippe Germani victi magis quam domiti erant. . . .

[But it is more difficult to retain than to create provinces;
they are won by force, they are secured by justice. Therefore
our joy was short-lived; for the Germans had been defeated
rather than subdued. . . .]

The reference "IV 12" must refer to an earlier system of numbering (and is strange, since the manuscripts refer to "duo libri").

25. Coleman, *Coleridge*, 115.
26. See chapter 9 below.

ment, but the divine right is through the Holy Spirit acting through the democratic electorate rather than through the Holy Spirit's installation of an absolute monarch.[27] In other words, the government rules in God's name by the dual nature of the English constitution. Bishops of the Church of England actively participated in the legislature, the king is crowned by the archbishop of Canterbury, and parish priests often act as magistrates. Coleridge's system, however, emphasizes that with this divine right come responsibilities and that the state must be able to support its actions on moral grounds, rather than merely on the grounds that those actions are the most expedient (as Canning did).

THE GORDIAN KNOT

Coleman's final, and perhaps most grievous, solecism occurs in her discussion of book 22 of *The Friend*. In this discussion, which takes place in her chapter "The Gordian Knot," she forces her own interpretation of the cleavage between public and private action onto Coleridge's discussion of the state acting rightfully through the Christian religion and concludes that "Coleridge's enthusiasm carries him over into the morality of the pagan world"; this she bases on an irrelevant definition of the pagan world from Isaiah Berlin, and she does so without citing Berlin's text, so there is no way to check whether Berlin's discussion was, in fact, relevant to Coleridge.[28] The entirety of the passage of *The Friend* that leads her to this conclusion is quoted below so that Coleridge may stand on his own legs.

> Lastly, it is chiefly to immediate and unequivocal attacks on our own Interests and Honor, that we attach the notion of RIGHT with a full and efficient feeling, prospects of Advantage and though there is a perverse restlessness in human nature, which renders almost all wars popular at their commencement, yet a nation always needs a sense of positive RIGHT to *steady* its spirit. There is always needed

---

27. See chapter 9 below for a detailed discussion of this paradigm and the Hookerian roots of it.

28. Coleman, *Coleridge*, 172–73.

some one reason, short, simple, and independent of complicated calculation, in order to give a sort of muscular strength to the public mind, when the power that results from enthusiasm, animal spirits, and the charm of novelty, has evaporated.

There is no feeling more honorable to our nature, and few that strike deeper root when our nature is happily circumstanced, than the jealousy concerning a positive Right independent of an immediate Interest. To surrender, in our national character, the merest Trifle, that is strictly our Right, the merest Rock on which the waves will scarcely permit the sea fowl to lay its Eggs, at the demand of an insolent and powerful Rival, on a shop-keeper's calculation of Loss and Gain, is in its' *[sic]* final, and assuredly not very distant consequences, a Loss of every thing—of national Spirit, of national Independence, and with these of the very wealth, for which the low calculation was made. This feeling in individuals, indeed in private life, is to be sacrificed to Religion. Say rather that by Religion, it is transmuted into a higher Virtue, growing on an higher and engrafted Branch, yet nourished from the same root that it remains in its' *[sic]* essence the same Spirit, but

Made pure by Thought, and naturaliz'd in Heaven; and he who cannot perceive the moral differences of national and individual duties, comprehends neither the one or the other, and is not a whit the better Christian for being a bad Patriot. Considered nationally, it is as if the Captain of a Man of War should strike and surrender his colours under the pretence, that it would be folly to risk the lives of so many good Christian Sailors for the sake of a *few yards of coarse Canvas!* of such reasoners we take an indignant leave. . . .[29]

Coleman interprets this passage in the following way.

For a brief moment here, Coleridge's enthusiasm carries him over into the morality of the pagan world, the world which, according to Isaiah Berlin, values above all else the "assertion of one's proper claims and the knowledge and power needed to secure their satis-

---

29. Coleridge, *Friend,* 2:305–6.

faction." Conscious that his rhetoric has betrayed him, and that he runs the risk of appearing antagonistic to Christian values, Coleridge cautiously reins his words back in and adds,

> Say rather that by Religion, it is transmuted into a higher Virtue, growing on an higher and engrafted Branch, yet nourished from the same root that it remains in its' essence the same Spirit, but
> > Made pure by Thought, and naturaliz'd in Heaven; (*TF* ii. 305–306)

This sudden turnabout is not very convincing, and as a way of countering the difficulties generated by his enthusiastic nationalism, he draws an important distinction between the spirit and the letter of the Law of Morality. This is the pivot on which all of Coleridge's distinctions turn; it is also the pivot which he hoped would give him sufficient flexibility to hold steady his claim that religious and nationalistic feelings flourish together under one universal and unchanging spirit.[30]

First, it must be made absolutely clear that nowhere in issue 22 of *The Friend* does Coleridge bring up the spirit and the letter. Furthermore, Coleman is wrong to view Coleridge's insistence on the state acting virtuously as an unconvincing turnabout. Coleridge argues here against constructive pacifism on the macro scale (state action) just as he previously argued against pacifism on the micro scale (personal action) in his discussion of the gentleman, his Quaker friend, and the highwayman. He argues against the idea that patriotism ought to be abandoned because of the Christian command to do no harm to one's fellow Christian, and he does this through irony. The irony and the point it makes should be taken at face value. Coleridge is making an argument for the establishment by dismissing pacifism on the grounds of classical Augustinian just-war theory—though incorporating a modern form of divine right theory in which the right flows from God to the entirety of the body politic rather than directly to the head of the body (the sovereign). All of this is consistent with both Augustine and Hooker's book 8. What actually happens in issue 22 is that for the first time Coleridge's classical Toryism comes into full voice. All of this is also inconsistent

---

30. Coleman, *Coleridge*, 172–73.

with Warburton's alliance theory of church and state, and though Warburton is not mentioned by name, other than in the scathing attack
quoted in the epigraph of this chapter, it is clear that Coleridge is implicitly arguing against the alliance model through his employment of
Hooker and Augustine. All of this is also consistent with Gladstone's
discussion of the moral nature of state action that views the state as an
individual actor, and it is likely that this particular passage substantially
influenced Gladstone when he read it in 1829.

This classical Toryism continues in full voice with Coleridge's defense of the British seizure of the Danish fleet. Again Coleman misinter-
prets it. Here her misprision centers on his discussion of the spirit and
letter of international law relevant to the seizure. The opening paragraph
of issue 24 of *The Friend,* entitled "The Law of Nations," reads:

> We may represent to ourselves this original free agency, as a right of
> commonage, the formation of separate States as an enclosure of this
> Common, the Allotments awarded severally to the co-proprietors
> as constituting national Rights, and the Law of Nations as the com-
> mon Register Office of their title deeds. But in all Morality, though
> the principle, which is the abiding *spirit [sic]* of the Law, remains
> perpetual and unaltered, even as that supreme reason in whom and
> from whom it has its' *[sic]* being, yet the *Letter* of the Law, that is, the
> application of it to particular instances and the mode of realizing it
> in actual practice, must be modified by the existing circumstances.
> *What* we should desire to do, the conscience alone will inform us;
> but *how* and *when* we are to make the attempt, and to what extent it
> is in our own to accomplish it, are questions for the judgment, and
> require an acquaintance with facts and their bearings on each other.
> Thence the improvement of our judgment, and the increase of our
> knowledge, on all subjects included within our sphere of action, are
> not merely advantages recommended by prudence, but absolute du-
> ties imposed on us by conscience.[31]

The agricultural image of enclosure is relevant to the domestic politics of 1809, when controversy over enclosure was still very much a live
issue. But this is not the heart of what Coleridge is imaging in the pas-

---

31. Coleridge, *Friend,* 2:321–22.

sage. He is referring to the Augustinian idea of the created world as a commonwealth of Christian society, accepting Augustine's idea of the commonweal from book 19, chapter 24, of *De Civitate Dei*. Augustine writes:

> If one should say, "A people is the association of a multitude of rational beings united by a common agreement on the objects of their love," then it follows that to observe the character of a particular people we must examine the objects of its love. And yet, whatever those objects if it is the association of a multitude not of animals but of rational beings, and is united by a common agreement about the objects of its love, then there is no absurdity in applying to it the title of a "people." And, obviously, the better the objects of this agreement, the better the people; the worse the objects of this love, the worse the people. By this definition of ours, the Roman people is a people and its estate is indubitably a commonwealth. But as for the objects of that people's love—both in the earliest times and in subsequent periods—and the morality of that people as it proceeded to bloody strife of parties and then to the social and civil wars, and corrupted and disrupted that very unity which is, as it were, the health of a people—for all this we have the witness of history; and I have had a great deal to say about it in my preceding books. And yet I shall not make that a reason for asserting that a people is not really a people or that a state is not a commonwealth, so long as there remains an association of some kind or other between a multitude of rational beings united by a common agreement on the objects of its love. However, what I have said about the Roman people and the Roman commonwealth I must be understood to have said and felt about those of the Athenians and of any other Greeks, or of that former Babylon of the Assyrians, when they exercised imperial rule, whether on a small or large scale, in their commonwealths—and indeed about any other nation whatsoever.[32]

In the nineteenth-century context, the entirety of Christendom should be one people united by a common object of their love. Coleridge is

---

32. Augustine, *City of God*, trans. Henry Bettenson (London: Penguin Books, 1984).

arguing that the commonwealth of the created world has been artificially divided by "separate states as an enclosure of this Common" and that the law of nations has been used as the administrative tool to conduct the use of this now partitioned common heritage. John J. O'Mera has suggested that this chapter of book 19 is the heart of the "charter of Christendom," and there is general agreement that *De Civitate Dei* is the fundamental starting point of Western Christian political thought.[33] Coleridge's point is that the modern law of nations is every bit as derivative of divine law as English law is and that action on the international scene requires the same moral considerations as action taken on either the micro scale of personal action or the macro scale of group action. The guide to this action within the now partitioned commonweal is the law, and it must be interpreted via the same Augustinian method that Coleridge had discussed on the personal level earlier: an examination of the letter of the law and the spirit of the law behind the letter. One must use one's reason to examine the law, and that reason will enable virtuous action. Coleridge has applied his original paradigm of virtuous action through reason to action in the international theater. The passage is completely consistent with the entire preceding discussion throughout the text of *The Friend*.

Coleman interprets Coleridge's passage rather differently, however:

> By the "Letter" of the Law, Coleridge means positive law, a body of legislation enforceable by authority; the "spirit," on the other hand, stands for the requirements of morality. The distinction in this passage between the letter and the spirit is paralleled by a further distinction between the realms of conscience and practicability. In emphasizing the need for attending to the particular circumstances and facts of a given case—the "how" and the "when" of our actions— Coleridge suggests that it is not enough for the dictates of conscience to be in harmony with a "perpetual and unaltered" law; they must also be practical and flexible enough to take into account the whole circumstances of a particular case.[34]

---

33. John J. O'Mera, *Charter of Christendom: The Significance of the City of God* (New York: Macmillan, 1961).

34. Coleman, *Coleridge*, 174.

It is strange that Coleman should stress the idea of particular circumstances here when fourteen pages later she will accuse Coleridge of "inexcusable sophistry" for attacking Canning on precisely the grounds of basing his argument on particular historical circumstances. Further, she has completely ignored the fact that Coleridge is referring to Augustine's Pauline doctrine by invoking the terminology of the spirit and the letter—stranger still when he has again made it clear that he has Augustine in mind by adopting Augustine's political theory of the commonweal of Christianity earlier in the passage. By invoking classical Augustinian terminology Coleridge is creating a further theological basis for his paradigm of reason facilitating virtue (drawn from Hooker) that he discussed earlier in *The Friend*; "For the letter killeth and the spirit giveth life," writes Paul. The ground of Augustine's theory—that the letter must be interpreted to find the spirit of the text—is simple and classic Augustinian hermeneutics as expressed in *De Doctrina Christiana* (a text that, because it is a manual for the interpretation of texts, it is fair to assume that a scholar of literature ought to be familiar with). By use of our reason we may interpret the spirit of the letter of the New Testament law and act virtuously as Christian patriots: here Coleridge again is referring back to the double root of the church and state in a modern theory of divine right. So Coleridge is not guilty of inexcusable sophistry at all; rather, he is insisting on a theologically grounded (Tory) polity.

The historical facts bear this out as well, for the action under consideration had significant repercussions for the British government and armed forces in 1809. In 1810 Napoleon would be on the verge of conquering Denmark. Britain's sole protection from the threat of Napoleon was its overwhelming naval superiority—but this relied on the British fleet keeping the French fleet locked down in their ports. As Alistair Horne describes the situation: "It had perhaps been morally reprehensible of Britain to bombard neutral Copenhagen (for a second time) in 1807, after Tilsit, but—not unlike Churchill's desperate attack on the Vichy French fleet at Oran in 1940 to prevent it falling into German hands—it showed that she had no intention of giving in."[35] Horne, however, adds, "Britain was also immensely rich, quite able to go on financing

---

35. Alistair Horne, *How Far from Austerlitz? Napoleon, 1805–1815* (London: Macmillan, 1996), 293.

coalition after coalition. In fact, she was getting richer as, with Napoleon locked up in Europe, she was able to mop up the outlying jewels of the French Empire in India and the Caribbean, and to exploit them for her own benefit. In turn, the capture of the last French Islands in the Caribbean released some seventeen British garrisons to reinforce Wellington."[36]

Most importantly, Napoleon had been considering an invasion of the British Isles since at least 1802 and had already constructed troop landing craft to transport his soldiers across the channel. He was even prepared to lose twenty-five thousand men in the crossing ("One loses that many in a day of combat anyway," he was reported to have said). Furthermore, he believed that breaking the British blockade of the English Channel for as little as eight hours would provide him enough time to land a sufficient force to make the invasion successful because there was no standing regular army *in England* capable of repelling an invasion.

France had been consistently unable to break the English blockade of the channel for the one day she needed because she lacked enough ships of the line. Had Napoleon seized the Danish fleet, an attempt would certainly have been more likely, and though French losses during an attempted crossing would have been immense, Napoleon *might* have been able to establish, at the very least, a solid beachhead of seasoned imperial guard, or perhaps Davot's renowned Third Corps. Troops such as these would have been able to hold off the British land forces for a very long period indeed. It was the French practice (one at which they were masters) to live off land they had captured, so no cross-channel supply lines would have been necessary to sustain the troops before they could be reinforced. In other words, Napoleon needed the Danish fleet for one day only and was prepared to sacrifice it to achieve his objective. Under these circumstances the seizure of the Danish fleet by the British navy was a necessary step in the maintenance of the blockade.[37] It is arguable that it was also necessary in order to relieve persistent fears about invasion on the part of the British public. Though vic-

---

36. Horne, *How Far from Austerlitz*, 296.
37. See David G. Chandler, "Copenhagen, Bombardment of," in *Dictionary of the Napoleonic Wars* (London: Arms and Armour Press, 1979), 105.

tory at Trafalgar had done much to calm the mood of the populace, fears of invasion remained—as the construction of Martello Towers after Trafalgar indicates. Previous to Trafalgar the fear of invasion had been very bad indeed: "Addington's war was to be essentially a defensive one in which the main threat was perceived to be invasion, where an increased militia and volunteer force would have an important role to play. Between 1803 and 1805 the invasion scare reached panic proportions, and the patriotic call to arms led so many to rally to the volunteer cause that proper arms and training could not be provided. . . ."[38] Coleridge's attack on Canning's defense of the seizure in the pages of his serial journal indicates in and of itself that fear of invasion was still a "live issue" for the British public in 1809—or at least that he believed it to be so for his subscribers.

Coleridge's point was that one hundred Danish ships sure to be under French command within two weeks were, in terms of their potency, one hundred ships of the line already arrayed against Britain: they were effectively already hostile rather than neutral. Coleridge also stressed that the ships had not been scuttled—as was the case in 1940 when the British navy, faced with the same dilemma scuttled a French fleet that was about to be captured by the German navy (at the loss of considerable Allied French life). The crews of the Danish fleet had been neither sacrificed nor taken prisoner; rather, the vessels and their munitions had been taken and manned by British crews. Though these facts may not seem theologically relevant to Coleman, they were very much so to Coleridge because his argument sought to emphasize the fact that, in addition to being within the confines of the *ius ad bellum* (a just war), Britain had remained within the confines of the *ius in bello* (a war conducted justly). Coleridge was arguing that Britain had acted within both the spirit and the letter of the laws of nations and that this action was not only moral but virtuous.[39] This was why he was so scathing in his attack on Canning. Canning was acting without moral considerations, while Coleridge believed that the action had been virtuous: in other words, Coleridge believed that Britain had acted virtuously at every opportunity

38. David Johnson, "Amiens 1802: The Phoney Peace," *History Today* 52, no. 9 (2002): 20–26.

39. Coleridge, *Friend*, 2:305–6.

and that Canning made no reference to the issue of virtue. Undertaking political action on the grounds of utilitarian philosophy was anathema to Coleridge: he required an older (Tory) Christian philosophical basis.

The Friend of 1809 is a microcosm of Coleridge's adult project of the fusion of theology and politics. Its text is best seen as a long discussion of theological polity—and indeed it was a journal, so the discussion questions of current events were to some extent unavoidably its focus. Deirdre Coleman has rightly noticed that the Gordian knot of the text is theological polity, and she has even noticed an influence from Hooker; her examination of this theological polity is, however, superficial at best and simply wrong in many instances. Having made his High Tory-ism evident with *The Friend* in 1809, Coleridge went on to write two Lay Sermons on the subject of Christian action in society. The point at which Coleridge became a professional theologian had arrived.

6

The Lay Sermons
The Christian's Actions in Society

THE STATESMAN'S MANUAL

This chapter discusses *The Statesman's Manual,* published in December 1816, and the second Lay Sermon, published in April 1817. These were the first overtly theological works Coleridge had written since the *Lectures on Revealed Religion.* Moreover, they mark the first instances in which Coleridge took an indisputably conservative *and* High Church stand in public. Previously he had taken conservative positions in political discussion, as when he defended the seizure of the Danish fleet, and such positions had been derived from religious principles. These were the first texts, however, in which he took a High Church position on religious issues—most demonstrably on education—and in purely religious documents. This claim will be illustrated by an exegesis of the text of the *Lay Sermons* and by a historical discussion of the Lancaster-Bell debate (to which Coleridge alludes in the text). Parallels with near-identical points made by John Keble in his Assize Sermon of 1833 will then be drawn to demonstrate that Coleridge's arguments were part of a conservative tradition that extended both before him and after him.

The Statesman's Manual was the first prose work written after Coleridge moved into Dr. Gillman's home in Highgate, London, where he would remain a resident for the rest of his life. Gillman was able at least to regulate both Coleridge's style of life and the dosage of his opium habit, and this may explain why the Lay Sermons demonstrate a cogency of rhetoric and linear thought that are not present in previous works—and most specifically in *The Friend.* In other words, there is a steadiness of thought present only in an embryonic form in the earlier works. More-over, in 1816 Coleridge moved from writing serial and occasional pieces to publishing more substantial works that stood on their own as com-plete endeavors. Though he continued to undertake freelance journal-istic work, he never again focused his full attention on it.

From 1816 onward, his work would be overtly rather than innately theological in nature. Every published work he wrote after 1816 (as well as the unpublished *On the Divine Ideas*) would be a theological text: *The Lay Sermons, Aids to Reflection, On the Constitution of the Church and State,* and *Confessions of an Inquiring Spirit* were the remaining works of his life, and each of them was a theological enterprise (the *Bi-ographia Literaria* had been finished in Bristol in 1815 and had been originally sent to a printer there). His theological position was gener-ally speaking a fairly conservative and High Church one. This is also evident from important ecclesiological essays in the *Literary Remains* (which, though written later than the *Lay Sermons,* are discussed below to reinforce the argument that from 1816 forward Coleridge was essen-tially a High Church theologian).

Precisely when, or how often, Coleridge returned to liturgical An-glican worship is unknown, but it is clear that as early as 1809 he consid-ered himself to be arguing a conservative, establishment position against a utilitarian one and that he died in the church that had baptized him. His annotations to the Book of Common Prayer demonstrate his com-mitment to the Church of England. Parts of these were written at least as early as 1827; the annotations to the Eucharist are dated December 14, 1827, and the notes to the Thirty-nine Articles are dated 1831; other notes are not dated, but the pervasive annotations suggest that he read the Prayer Book often. He wrote notes on "The Sacrament of the Eucha-rist," "Companion to the Altar," "The Communion Service," "The Mar-riage Service," "The Communion of the Sick," the liturgy for both the eleventh and the twenty-fifth Sundays after Trinity, and Psalms 8, 68, 72, 74, 82, 87, 88, 104, 105, 110, 118, and 126.[1] His annotation to one of the Thirty-nine Articles appears below:

> XX. [article number] It is mournful to think how many recent
> writers have criminated *[sic]* our Church in consequence of their

---

1. These annotations are taken from Coleridge, *Complete Works.*

own ignorance and inadvertence in not knowing, or not noticing, the contra-distinction here meant between power and authority. Rites and ceremonies the Church may ordain *jure proprio:* on matters of faith her judgment is to be received with reverence, and not gainsaid but after repeated inquiries, and on weighty grounds.

Well! I could most sincerely subscribe to all these articles. September, 1831.[2]

Here Coleridge indicates that he is beyond all question a Conformist. It is also important to note how warmly he speaks of the Church of England as "our church." So it is clear that by at least 1827—and all the evidence points to this being the case much earlier as well (see below)—Coleridge considered himself to be a communicating member of the Church of England and no longer a Unitarian. In fact, the short chronology that appears in each introduction to the Bollingen series states that on May 10, 1827, Coleridge took his first communion since Cambridge and suggests that this was prompted by a serious illness.[3] This information does not appear at all in Valerie Purton's *Coleridge Chronology* (probably the most reliably definitive secondary source of specific events in Coleridge's life) or in Chambers's biography (which is the most well-footnoted piece of history), nor do any of the letters of the summer of 1827 mention this—and a great deal of the epistolary material from that summer is theological in nature. (Coleridge was engaged with H. F. Cray—who had been named curator of books for the British Museum—in a prolonged discussion of the Bible, and though in the period following May 10 there is a gap in the correspondence until May 28, a letter written on that day to Cray discusses the book of Revelation, and the subject of Apocalypse, in detail without mentioning the church.) But though the Bollingen chronology is not footnoted, there is no good reason to disbelieve that Coleridge did take communion in 1827—and indeed the fact that the annotation to the Eucharist in the Prayer Book was written in the same year gives this some circumstantial credence.

The *Lay Sermons* became the first in a series of works written with the Anglican communion specifically in mind. The two texts should therefore be seen as the embarkation point of an Anglican project. Each

---

2. Coleridge, *Complete Works*, 5:28.
3. See, for instance, Coleridge, *Friend*, 1:xxxiii.

was written *within* the Church of England tradition and designed to educate persons in the practice of Conforming Anglicanism. Each displays elements of Coleridge's larger theological project, as first described in *The Friend* of 1809 and developed in the later works. The two sermons seek a synthesis of polity and piety; the social hermeneutics of Coleridge's mature theological project is clearly identifiable.

To use the image of cards: the Conformist hand that Coleridge was playing for most of his adult life was first tipped in a fairly subtle way. The text of *The Statesman's Manual* is subtitled "The Bible the Best Guide to Political Skill and Foresight" and is "Addressed to the Higher Classes of Society,"[4] though importantly Coleridge said in a letter to George Frere: "The Title to the present ought to have been, and I had so directed it—addressed to the Learned and Reflecting of all Ranks and Professions, especially among the Higher class."[5] *The Statesman's Manual* is, as far as it is anything generic, a treatise on education—and education was a theme to which Coleridge returned again and again in his religious writings. Coleridge's general point within the text is that to implement the scheme of charity and Jubilee presented in the Bible— that is, to form a Christian nation (commonwealth) on the patterns prescribed by the Bible and Augustine, as discussed in *The Friend*—the higher classes (or "the reflecting of all classes") should implement a biblical commonwealth through the education of the nation. It is an inchoate form of Coleridge's idea of the clerisy.[6]

> We hear, at least, less of the jargon of this *enlightened age*. After fatiguing itself, as performer or spectator in the giddy figure-dance of political changes, Europe has seen the shallow foundations of its self-complacent faith give way; and among men of influence and property, we have now more reason to apprehend the stupor of despondence, than the extravagancies of hope, unsustained by experience, or of self-confidence not bottomed on principle.

---

4. Samuel Taylor Coleridge, *Lay Sermons,* ed. R. J. White, vol. 6 of *The Collected Works of Samuel Taylor Coleridge,* Bollingen Series 75 (Princeton: Princeton University Press, 1972), 3. Subsequent citations to this work are given parenthetically in the text.

5. Coleridge, *Collected Letters,* 4:695.

6. See chapter 9 below.

In this rank of life the danger lies, not in any tendency to innovation, but in the choice of the means for preventing it. And here my apprehensions point to two opposite errors; each of which deserves a separate notice. The first consists in a disposition to think that as the Peace of Nations has been disturbed by the diffusion of a false light, it may be re-established by excluding the people from all knowledge and all prospect of amelioration. O! never, never! Reflection and stirrings of mind, with all their restlessness, and all the errors that result from their imperfection, from the *Too much,* because the *Too little,* are come into the world. The Powers, that awaken and foster the spirit of curiosity, are to be found in every village: Books in every hovel. . . . Here as in so many other cases, the inconveniences that have arisen from a thing's having become too general, are best removed by making it universal. (39)

Coleridge desired a national education, and he was careful to note that the mere instruction of literacy and arithmetic was not itself an *education.* He sought a nation of more than merely literate *hoi polloi:* he desired a society that would be taught to use its reason—one composed of persons who were able to reflect upon their decisions. Now, this itself is not so remarkable, but what is worthy of comment is the manner in which Coleridge wished this education to take place. "Education," he argued, "consists in *educing* the faculties, and forming the habits; the means varying according to the sphere in which the individuals to be educated are likely to act and become useful" (40). Through a system of education, Coleridge believed, the populace could become better Christians. So education was integral to Coleridge's idea of a Christian nation—even at this relatively early stage (in a far less clearly defined form than it would later be in *On the Constitution of the Church and State,* where he advocated an education through the state church—the clerisy). Moreover, it was the theme of education that tipped the High Church hand Coleridge had decided to play: for during his discussion of education in general he chose to enter the Lancaster-Bell educational methodology debate, vehemently upon the side of Dr. Bell. Some explanation of that debate is necessary.

The system of mutual tuition, in which older boys and girls were used as prefects to conduct and correct lessons to groups of younger students while the master walked through the class and checked the work of all the prefects, was developed independently by two men virtually simultaneously. Some eight thousand miles separated Joseph Lancaster (a midlands Quaker) and Dr. Bell (a Church of England missionary in India) at the point when the systems were conceived—but the method was identical. The amount of ink and breath that was wasted arguing about the differences in minutiae of the teaching tools, such as individual lesson cards versus a large placard that all could read from a short distance, was absurd. The two systems were for all practical purposes identical save in one respect: one was invented by a Quaker in England (Lancaster) and the other by an Anglican missionary priest in India (Bell). The number of venomous comments published against Lancaster by persons as high up within the establishment as Bishop Herbert Marsh is indeed remarkable, considering that the schemes were *pedagogically* identical. Coleridge shared the Anglican preference for Bell, but his praise of the system contained a sting in the tail: "I cannot but denounce the so called Lancastrian schools as pernicious beyond all power of compensation by the new acquirement of Reading and Writing.—But take even Dr. Bell's original and unsophisticated plan, which I myself regard as an especial gift of Providence to the *human race;* and suppose this incomparable machine, this vast moral steam-engine to have been adopted and in free motion throughout the Empire; it would yet appear to me a most dangerous delusion to rely on it as if this of itself formed an efficient national education" (43). Though Coleridge was immensely complimentary to Bell's system, calling it a gift of providence, his own concerns about the difference between education and literacy, his conviction that education involved reason and not merely the tools of reading and arithmetic, are equally evident. He was concerned that even a system of which he approved, such as Bell's, should not be implemented on its own. To Coleridge, for whom education was a matter of educing the faculties and "forming the habits by which they were educed," Lancaster's system was dangerous because there was an opportunity for it to form *Quaker* habits in destitute Anglican children who were attending Lancaster's charity schools as the only available means of obtaining an education.

Both systems were practiced out of manuals. A typical manual of Bell's system was compiled in 1820 by W. Buckwell, incumbent of Langnor, in Staffordshire, and of Earl Stearndale, in Derbyshire, under the title *A Small Manual for the Use of Village Schools (in Which an Attempt Is Made to Assist Plain Country School Masters and Mistresses to Under-*

stand and to Adopt the Rev. Dr. Bell's System of Instruction).[7] Though the manual was four years younger than *The Statesman's Manual,* it was merely a codified printing of lessons that Dr. Bell had himself described in his book *The Madras System of Education.* That is to say, it contained different sections of the *Book of Common Prayer* (mostly the Catechism, the Creeds, and biblical passages) transcribed into short "gobbets" for the consumption of schoolchildren. This was the difference between Bell's system and Lancaster's: that the "habits" (the pieces of text children learned to read) that were used to educe the mental faculties in Bell's system were drawn from the Anglican catechism and creeds. Lancaster, on the other hand, used for his texts patriotic passages, such as the national anthem. For instance, Lancaster used the words "God Save The King" as the first sentence children were taught to write. He was a patriotic and deeply charitable man and was responsible for the education of hundreds of thousands of poor children, but he was attacked virulently because he chose not to use moral passages from the Book of Common Prayer as his set texts. When Lancaster cited biblical passages he did so in a denominationally neutral way, by no means privileging a Quaker interpretation. Yet the mere fact that he was a Quaker was enough to condemn him in the eyes of High Church Anglicans.[8] By his vehement support of Bell, Coleridge made it very clear indeed that he was firmly and inexorably identified with the side of the established church—and the High Church establishment at that, which viewed Lancaster's system as very dangerous because it placed a Nonconformist in the position of teaching biblical passages to the children of Conformists, and, as Bishop Marsh had earlier made plain, distributing the Bible without the Prayer Book was unacceptable to the High Church faction.[9]

In his early years, and indeed occasionally up to his departure for Malta, Coleridge had spoken of the Quaker community with some

---

7. There doubtless were others, but this is the only one that I have been able to locate.

8. See below.

9. Marsh's pamphlet went through multiple editions; one surviving is "An Inquiry into the Consequences of Neglecting to Give the Prayer Book with the Bible . . ." (printed in Cambridge, 1812). For the authoritative treatment of pamphlet survival, see "Towards a Bibliometric Analysis of the Surviving Record 1701–1800," in *The Cambridge History of the Book in Britain,* vol. 5, *1695–1830,* ed. Suarez and Turner, 39–65.

respect, though he seems to have disliked its antiliturgical practices. In a letter to John Prior Estlin written on December 7, 1802, he had even gone so far as to suggest that it was the faith closest to his own principles: "I approve altogether & embrace entirely the *Religion* of the Quakers, but exceedingly dislike the *sect*, & their own notions of their own Religion."[10] Here in *The Statesman's Manual*, in 1816, Coleridge answered definitively the question of which communion he belonged to. Coleridge also seemed to be unaware of the inconsistency of attacking Lancaster in a text in which the fundamental building block of his argument was Christian charity (it was the Quaker principle of charity that had motivated Lancaster to found his charity schools). Coleridge's commitment was clearly not to charity in general, then, but to charity under the auspices of the established church—a High Church position.

Within *The Statesman's Manual* one of his primary purposes was to make plain his view that the educated and upper classes of society had as their responsibility the education of the remainder of society—a theme that he would discuss in great detail during his discussion of the clerisy as a national educating faculty operating through the parish in *On the Constitution of the Church and State*. Yet he was unwilling to select his educators from any source other than the established church.

There is an interesting parallel between the views expressed in Coleridge's Lay Sermon and Keble's Assize Sermon of 1833. This is not to suggest a causal relationship or a direct influence, but it is noteworthy that Coleridge's religious concerns (as expressed in the Lay Sermons) were pervasive enough to be expressed some eighteen years later in the launch of the Oxford Movement. Keble wrote:

> What are the symptoms, by which one may judge most fairly, whether or no a nation, as such, is becoming alienated from God and Christ? . . .
>
> One of the most alarming, as a symptom, is the growing indifference, in which men indulge themselves, to other men's religious sentiments. Under the guise of charity and toleration we are come almost to this pass; *that no difference, in matters of faith, is to disqualify for our approbation and confidence, whether in public or domestic life.* Can we conceal it from ourselves, that every year the practice is becoming more common of trusting men unreservedly in the

---

10. Coleridge, *Collected Letters*, 2:892–93.

most delicate and important matters, without one serious inquiry, whether they do not hold principles which make it impossible for them to be loyal to their CREATOR REDEEMER, and SANC-TIFIER? Are not offices conferred, partnerships formed, intimacies courted,—nay, (what is almost too painful to think of,) do not parents commit their children to be educated, do they not encourage them to intermarry, in houses, on which Apostolical Authority would rather teach them to set a mark, as unfit to be entered by a faithful servant of CHRIST?[11]

So, the parallel is clear; Keble labeled education as among the most important in a list of those symptoms of apostasy "almost too painful to think of." Education, and the responsibility for the upper classes to oversee its correct dissemination, was a prime focus of *The Statesman's Manual,* and Coleridge's stance on the Lancaster-Bell debate showed just how important he felt it was for the Church of England to have the prime responsibility—one might say the only facility—to provide education to the majority Conformist population. Clearly, church school education was a vital part of Coleridge's blueprint for the Christian commonwealth that he believed was England's final cause; the control of ideas through state education served to protect the truth and to ensure that it would be passed on to the next generation in an untainted form. These were classical conservative, High Church, views that Keble was to bring up eighteen years later, and with which Coleridge, along with Marsh and other high churchmen, was preoccupied; they also hark back to disputes, chief among them the Sacheverell trial, during Queen Anne's reign: a subject that will be discussed at length.[12]

THE SECOND LAY SERMON

The second Lay Sermon was "Addressed to the Higher and Middle Classes on the Existing Distresses and Discontents" (119). The distresses and discontents to which Coleridge alluded were, of course, political.

---

11. John Keble, *National Apostasy Considered in a Sermon Preached in St. Mary's, Oxford, before His Majesty's Judges of Assize* (Oxford: Printed by S. Collingwood Printer to the University for J. H. Parker, 1833), 11, 15. Emphasis and use of all caps in original.

12. See chapters 9 and 11 below.

Within Coleridge's idea of the Christian society the Christian duty of the upper class—the university educated—was to educate hoi polloi; the Christian duty of the middle classes—merchants, businessmen, and clerks—was to create an infrastructure that might provide them with sufficient sustenance; this was to be done through charitable action and charitable monitory donations on the part of the merchant and business classes. This was the subject of the second *Lay Sermon*, the best précis of which is contained in the concluding paragraph.

> Our manufacturers must consent to regulations; our gentry must concern themselves in the *education* as well as in the *instruction* of their natural clients and dependents, must regard their estates as secured indeed from all human interference by every principle of law, and policy, but yet as offices of trust, with duties to be performed, in the sight of God and their Country. Let us become a better people, and the reform of all the public (real or supposed) grievances, which we use as pegs whereon to hang our own errors and defects, will follow of itself. In short, let every man measure his efforts by his power and his sphere of action, and do all he can do! Let him contribute money where he cannot act personally; but let him act personally and in detail wherever it is practicable. Let us palliate where we cannot cure, comfort where we cannot relieve; and for the rest rely upon the promise of the King of Kings by the mouth of his Prophet, "BLESSED ARE YE THAT SOW BESIDE ALL WATERS." (230)

The Lay Sermon was actually a rather clotted philosophical attack upon the lack of charity within England's industrial and mercantile society. It was not so much an attack upon industrialization itself as an attack upon excesses of commercialization: "OVERBALANCE OF THE COMMERCIAL SPIRIT IN CONSEQUENCE OF THE ABSENCE OF WEAKNESS OF THE COUNTER-WEIGHTS; this overbalance . . . displaying itself 1. in the COMMERCIAL WORLD itself; 2. In the Agricultural; 3. In the Government; and, 4. In the combined Influence of all three on the more numerous and labouring Classes" (169). In essence Coleridge was describing a culture of selfishness, the excesses of which he believed could be countered only by "the slow progress of intellect, the influences of religion, and irresistible events guided by Providence"—reason facilitating virtue. John Colmer, in his book *Coleridge, Critic of Society,* sees the second Lay Sermon as addressing economic issues—though he lays more stress on the implications of the work for agriculture: "In the first part Coleridge seeks to delineate the features of those who claim that they are able to prescribe an immediate cure for the complex distresses of the country. These are the popular demagogues and political empirics, and with the aid of a passage from Isaiah he heaps a torrent of denunciation on their heads. The middle and by far the longest section is taken up with an analysis of the ultimate causes of the present social disorders. The last section is the shortest and the weakest. Consisting of only two pages it prescribes the remedies."[13] For Colmer, the last section, though the weakest, is also in some ways the most practical: "Nevertheless, at the very end of the second *Lay Sermon* Coleridge does offer one definite and practical solution to the sufferings brought about by the process of industrialization. 'Our manufacturers must consent to regulations,' he declares and a year later he wrote circulars to rally opinion behind Sir Robert Peel in his attempt to legislate on behalf of the children in the cotton mills."[14] Because the longest section of the text, the middle third according to Colmer, is speculative economics, which Colmer points out are remarkably good for their time, there is not much religious material in the second Lay Sermon.[15] But a large section of this middle third is spent arguing against the Poor Laws of the time. As Colmer puts it, Coleridge "was certain that the Poor Laws exerted a demoralizing effect both on the poor and on the classes who were responsible for their continuance."[16] Coleridge felt that the economics of the period generally, and the Poor Laws specifically, were uncharitable and therefore un-Christian. His opposition to them was moral, and though he did not advocate the egalitarian alternative he had advocated as a young man when he called for the abolition of property, he was still genuinely concerned about the plight of the poor and offered what he saw as a serious alternative: namely charity. The point of Coleridge's system is that it took the maintenance of the indigent and destitute out of the realm of the state and placed it within the realm of the church. Most people thought the Poor Laws too generous, and Coleridge wanted to shift the "burden" from the macro scale of the state acting for society

13. John Colmer, *Coleridge, Critic of Society* (Oxford: Clarendon Press, 1959), 139.

14. Colmer, *Coleridge,* 140.

15. Colmer, *Coleridge,* 143–50.

16. Colmer, *Coleridge,* 144.

to the micro scale of individual Christian persons acting charitably. He was not against the free market (far from it), but he did not see the market as a vehicle for producing a minimum standard of living, as Thomas Chalmers did.[17] To repeat: he was against excessive mercantilism and believed that the church provided the best set of brakes to slow the rapid rise of inequality produced by rapid industrialization and England's transition from a predominantly agrarian society to a predominantly industrial one. He was refining the discussion of the commonwealth made in *The Friend*, where he had used the image of enclosure, to a more practical plan of implementation.[18]

What is important is that the second Lay Sermon displays the recurring theme of reason leading to virtuous action through reflection just as *The Statesman's Manual* did. Colmer was not quite correct in the following quotation; the point is actually that the "church" *comprised* the population of England, so if the distresses of the poor would be relieved *personally* (individually, or on the micro scale) then it would indeed be the "church" that "administered" poor relief—by its fostering of charity in individual Christians through the clerisy. "Clearly in his later life Coleridge did not anticipate that the Church should replace the State as the organization responsible for the administration of a complicated system of poor relief. He hoped that the distresses would be relieved personally by its members acting in the spirit of Christ and not in accordance with the laws formulated by the new school of political economists. A disbelief in the efficacy of private charity and a total reliance on a system of state measures was 'the essence of the new blasphemy,' he declared."[19] Obviously, Coleridge did not anticipate a situation where the church took on the role of the modern civil service by dispensing a dole: to say this is unnecessary and silly—of course the concept would be completely alien to him. The point that Colmer does not seem to recognize is that Coleridge's discussion of the actions of the church on the micro scale of *individual* action also constitutes a discussion of its actions at the level of the macro scale of *civil* action: *this is the entire point of discussing the church and state as an organic unity composed of the same individuals.*

---

17. See chapter 11 below.

18. See chapter 5 above.

19. Colmer, *Coleridge*, 145.

The theme of reason facilitating virtue would dominate *Aids to Reflection*, and it was a theme that recurred over and over again in *The Statesman's Manual*. The skeleton of Coleridge's social plan was to use the university educated (i.e., the clerisy) to educate the nation, and by the word *educate* he had not merely meant "to make literate" but rather to *educate:* to cultivate reason, and thereby to facilitate virtuous action. That educated nation he envisioned would in turn make the "slow progress of the intellect" that would in turn facilitate the influences of Christianity and its foundation in charity. Hence the irresistible events guided by providence would build a commonwealth where Englishmen would become "a better people, and the reform of all public (real or supposed) grievances, which we use as pegs whereon to hang our own errors and defects, will follow of itself."

The second sermon was very much within the context of the Church of England: it was a sermon advocating a social program within the context of a Christian nation and was preached to a nation sitting within a single theoretical Church. The sermon viewed all of England as one Christian community that could be brought closer to Coleridge's chosen telos, the Christian commonwealth, through a communal cooperation in which the upper classes gave to as much as they gained from the working classes.

Throughout the *Lay Sermons* a theology was preached that was built upon a plan that had been described in rudimentary form in *The Friend* of 1809 and was consistent with the plans that would be advocated in Coleridge's later work. The text shows Coleridge, as a conforming member of the Church of England, implementing the Anglican theological tradition and drawing a more thorough (but still incomplete) plan for a religious society than he had been able to sketch in *The Friend*. Coleridge displayed High Church concerns similar to those that Keble and the Tractarians would express in the 1830s.

The Lay Sermons were the first of several attempts at setting out the scheme that Coleridge would call his lifetime's work, which may be best described as the nexus of political, philosophical, and religious ideas. It was a project that would take a number of different refined forms, each of them more refined in its particular focus—as each of the remaining chapters of this work will show.

7

Aids to Reflection
Dissecting the Changeling

He had fought his way back to Anglicanism.

—J. W. Wand, *The Second Reform*

J. W. WAND WRITES OF COLERIDGE'S WRITINGS THAT "IN POETRY his best known work is the *Ancient Mariner*, with its equally strong sense of the numinous and of the aesthetic quality of nature. In philosophy he is best remembered by his *Aids to Reflection*, which is a collection of aphorisms largely derived from Archbishop Leighton. It establishes much the same position as the poem by asserting that facts cannot be conceived without value."[1] *Aids to Reflection* (1825) is important to my argument in a basic way: it was a "collaboration" between Coleridge and a number of Anglican thinkers (chiefly Leighton). Yet it is also surprisingly unimportant to our topic because the sections that Coleridge wrote himself are concerned with the project of idealism and were influenced primarily by Schelling and the neo-Platonists. The paradox of *Aids to Reflection* is that while it was a landmark in the process by which Coleridge absorbed elements of the Anglican tradition (thereby continu-

---

1. J. W. Wand, *The Second Reform* (London: Faith Press, 1953), 53.

ing his realignment with the orthodox Church of England), this landmark status is true only of the first section of the work—the form the project was originally envisioned to take. The later sections of the work, where Coleridge aphorizes more contemporary material than Leighton, is irrelevant to Coleridge's relationship with the Anglican Church—though Douglas Hedley's work argues that it is very much relevant to the overall Coleridgean project of a theological polity.[2]

DISSECTING THE CHANGELING

This paradox is substantially unraveled through an examination of the "Advertisement" to the first edition of *Aids to Reflection*; it was never reprinted, and this is a pity, for it gives a good insight into how Coleridge himself viewed the work:

> In the bodies of several species of Animals there are found certain Parts, of which neither the office, the functions, nor the relations could be ascertained by the Comparative Anatomist, till he had become acquainted with the state of the Animal before birth. Something sufficiently like these (for the purpose of an illustration, at least) applies to the Work here offered to the Public. In the introductory portion there occur several passages, which the Reader will be puzzled to decypher, without some information respecting the original design of the Volume, and the Changes it has undergone during its immature and embryonic state. On this account only, I think myself bound to make it known, that the work was proposed and begun as a mere Selection from the Writings of Archbishop Leighton, under the usual title of The Beauties of Archbishop Leighton, with a few notes and a biographical preface by the Selector. Hence the term, *Editor,* subscribed to the notes, and prefixed alone or conjointly to the Aphorisms, accordingly as the Passage was written entirely by myself, or only modified and (*avowedly*) [emphasis in original] interpolated. I continued the use of the word on the plea of uniformity: though like most other deviations from propriety of

---

2. See below.

language, it would probably have been a wiser choice to have omitted or exchanged it. The various Reflections, however, that pressed on me while I was considering the motives for selecting this or that passage; the desire for enforcing, and as it were integrating, the truths contained in the Original Author, by adding those which the words suggested or recalled to my own mind; the conversation with men of eminence in the Literary and Religious Circles, occasioned by the Objects which I had in view; and lastly, the increasing disproportion of the Commentary to the Text, and the too marked differences in the frame, character, and colors of the two styles; soon induced me to recognize and adopt a revolution in my plan and object, which had in fact actually taken place without my intention, and almost unawares. It would indeed be more correct to say, that the present Volume owed its accidental origin to the intention of compiling one of a different description, than to speak of it as the same Work. It is not a change in the child, but a changeling.

Still, however, the selections from Leighton, which will be found in the prudential and moral Sections of this Work, and which I could retain consistently with its present form and matter, will both from the intrinsic excellence and from the characteristic beauty of the passages, suffice to answer two prominent purposes of the original plan; that of placing in a clear light the principle which pervades all Leighton's Writings—his sublime View, I mean, of Religion and Morality as the means of reforming the human Soul in the Divine Image (*Idea*); and that of exciting an interest in the Works, and an affectionate reverence for the name and memory, of this severely tried and truly primitive Churchman.[3]

In the light of Coleridge's delineation of the finished *Aids to Reflection* as a "changeling"—a work that changed into something it originally was not intended to be—the argument about it being of paradoxical importance will become more clear. In other words, as will be demonstrated further below, *Aids to Reflection* actually contains two separate

---

3. S. T. Coleridge, "Advertisement," in *Aids to Reflection in the Formation of a Manly Character on the Several Grounds of Prudence, Morality, and Religion* . . . (London: Taylor and Hessey, 1825).

Table 1. Diagramming the Changeling

Section	Leighton	Coleridge	Both	Others
Introduction			29	2
On Sensibility		1		
Prudential Aphorisms	1	2	1	
Moral and Religious Aphorisms	34	3	14	
Aphorisms on Spiritual Religion			1	5[a]
Aphorisms on That Which Is Indeed Spiritual Religion	5	8	2	9[b]
Conclusion			The Entirety	

a. Four by Henry More and one by John Hacket.

b. One by Burnet and Coleridge, one by Hooker, five by Jeremy Taylor, one by Luther, and one by Field.

works: a manual, or primer, for young clergymen constructed from Leighton with commentary by Coleridge, and a broader idealist project constructed by Coleridge with occasional aphorisms taken from other sources (Leighton and others).

Aids to Reflection consists of approximately 118 aphorisms, of which Coleridge wrote 44 (counting the undivided section of the work "On Sensibility" as one aphorism).[4] Leighton supplies 40 of the total number. Coleridge and Leighton in concert (i.e., Coleridge embroidering on a piece of prose from Leighton rather than commenting after a passage from Leighton) account for a further 19 aphorisms. Other authors supply 14 as follows: Henry More, 4; John Hacket, 1; Gilbert Burnet (with Coleridge), 1; Richard Hooker, 1; Jeremy Taylor, 5; Luther, 1; Richard Field, 1. Table 1 shows which author supplied what to which section of *Aids to Reflection*.

---

4. This count does not separate comments from original aphorisms—and adopts the numbering system used by Coleridge.

Dissecting the changeling in this way shows that the original project of a primer for young clerics was constituted by the "Moral and Religious Aphorisms" and to an extent by the "Aphorisms on That Which Is Indeed Spiritual Religion." That this latter section was a part of the original is demonstrated by the fact that of the five aphorisms attributed to Leighton, two (nos. 2 and 24) are approximately fifteen pages each, while one very long section by Coleridge (a twelve-page section of commentary by Coleridge on aphorism no. 8) is a treatise "On the Difference in Kind of Reason and the Understanding," which is clearly part of the changeling spliced into the original project. The changeling, then, consists of "Introduction," "On Sensibility," "Aphorisms on Spiritual Religion," odd bits of "Aphorisms on That Which Is Indeed Spiritual Religion" (especially the section on reason and the understanding), and the "Conclusion."

The epigraph to this chapter has been chosen for two reasons. First, Bishop Wand was a careful and penetrating commentator on the history of the Church of England in the first half of the nineteenth century, and one who anticipated the conclusions of contemporary revisionists like Nockles in an embryonic form some forty years ago; he therefore serves as an excellent example of an informed but detached commentator.[5] Second, Wand fell into the subtle error of not "dissecting the changeling." In other words, though he noted that the aphorisms that constitute *Aids to Reflection* are "largely derived from Archbishop Leighton," he drew his interpretation of the work as a whole from the "changeling project"— that section of the text written solely by Coleridge.[6] This is a paradigm of interpretation that has been followed by most commentators on *Aids to Reflection* (including Douglas Hedley, whose work will be discussed below). Though there has certainly been some valid interpretation of *Aids to Reflection* taken as a whole, it *is* important to note that there are two distinct projects within the work. Most, if not all, commentators on the work have failed to make this distinction. Moreover, the distinction is of particular importance to the ecclesiastical historian: for if he does not make it, Anglican elements of *Aids to Reflection* are swallowed

---

5. Wand is not a Coleridgean, though he argues that Coleridge was the real progenitor of the Lux Mundi school.

6. Wand, *Second Reform*, 53.

by the idealist project (in the form of the introduction, conclusion, and pieces of the later sections) that brackets the primer—constituted by the sections composed primarily of Leighton's writings.

LEIGHTON

Coleridge was not alone in his enthusiasm for the thought of Robert Leighton, though scholars do not seem to have been aware of this. A staggering seventy editions of various works by Leighton were published between 1748 and 1910, and more astonishingly still, sixty-eight of them were produced during the nineteenth century. Forty-one editions of Leighton's *Whole Works* were published in London, Edinburgh, and New York City between 1748 and 1875, and twenty-six editions of *Selections and Occasional Writings* in London and New York City between 1805 and 1884, along with three editions of the *Rules and Instructions* in 1795, 1838, and 1910. So when Coleridge chose to use Leighton as a starting point for his primer, he saw himself as riding a wave of orthodoxy that had not yet crested. This is important because it illuminates the hand he believed he was playing. He originally viewed his project as the creation of a primer of orthodoxy for young men in the Church of England.

The *Whole Works* was usually produced in four volumes, though there were a substantial number of editions produced in two volumes— and even a few where the *Whole Works* was printed in one volume. *Aids to Reflection* was produced entirely from the 1820 London edition "Printed for Ogle, Duncan, and Co.; John Hatchard and Son; L. B. Seeley; and Parker, Oxford, and Deighton, Cambridge."[7] Several manuscript notes have been preserved on the opening leaves of the edition;

---

7. British Library catalog no. C126h1. This is listed under books owned by S. T. Coleridge in the catalog. The British Library acquired the set of four volumes by donation from the Pilgrim Trust. The edition has been rebound twice, once in what appears to be a late Victorian leather cover (no date has been recovered for this rebinding) on which is written "Leighton's Works Volume I (II, III, IV)—MS. Notes by S. T. Coleridge." This cover has been preserved in thin spine panels that bear only the writing. The British Library had the volumes conserved with new boards bound in plain blue cloth.

one of these was penned by "E. H. C." (Ernest Hartley Coleridge), with the date of May 16, 1896, and is almost certainly from new leaves inserted by the first rebinding. This annotation reads: "These notes are not published. Those published in the Literary Remains- Were written in Gillman's copy—4 vols 1819. This copy must have been used in the compilation of the Aids to Reflection—and the original homes of H *[sic]*. Moral aphorisms are pointed out. (e.g. M. aph. xvii)[.]" In other words, Coleridge had joined an already evolving trend of interest in Leighton when he purchased his own edition in 1820. He had already marked Gillman's copy, and he seems to have wanted a clean copy from which to organize the primer that *Aids to Reflection* was originally intended to be.

The publication details of the 1820 edition emphasize the availability of Leighton's texts at the time Coleridge began preparing *Aids to Reflection*. As mentioned above, the 1820 edition was printed for five booksellers: three from London; Parker of Oxford; and Deighton of Cambridge. This follows on from the 1819 edition, which was advertised as "The Jenuine *[sic]* Works of Robert Leighton, Preface by P. Doddridge, Corrected; Life of Leighton by E. Middleton." Obviously the corrected edition sparked the quintuple production of 1820. That Leighton's popularity was gaining momentum quickly (even before Coleridge's influence) is demonstrated clearly by the fact that five booksellers were cooperating to produce an edition five years before *Aids to Reflection* was published, and also by two other extant editions of the *Whole Works* published between 1820 and the point at which *Aids to Reflection* could conceivably have begun to have had a positive impact on the popularity of Leighton's writings—bringing the total number of nineteenth-century editions that preceded the possible influence of *Aids to Reflection* to eight, coupled with four editions of the "Selections" to make twelve total printings preceding the influence of *Aids to Reflection*. Characteristically, by the time Coleridge had come to publish *Aids to Reflection* (some five years later), his interest in Leighton had waned slightly—to the point where his primary project in the work had become idealism rather than the dissemination of Leighton's wisdom—which is why he called *Aids to Reflection* a changeling. But whatever the final form of the book, the central question remains: what Leighton's influence on Coleridge was and what *Aids to Reflection* tells us about his relationship to the Anglican Church.

Both these questions will, I believe, be answered by the sections of *Aids to Reflection* that constitute the primer. The only scholar who has

so far addressed the new material by Coleridge in detail is Douglas
Hedley in his *Coleridge, Philosophy and Religion: "Aids to Reflection"
and "The Mirror of the Spirit."* With the exception of one acknowledgment quoted below, Hedley is firmly in the camp of those who see *Aids
to Reflection* as a unified work with a cogent focus, namely the development of idealism out of a Platonic tradition. In this interpretation,
however, Leighton falls by the wayside (Hedley does not even mention
Leighton's name until forty-five pages into the book). Furthermore,
throughout his interpretation of *Aids to Reflection*, Hedley quotes almost entirely from material written by Coleridge. This is by no means
an *incorrect* way to approach *Aids to Reflection*. In fact it is not a thousand miles away from the way in which the text is approached here, because whereas Hedley unconsciously excises the primer and discusses
only "the changeling" that *Aids to Reflection* became, this book consciously dissects the primer out of the text and focuses on it. A brief examination of Hedley's book, the authoritative work on *Aids to Reflection* (and on Coleridge's philosophy generally), will show that the final
focus of the text was an attempt to demonstrate the unity of philosophy and theology; this is of only tangential relevance to the discussion of
Coleridge and the Church of England (though it is the entire project of
On the Divine Ideas).[8] Indeed, Hedley himself makes much the same
point in a different way.

> The final form of *Aids to Reflection* with its long passages of Cole-
> ridgeian metaphysics does not cohere easily with the original intent
> to produce a collection of "beauties," that is, short excerpts of strik-
> ing prose from Leighton. The final product was much more than a
> homage to Leighton, and in fact many of the most important quo-
> tations come from other writers. Coleridge shows some discomfort
> in his attempt to maintain the aphoristic plan of the work while evi-
> dently attempting something much more ambitious than the origi-
> nal concept, and much more difficult to sustain as aphoristic. The
> fact that *Aids to Reflection* started as a relatively minor project and
> became something close to the projected "Assertion of Religion" is
> of considerable importance for our judgment of the real significance
> of the aphorism. The change in plan took place while the work was

---

8. See chapter 8 below.

being printed, and this led to Coleridge employing rather artificial devices "Preliminary" or "Note Prefatory" or "Comment" to sustain the impression that the aphoristic structure had been maintained (cf. Aids Lviii–lxxi). Nevertheless, we cannot simply attribute Coleridge's use of the aphorism to contemporary fashions and his problems with the technical production of his text.[9]

The fact that the final form of *Aids to Reflection* closely resembled the "Assertion of Religion" or the project undertaken in *On the Divine Ideas* is significant, but since the project attempted within *On the Divine Ideas* exists only in an inchoate form, it is best examined in the next chapter, which focuses on the text of the *On the Divine Ideas*. Both *Aids to Reflection* and *On the Divine Ideas* are fragmentary, the earlier work because of its aphoristic form and the later work because it is unrevised. Even taken together they fall far short of giving a cogent voice to Coleridge's attempt to demonstrate what he called "the assertion of Religion" (i.e., the idea that philosophy was impossible without its influence).

Hedley believes that Coleridge "discovered" Leighton during a spiritual crisis in 1813–14. This view is based on the presence of a few skeletal annotations to a copy of the 1748 edition; the copy itself has not been located, and the annotations have been preserved in the form of a manuscript copy in the hand of Alfred Elwyn, who maintained to Henry Nelson Coleridge that it was S. T. Coleridge's hand (these annotations are also suggested to be earlier than 1819). Whether or not this is true, and there is no real reason to disbelieve it, the formative influence obviously came during the period 1819–20, when Coleridge annotated two separate copies of the *Whole Works*. The purported marginalia of the 1748 edition are characteristically Coleridgean in such vocative comments as "Father in heaven have mercy on me! Christ, Lamb of God have mercy on me! Save me Lord! or I perish. Alas, I am Perishing."[10] Some of the

---

9. Douglas Hedley, *Coleridge, Philosophy and Religion: Aids to Reflection and the Mirror of the Spirit* (Cambridge: Cambridge University Press, 2000), 89.

10. The Bollingen editors cite this as marginalia to the passage of Leighton: "If any one's Head or Tongue should grow apace, and all the rest stand at a Stay, it would certainly make him a Monster; and they are no other, that are knowing and discoursing Christians, and grow daily in that, but not at all in Holiness of

other marginalia are slightly more discursive but are not informative. Clearly the serious study of Leighton was undertaken in 1819 and 1820. What is perhaps most important is that Coleridge began the project of *Aids to Reflection* as an instructional manual for young clergy: *assenting* clergy. Two quotations will suffice to demonstrate this point.

The first is from the flyleaf of Coleridge's 1820 edition of Leighton: "We might compare Leighton in his appearance and character as an archbishop of the short lived Protestant Episcopal Church of Britain (the Scoto-anglican *[sic]* church by law established under the Stuart Dynasty) to the bright Star in Cassiopeia; but with this difference, that in the latter instance the star disappeared, the constellation remaining, in the former the Constellation vanished, no longer numbered among The Heavenly houses While the Star remains in undiminished magnitude, and unwaning tho' solitary splendor." There is ample reason to believe that in 1820 and thereabouts Coleridge was infatuated with Leighton, and so when he ranked Leighton as the most divine of the English divines he surely meant it (at least at the time).

The second quotation comes from the section of *Aids to Reflection* that is most definitively part of the primer, the "Moral and Religious Aphorisms." Below are aphorisms 21 (Leighton), 23 (Leighton), 24 (Leighton and Coleridge together), and 25 (Coleridge); where a title appears in all caps, it is by Coleridge.

[Aphorism 21, Leighton:]

The most approved teachers of wisdom, in a human way, have required of their scholars, that to the end their minds might be capable of they should be purified from vice and wickedness. And it was Socrates' custom, when any one asked him a question, seeking to be informed by him, before he would answer them, he asked them concerning their own qualities and course of life.

[Aphorism 23, Leighton:]

THE SUM OF CHURCH HISTORY

In times of peace, the Church may dilate more, and build as it were into breadth, but in times of trouble, it arises more in height;

Heart and Life, which is the proper Growth of the Children of God." They do not, however, say how they identify this, (or any other note) with a passage of Leighton. They simply list this as being from vol. 1 of the 1748 edition, p. 213.

it is then built upwards; as in cities where men are straightened, they build usually higher than in the country.

[Aphorism 24, Leighton and Coleridge:]

WORTHY TO BE FRAMED AND HUNG UP IN THE LI-BRARY OF EVERY THEOLOGICAL STUDENT

Where there is a great deal of smoke and no clear flame, it argues much moisture in the matter, yet it witnesseth certainly that there is fire there; and therefore dubious questioning is a much better evidence, than that senseless deadness which most take for believing. Men that know nothing in sciences, have no doubts. He never truly believed, who was not made first sensible and convinced of unbelief.

Never be afraid to doubt if only you have the disposition to believe, and doubt in order that you may end in believing the truth. I will venture to add in my own name and from my own conviction the following:

[Aphorism 25, Coleridge:]

He, who begins by loving Christianity better than truth, will proceed by loving his own sect or church better than Christianity, and end in loving himself better than all.[11]

This selection from "Moral and Religious Aphorisms" gives a good feeling for the manner in which the primer was constructed. It consists of pearls of wisdom from Leighton, some with internal comments from Coleridge; aphorisms that Coleridge adds in this section are invariably continuations of points raised by Leighton. These, like so many monads, stand on their own without a necessary connection to either what has gone before or what comes after. There is no coherent argument within the primer; it is purely aphoristic. The quoted passages also are very representative of the subject matter of the primer; the aphorisms in this section discuss the need for a moral predisposition on the part of the young theologian. In these two ways the primer is very different from the rest of *Aids to Reflection,* in that it is both more expository and more "orthodox" and therefore less controversial. This is not to say that the theology of the finished *Aids to Reflection* is *un*-orthodox, or heretical, but rather

11. Samuel Taylor Coleridge, *Aids to Reflection,* ed. John Beer, vol. 9 of *The Collected Works of Samuel Taylor Coleridge,* Bollingen Series 75 (Princeton: Princeton University Press, 1993), 105–7.

that it is a deeply speculative and mystical theology—investigating the spiritual encounter with the Divine and the relationship of that encounter with human reason.

So what may be concluded about Leighton's influence on Coleridge? First, it was transitory. Coleridge was influenced by Leighton for a demonstrably bracketed period of time: about five or six years beginning in 1819. Second, it was hermeneutical—in the Greek sense of the word, not the modern theological one—rather than constructive: Leighton brought the message of Anglican theology back to Coleridge in the same way as Hooker brought the proper dynamics of church and state to him. Leighton helped Coleridge to express ideas and considered opinions that he already held. The most striking proof of this paradigm is in the margin of Leighton's *Commentary on I Peter i.8–9* in the 1820 edition, where an annotation by Coleridge of over one thousand words criticizes Leighton's misunderstanding of the difference between the reason and the understanding. The long discussion of this question in the section of *Aids to Reflection* entitled "That Which Is Indeed Spiritual Religion" is an important and fundamental part of his project of the assertion of religion, and though Coleridge believed Leighton was wrong about these two faculties so paramount to his speculative theology, the note is still full of admiration for Leighton's discussion of moral theology. The point here is that Coleridge was using Leighton to elucidate a point of moral theology but that when the project expanded into its changeling form (while retaining the aphorism for its morally didactic utility) he pointed out that Leighton's ideas were not entirely consistent with his own changeling project. In other words, two separate programs were being followed, and this annotation was penned during the early stages of the production of *Aids to Reflection*. It would be difficult to find a more convincing argument for the position that Coleridge undertook two distinct projects within the corpus of what was published as *Aids to Reflection* and that Leighton was a part of the original primer only and not the changeling project: "the assertion of Religion."

So the conclusion to be taken away from *Aids to Reflection* at this point is uncomplicated: the project of the "primer" based on Leighton was of monumental importance for the simple reasons that in 1819–20 Coleridge was interested in providing a primer for young Anglican clergymen and intended to use Leighton's work, part of the Anglican tradition (and a part of the Scottish Anglican tradition at that, thus further demonstrating that the concerns over the Act of Union that had created difficulties for Sacheverell and Warburton in the first thirty years of the eighteenth century no longer existed by the time Coleridge was writing), in concert with his own to construct this primer. When he began the project he believed Leighton was the most penetrating and beautiful commentator on moral theology whom he had ever read. But as the book progressed from moral theology to speculative theology, Coleridge would abandon Leighton in favor of other Anglican divines and also in order to develop his own independent ideas.

In the case of both projects attempted within *Aids to Reflection*, however, Bishop Wand is correct in his assertion that with its publication Coleridge had "fought his way back to Anglicanism": by publishing a book written in concert with Leighton, he made himself a part of the Anglican theological tradition in a way that he had not done before.

8

On the Divine Ideas

Coleridge's Systematic Theology

The Received Text

For most of his mature working life, certainly for the last two decades of his life, Samuel Taylor Coleridge spoke repeatedly, in both his letters and his table talk, of constructing a substantial work that would demonstrate Christianity as "the one true philosophy." His own daughter, Sara, in a letter written to her friend Mrs. Plummer in October 1834 (some two months following her father's death), makes clear that she believed this to be the primary focus of her father's work.

> We feel happy, too, in the conviction, that his writings will be widely influential for good purposes. All his views may not be adopted, and the effect of his posthumous works must be impaired by their fragmentary condition; but I think there is reason to believe, that what he has left behind him will introduce a new and more improving mode of thinking. . . . It is not to be expected that speculations which demand so much effort of mind and such continuous attention, to be fully understood, can ever be *immediately* popular. . . . Heraud, in his brilliant oration on the death of my father, delivered at the Russell Institution observes that religion and philosophy were first reconciled—first brought into permanent and indissoluble union in the divine works of Coleridge; and I believe the opinion expressed by this gentleman, that my father's metaphysical theology will prove a benefit to the world, is shared by many persons of refined and

searching intellect both in this country and in America, where he has some enthusiastic admirers; and it is confidently predicted by numbers that this will be more and more felt and acknowledged in course of time.[1]

Sara's discussion serves well as an introduction to this chapter, which argues that Coleridge's *Opus Maximum* is a cogent metaphysical theology built on a vitalist model.[2] Her prophetic comment that the posthumous works' "fragmentary condition," which demands "so much effort of mind and such continuous attention," will keep them from becoming immediately popular is also astute—though it is difficult to believe she would have envisioned that it would take nearly 170 years for an edition of his metaphysical theology to emerge. Nor is it likely that Sara could have foreseen that after that time there would still be questions surrounding the ordering of the fragments themselves—how could she if she was among persons who knew Coleridge's own intentions of the order (which have been lost)?

It is widely believed by Coleridge scholars (it would not be an exaggeration to say it is agreed) that Coleridge failed in the attempt to produce, in any recognizable form, a work that portrayed Christianity as the one true philosophy. Though (characteristically) he made a number of attempts to create such a system, he became distracted with other projects (ranging from *Aids to Reflection* to *Logic, On the Constitution of the Church and State,* etc.) and left only a group of fragmentary and either truncated or aborted attempts to construct this system—these are the "fragments" published in the volume of the *Collected Works* entitled *Opus Maximum.* In fact, this view is accurate for only one of the four fragments (fragment 4: the earliest). Fragments 1, 2, and 3 contain a systematic theology, in sixteen logically progressive chapters, which, though it may not be polished, or constitute the entire extent to which Coleridge hoped to expand the work eventually, is certainly cogent, detailed, and "complete" as it stands. At the very least the received text as

---

1. Sara Coleridge, *Memoir and Letters of Sara Coleridge,* 2 vols., ed. Edith Coleridge (London: Henry S. King, 1873), 113–14.

2. See below for a precise definition of *vitalism* as the term is used in this chapter.

we have it is a "finished" draft of the first volume of a work that Coleridge *might* have intended to expand into other volumes—though it ought to be noted that Coleridge produced no multivolume work. The work is titled *On the Divine Ideas.*

REDACTING THE FRAGMENTS

The cogency of the work can be seen and understood only when the fragments are redacted differently from the order in which Thomas McFarland believed they were drafted. Even Nicholas Halmi respectfully points out that there are questions about the order:[3] "[The fragments] are presented in the order preferred by the senior editor, although it is not the order of composition, insofar as that can be determined from physical evidence (e.g. watermarks) and textual evidence (e.g. borrowings from Coleridge's other writings). Although none of the manuscripts can be dated with precision, Fragments 1–4 were dictated mostly *[sic]* likely between 1819 and 1823, while the holograph Preface was written no earlier than 1828 and more likely in 1832."[4]

It is the premise of this chapter that the proper order in which the fragments should be read, the order in which *Coleridge* intended them to be read, is 3, 1, 2. This view is supported not only by both higher and lower literary criticism (not to mention good historical methodology) but by the logical progression of the theological system, which takes the premise of fragment 3, God understood as the Absolute Will, uses it as the central hermeneutic by which the entire system is to be constructed and examined, and then progresses through consequent philosophical and theological issues and doctrines.

What emerges in the final four chapters of the work when viewed in this order (i.e., approximately the second half of fragment 2) is an a priori

---

3. The ordering of the fragments is a live issue, as Murray Evans has pointed out.

4. Nicholas Halmi, "Editorial Practice," in *Opus Maximum,* by Samuel Taylor Coleridge, ed. Thomas McFarland with Nicholas Halmi, vol. 15 of *The Collected Works of Samuel Taylor Coleridge,* Bollingen Series 75 (Princeton: Princeton University Press, 2002), xx.

vitalist system of philosophy centered on the Absolute Will (equated to God and scripturally grounded in the Hebraic concept of the Elohim) as the vital animating element of the system through the eternal expression of the primary act of the Divine Will: the "I AM." Overlapping and interlaced with this discussion (and pursued in the first five chapters of the work as well) is a philosophical theology that presents the Trinity as the one and only logically possible form that the Divine could take. Chapters 8 through 13 are a focused presentation of Coleridge's theological anthropology, or doctrine of Man, with chapter 13 providing the bridge from the discussion of humanity itself to the discussion of humanity *as a part of nature* and introducing the discussion of Coleridge's vitalist system of philosophy. All the chapters continually refer to the concept of God as the Absolute Will. In other words, the system presents Christianity as a philosophy, and Trinitarian Christianity founded on the conceit of Absolute Will as the one possible "True Philosophy."

In fact, though, there is less divergence between this redaction of the fragments and that of McFarland than there might appear to be on the surface. There is complete agreement that fragment 4 is the earliest, that fragment 2 follows directly from fragment 1, and indeed, that the range of dates he and Halmi give for the composition of fragment 3 (1822–23) is consistent with the possibility of placing it before fragment 1 (which is dated between 1820 and 1823). Furthermore, McFarland and Halmi hang their dating of "probably 1822–3" solely on speculative evidence: the assumption that a comment on the *Memoirs of Thomas Halyburton* (written in Coleridge's own hand) from a separate notebook indicates that this comment was written on July 29, 1822.[5] Yet McFarland remarked in 1977 that the addresses of Ralph Wedgwood, Thomas Monkhouse, and John Watson are written (by Coleridge) on the inside of the front cover and that these can be dated "probably between Dec 1820 and Jan 1821."[6] It makes little sense that Coleridge wrote the addresses of three friends on the inside cover of a notebook he would not use for a further two years. The anecdotal evidence is contradictory.[7]

---

5. McFarland and Halmi, notes to Coleridge, *Opus Maximum*, 214.
6. McFarland and Halmi, notes to Coleridge, *Opus Maximum*, 214.
7. The only surviving letter written to any of the three men between 1820 and 1825 is a letter written to Thomas Monkhouse on June 24, 1840.

In short, this cross-referencing to the separate notebook (CN iv 4909) is probably too threadbare a piece of evidence to overwhelm, first, the logical progression of the three fragments; second, the classically Coleridgean introduction to the entire project that the first two paragraphs of fragment 3 constitute; third, the fact that fragment 3 begins with a title "ON THE DIVINE IDEAS," written entirely in capital letters; and fourth, the fact that fragment 3 consists of two chapters, the second of which discusses the impossibility of demonstrating the existence of God through scientific methodology (see below), while fragment 1 begins chapter 3 and the second sentence of the first paragraph reads: "We have spoken of *Science, or of* Sciences, in the severest sense of the word, vis. Those superstructures of the pure intellect in which the speculative necessity reigns throughout and exclusively, the act of reasoning and imagining being the only practical ingredient, or that alone in which any reference is made to the Will, and even in this to the Will in that sense only in which it remains utterly undetermined. . . ."[8] That passage is a perfect description of the lion's share of the content of the second chapter of fragment 3. In other words, the "lost two chapters" of fragment 1 are in fact fragment 3.[9]

Fragment 4 does not fit into the system; it is an inchoate, or embryonic, version of the philosophical positions and ontological presentations of Christian doctrines that exist in the sixteen chapters of *On the Divine Ideas* (from here throughout that title refers to the work as a whole and not simply to fragment 3), and it indeed is a fragment. Fragment 4 is best understood as analogous to a detailed and focused notebook in which Coleridge worked out unpolished sections of his system, to which he gave a proper finish in the received form of *On the Divine Ideas.* Hence it is not surprising that McFarland found analogous, or overlapping, material with the discussion undertaken in the second chapter of fragment 3; but it was misguided of him to suggest that it should be viewed as the completion of that chapter (and oddly inconsistent with his simultaneous argument that fragment 4 was the earliest fragment of the work).

---

8. Coleridge, *Opus Maximum,* 5. Subsequent page citations to this work will be given parenthetically in the text.

9. Even if fragment 3 was written in August of 1822, fragment 1 could still have been written in the later months of that year and subsequent months of 1823.

Because of its fragmentary nature (and because the force of this chapter is to argue that a coherent and logically cogent system exists in the received text of fragments 3, 2, and 1, and that fragment 4 was a forerunner to them), textual exegesis of fragment 4 will not take place in this chapter. Fragment 4 may be informative when viewed as a "foregoer" or "pathfinder"—drafts of arguments that Coleridge would polish in the work itself (or even, given a most sympathetic reading, as subsidiary commentary on the system by Coleridge—though this is difficult to square with its being the earliest composed notebook), but it is informative *only* in a subsidiary fashion. For example, the attack on mechanistic philosophy on pages 295–96 of the text is indeed informative as a stronger, more snide, and less polished presentation of Coleridge's views on mechanism (it may even be a more true presentation of his feelings), and Coleridge's discussion of pneumatology and linking of it to basic chemistry (metallurgy) on page 320 may make even clearer his intention of uniting God with nature in a vitalist system of theology. Neither of these passages, however, is as elegant or, more importantly, as logically tight as the presentation of each of these subjects in *On the Divine Ideas*. *On the Divine Ideas* was written over a long period; Coleridge compiled virtually all of his published works over at least two years. Though I agree with the view that this fragment is the earliest of the four, I find McFarland and Halmi's methodology and reasoning behind dating fragment 4 as the earliest unconvincing. The reasons why I find this dating unconvincing have consequent and significant relevance to the acceptance of their dating of fragment 3. My concerns here are that for a second time McFarland and Halmi have used the similarity of a passage of the text of the fragment with material in a single manuscript entry in separate bound notebook (CN iv 4775–76), then relied entirely on the dating of this separate entry by Kathleen Coburn (and Coburn's dates themselves are not beyond question). In other words, the evidence by which McFarland and Halmi assign the fragment the date of 1819 is threadbare at best—and certainly not compelling. Finally, McFarland's attempt to buttress this date by suggesting that "a reference on f 8 to 'the growth of a tulip in 1819' suggests that year as the *terminus a quo* of the fragment's composition" is, frankly, *specious*. It is specious because the entire sentence reads: "The assumed priority, therefore, would at best be but an historical accident, with no more causitive connection than the age <birth> of George the Third <in 1750> to the growth of a tulip in

1819." Finally, the third argument that "the list of chemical symbols on ff 193–4 is very similar to one in a notebook entry of June 1819" is also less than overwhelming. So, I find the remorseless reliance on the Notebooks to date the fragments less than either entirely convincing or *historically reliable*—and as I have demonstrated above, at times it can be contradictory.

The work as we hold it (the received text of fragments 1–3) is complete, if not "finished" (or, to use a more literary term, "revised"); the argument that Coleridge himself considered it so is reinforced by the fact that he wrote a preface to it. (Hegel, for instance, famously wrote the preface to his *Phenomenology of Spirit* only after he had completed the work.) Coleridge's "preface," though, is problematic: far from being a summary of the work, it is extremely short and (characteristically for Coleridge) cryptic in the best light. While establishing one point (that Coleridge believed he had finished constructing his system), it creates other subsidiary confusions that draw one away from the yield of its composition. In it he wrote that his "system is divided into three unequal parts, each of which forms an independent work—the whole comprised in five Volumes. Two of these, and the larger part of the third, are prepared for the press—and <of> the remainder the materials & principal contents exist in Sybilline MSS—" (4). It appears that McFarland took this statement in the preface to refer, on the micro scale, only to the unpublished works constituting the *Opus Maximum*; in this case it becomes clear why he adopted the narrow interpretation that the fragments 1 through 3 were the "two [volumes] . . . and the larger part of the third" prepared for the press and that fragment 4 was the "Sybilline MSS" holding further unfinished promise rather than seeing this earliest fragment as a mere draft of the work. But there are other options if one examines the statement from the preface on a macro scale: "the larger part of the third [volume]" might be *Confessions of an Inquiring Spirit,* or it might be the entire *On the Divine Ideas* or (fragments 3, 1, and 2): the inclusion of these fragments within the greater system is supported by the appearance of an inchoate version of the "Pentad of Operative Christianity" (a diagram from *Confessions of an Inquiring Spirit* that summarizes Coleridge's theology; see chapter 10) at the bottom of the page on which the preface is written). If either of these is the case, I suspect that the two published parts are *On the Constitution of the Church and State* and *The Lay Sermons*—the former of which was published about the time the preface was written (at least in the same year; we do not know exactly when the preface was written).[10] Even if *On the Divine Ideas* is only the "Sybilline MSS," or if McFarland is correct and Coleridge was referring only to the unpublished materials now known as fragments 1–4, the preface still makes it clear that Coleridge considered his system of "Deo Homine et Natura" to exist. Apparently his daughter Sara, her family, and her father's companions believed this as well. The point is not esoteric decoding of, and speculation on, what Coleridge meant by his "five volumes"; the point is that in 1828/32 he believed he had a cogent system and wrote a preface to it, and in any of the possibilities outlined above *On the Divine Ideas* constitutes the philosophical theology—the ontology.

On the Divine Ideas has been identified as a "vitalist" project, so it is important to clarify both what is generally understood by the term in philosophical circles and what is specifically meant when it is used here in reference to Coleridge. The *Routledge Encyclopedia of Philosophy* provides a concise and uncontroversial definition:

> Vitalists hold that living organisms are fundamentally different from non-living entities because they contain some non-physical element or are governed by different principles than are inanimate things. In its simplest form, vitalism holds that living entities contain some fluid, or a distinctive "spirit." In more sophisticated forms, the vital spirit becomes a substance infusing bodies and giving life to them or vitalism becomes the view that there is a distinctive organization among things. Vitalist positions can be traced back to antiquity. . . . Vitalism is best understood, however, in the context of the emergence of modern science during the sixteenth and seventeenth centuries. Mechanistic explanations of natural phenomena were extended to biological systems. . . . Vitalism developed as a contrast to this mechanistic view. Over the next three centuries, numerous figures opposed the extension of Cartesian mechanism to biology, arguing that matter could not explain movement, perception, development or life.[11]

---

10. I suspect this because the works discuss "The Christian Nature of Society" and "The Christian's Actions in Society" respectively.
11. Edward Craig, gen. ed., *Routledge Encyclopedia of Philosophy* (London: Routledge, 1998), 9:639–40.

Coleridge integrated a vitalist natural philosophy into his system of theology to create an ontology in which God (defined as the Absolute Will) was the "spirit" that animated the living.[12] The mechanism that he was opposing was utilitarian in its ethics and static in its metaphysics: a stance that removed the participation of the Divine from the immediacy of action and the permeation of the now. The mechanistic system most particularly in vogue at the time when *On the Divine Ideas* was written was that of Paley—and though within this work Coleridge was not necessarily attacking Paley specifically, he was attacking the sterility of utilitarianism and mechanism generally (and thus certainly Paley by implication):[13]

> The scheme of <pure mechanism,> which under all disguises, tempting or repulsive, christian or infidel, forms the groundwork of all these systems of <modern> moral and political philosophy, political economy, and education, which by manufacturing mind out of sense and sense out of sensation, which reduces all form to shape and all shape to impression from without, leads . . . to its own confutation, and scorpion-like, destroys itself, while the tail turning round in its tortures, infixes the poisoned sting in its head—inevitably leads to it, <I say,> if only it be forced by a stern logic <in>to all its consequences. (145–46)

Coleridge conceived a system in which each action was a manifestation of the particular will and each act of will was a manifestation of the Absolute Will: God became the indwelling ground of all will and as such the indwelling ground of each conscious act: the animating principle of each moment of life. This idea was coupled with human reason as the *Imago Dei.*

---

12. Readers unfamiliar with the place of vitalism within the history of natural philosophy or science of the seventeenth and eighteenth centuries are urged to look up the *Routledge Encyclopedia*'s full treatment of the term, as it gives a trenchant and detailed discussion in the context of the history of science, specifically physiology, chemistry, and biology, that is also concise and elegantly accessible.

13. For the most thorough treatment of Coleridge's attack on Paley, see Hedley, *Coleridge.*

What then is the ground of this coincidence between reason and experience? Between the laws of the sensible world and the ideas of the pure intellect? The only answer is that both have their ultimate ground, and are ultimately identified in, a supersensual essence, the principle of existence in all essences and of the essences in all existence, or the Supreme Reason that constitutes the objects templates and <then> by the powers thus constituted, viz. The divine Ideas, gives being to the whole phaenomenal universe . . . and it needs only remind the reader that the original postulate . . . was that of a responsible Will from which the reality of a Will generally became demonstrable. (163–64)

From where Coleridge's influences to use the will as the focus of his system came is an unsettled question: the cynic might answer, "the Christian tradition of rational thought," and that answer is likely to be as close to the truth as any other, though it is also unlikely that Schelling's captivation with the subject of the will can be discounted as a constructive influence. Schelling's concentration on the subject of the will began with his discussion of it in *On Human Freedom,* published in 1809 (a particular work the conclusions of which Coleridge vehemently disagreed with), and from that point on the subject of the will remained in the center of Schelling's philosophy. Coleridge mentions Schelling during his discussion of the economic trinity at the very end of fragment 2 (the very end of chapter 16). There he warns readers against understanding any concept of succession in the term *becomes* (when referent to the idea that the will of the Father "becomes" the will of the Son), as "in the recent writings of Schelling and his followers, as often as they attempt to clothe the skeleton of the Spinozistic pantheism and breathe a life thereinto" (204–5). It is also likely that Schopenhauer's exhaustive and idealistic discussion of the will as the center of encountered reality (in both *The Fourfold Root* and *The World as Will and Representation*) was an influence in some form—though there is less forensic bibliographical evidence to demonstrate this influence than there is with Schelling. Where Coleridge made the idea his own was by moving from the philosophical realm to pure theology by equating the Absolute Will with the Elohim—the Hebraic concept of the animating and eternal breath of God—and marrying it to the concept of the creative "I AM" (in the Gospel of Mark the *ego eimi*).

This perfect union of personeity and the absolute Will is, the reader will have already noticed, strongly marked in the Mosaic History, here quoted only as the most ancient documents of the human mind. When the sublime writer is speaking of the supreme Will, he is named Elohim, i.e. the self-existent, the strengths or all strengths or efficient powers contained in one unoriginated, the Origin and perpetuation of all. But the yet higher revelation he reserves for the Jehovah himself, "I am," and as the consequence of this, "I am the Lord thy God." (164–65)

Within the scope of this chapter it is impossible to discuss the entire text of all three fragments. The only comprehensible way to demonstrate how the text of *On the Divine Ideas* holds together as a united system is to set out a précis of each of the sixteen chapters (with absolutely minimal commentary) and then to use quotations drawn from throughout the text to allow Coleridge to make his own argument. Only once the reader has a picture of the system in his or her mind can exegesis of the text be made to support the interpretation.

The following sixteen précis give the skeleton of Coleridge's argument in each chapter; these are accompanied by the page numbers of each of the chapters in the *Collected Works* (Bollingen ed.) *Opus Maximum*, as well as any title that Coleridge gave the chapter. Coleridge gave numbers but not titles to the chapters contained in fragment 1, though he titled five of the eight chapters contained in fragment 2. Chapters 1 and 2 are the text of the notebook termed fragment 3; chapters 3 through 8 are the text of the notebook termed fragment 1; and chapters 9 through 16 are the text of the notebook termed fragment 2.

THE SYSTEM PRESENTED: THE SIXTEEN CHAPTERS
AND THEIR CONTENT

Chapter 1, pages 215–47, "On the Divine Ideas." (Written in a substantially larger hand than the lines that follow it, centered, and underlined in the holograph, this title is more substantially emphasized than Coleridge's other chapter titles, suggesting that it is the title of the entire work.) Coleridge's cosmology is presented, followed by his cosmogony. It is argued that the Divine is the Absolute Will; that as individual will differentiates itself from Absolute Will, the ontological fall takes place; and that the Absolute Will is protected from the charge of being the origin of evil because differentiation into the particular existed in the Absolute Will only "in potentiality."

Chapter 2, pages 248–90 (no title). That the necessity of viewing evil thus originated as the differentiation of particular will is demonstrated (a position clearly heir to and structurally influenced by Kant's discussion of radical evil differentiated from natural evil in *Religion within the Limits of Reason Alone*).[14] Possible alternative cosmologies to his own are shown to be false; the complete originality of the Trinity as a Christian doctrine is demonstrated; and all *apparent* precursors to the Christian Trinity (particular the Plotinian) are dismissed as influences. The second half of the chapter concentrates on the eradication of the possibility of giving a scientific proof of the existence of God: this is refuted on the grounds that science exists in the realm of the understanding, rather than the reason, and hence includes a presupposition in all of its postulates and proofs.

Chapter 3, pages 5–11 (numbered by Coleridge but not titled). The incapacity of a scientific proof of God is reiterated, married to the concept of the will (both absolute and particular), and the necessary consequence of moral responsibility is demonstrated. The consequent reality and essential difference of moral good and evil are delineated.

Chapter 4, pages 12–16 (numbered by Coleridge but not titled). The purity of the faculty of reason as an attribute of the divine and its inextricable connection to this antecedent element (the Absolute Will or God) are reemphasized. This is the point in the work where Coleridge formally dismisses a posteriori evidence on a *purely philosophical* level, discussing the actual being of a responsible will.

Chapter 5, pages 16–24 (numbered by Coleridge but not titled). The actual being of particular wills is discussed and examined as separate from the Absolute Will. This is the beginning of Coleridge's theological anthropology or doctrine of Man.

Chapter 6, pages 24–48 (numbered by Coleridge but not titled). In this continuation of the theological anthropology, the concepts of self-

---

14. Later in the work, in chapter 6 (contained in fragment 1), Coleridge wrote, "Faith (faith, which is used here in the same sense as Kant uses the Will, as the ground of all particular acts of willing) is a *total* act of the soul: it is the *whole* state of the mind, or it is not at all!" (43).

love, sensuality, pleasure, and pain are discussed. The self that loves is decisively differentiated from "self-love." In the second half of the chapter the concept of the self is married to the concepts of the will and moral responsibility (in other words, the discussion undertaken in chapters 3 and 4 is joined with the discussion of chapters 5 and 6).

Chapter 7, pages 48–57 (numbered by Coleridge but not titled). All the discussion that has taken place to this point is recapitulated: the statements on the human condition in the encountered creation are gathered and clarified, and a shift takes place from a purely theological discussion back into a philosophical theology. The chapter ends with a long quotation from Jeremy Taylor.

Chapter 8, pages 57–79, "Faith and Conscience" (numbered and titled by Coleridge). The concept of self-consciousness is tied to the concept of the will, and then the particular will to the divine Absolute Will. It is argued that the concept of the "I" or the "self" can be self-identified or differentiated from the world around it only through the will. "Man knows himself to be because he is a man, but he is a man because God is and hath so willed it. It is the great 'I am' only who is because he affirmeth himself to be" (67). This chapter also begins Coleridge's project of building a vitalist system of natural philosophy by formally differentiating his philosophy from the "mechanico-corpuscular system" (73). This, he makes clear, is because in his system reason (rather than the understanding) supplies the only guiding light to the conscience, and reason is a projection of the Divine Will.

Chapter 9, pages 80–96 (neither numbered nor titled by Coleridge). Coleridge's doctrine of the *Imago Dei* is presented. The image of God is in human reason as the synthesis of the concepts of identity and the absolute: in fidelity to the Absolute Will through informed actions (specific acts of the particular will) in accordance with the Absolute Will. When reason is usurped by the understanding, the personal will rebels against the Absolute Will and the acting individual descends into the level of the sensuous. Faith is the obedience of the individual will to reason; therefore it is fidelity to both God and oneself.[15]

---

15. It is arguable but far from certain that Coleridge was drawing at least the shadow of a doctrine of the Atonement through the heavy emphasis on faith as fidelity to both the Divine Will and the particular will and the identification of reason (the guide by which the particular will must act to be faithful) as the synthesis of the individual and the absolute.

Chapter 10, pages 96–119, "On the Existential Reality of the Idea of the Supreme Being, i.e. of God" (titled but not numbered by Coleridge). An apophatic (*via negativa*) approach to defining the attributes of the Deity is delineated. On the surface this chapter seems a disappointing "gearing down" from his discussion of the will in the preceding chapter. There appears to be a break in logical flow, but this is not the case. The hermeneutic of apophaticism becomes the key to distinguishing the idea of "personeity" (distinguishing the *particular* from the *absolute:* the individual will from the Divine Will); Coleridge will use it to incorporate the vitalist philosophy in chapters 14 and 15 into his theological system.

Chapter 11, pages 119–27, "Of the Origin of the Idea of God in the Mind of Man" (titled but not numbered by Coleridge). It is argued that the origin of the idea of God begins with love: a child's love for a parent. Originally the child is conscious of only one self in the relationship: the parent. The parent is comprehended as all that is other than the infant. The love for the parent is "elevated to the universal Parent." Important in this short chapter are the opening paragraphs, which place humanity in the context of an ever-evolving natural system: here for the first time the subject of nature is introduced. (Clearly Coleridge was familiar with the theories of Erasmus Darwin.)

Chapter 12, pages 127–33, "On the Present General Education of Man in Relation to the Idea of God" (titled but not numbered by Coleridge). The idea that the apophatic approach to the idea of God can be demonstrated in the development of self-consciousness in a child is expanded in this short chapter. Coleridge argues that only in the absence of the mother is the idea of a self developed by the child to conceive of the mother. It is then applied to the child itself as the periods of the mother's absence from him increase.

Chapter 13, pages 133–50 (neither numbered nor titled by Coleridge). The philosophical argument of the chapter is twofold: it expands the development of the child still further from mere self-consciousness into the concept of "personeity" (the natural progression of the reason in the child), and it discusses the "artificial education" of the mind—that is, the development and cultivation of the understanding. Coleridge argues that through this process of artificial education the *idea* of life is translated into the concept of "power." This discussion of the understanding and of the artificial education is how Coleridge begins to elucidate his vitalism (using the idea of life) and where he begins a frontal assault on mechanistic philosophy (145).

Chapter 14, pages 150–66 (neither numbered nor titled by Coleridge). The vitalist system of created nature is expanded; its vital element is identified as the indwelling of the Divine Will. Coleridge demonstrates its scriptural grounding and distinguishes his system from deism and pantheism. He uses the concept of the will to join reason and experience through the "Divine Ideas" (163–64): the Absolute Will is the source of the idea of personeity and is unified with history in the Mosaic history (returning to the scriptural focus of the chapter). The Will is identified as the Elohim: the spirit of God.

Chapter 15, pages 166–77 (neither numbered nor titled by Coleridge). On pages 166–67 the vitalist philosophy is linked back (and riveted to) the hermeneutic of apophaticism: the approach allows Coleridge the ability to leave everything that cannot be identified and defined as the vital element—Absolute Will. If a thing can be defined it has a personeity, or a being without personeity (as in plant life); therefore a thing that can be defined is either an individual will with moral responsibility or a definable part of nature perceivable through the sensuous impulses. Everything else is God: the Absolute Will animates all as the Elohim through the act of pure will contained in the originating "I AM."

Chapter 16, pages 177–213, "Ideas Flowing out of the Divine Personeity" (titled but not numbered by Coleridge). Coleridge's Christology is delineated and the personeity of the Holy Spirit is discussed. Man's responsibility for his own fallen nature is explained, and the Divine Ideas are identified as the three persons of the Trinity. The theological system comes full circle, having traveled through a discussion of both the nature and fallen state of Man and his place in the overall creation constituted by nature, and is knitted back into its starting point: the Divine Ideas.

TEXTUAL EXEGESIS OF THE SYSTEM

One of two central premises of *On the Divine Ideas* is that what is absolutely true is eternal (whether the Divine Being or the mathematical fact that in every triangle the sum of the angles is 180 degrees) and that these truths can be arrived at only through reason. The other central premise of Coleridge's systematic theology is that God is Absolute Will. As he does elsewhere, Coleridge distinguishes reason from understanding. The distinction is probably more simple, though no less substantial, than Coleridge presents it as being: reason provides only knowledge that can be gained a priori, while the understanding provides only knowledge that can be gained a posteriori. The understanding is dependent upon the senses and human perception and therefore cannot provide truths that are eternal. A discussion of the Divine or its attributes can be undertaken only through reason.

A substantial portion of the first paragraph of the first chapter is quoted in several passages below to demonstrate that it is proleptic of Coleridge's full system rather than merely a part of it.[16] This indicates that Coleridge had a fairly complete idea of what he intended to write when he began. What may first appear to be apostrophe is actually a prolix way of stating that throughout the system his discussion of the Divine Will takes an a priori path.

> I cannot commence this subject more fitly than by disclaiming all wish and attempt of gratifying a speculative refinement in myself, or an idle + presumptuous curiosity in others. I leave the heavenly hierarchy with all their distinctions "Thrones, Dominations, Princedoms Virtues Powers," Names Fervours, Energies, with the long et cetera of the Cabbalists and degenerated Platonists to the admirers of the false Dionysious, and the obscure students of Cornelius Agrippa. All pretence, all approach to particularize on such a subject involves its own confutation: for it is the applications of the understanding through the medium of the fancy to truths of which the reason exclusively is both the substance beheld + the eye-beholding or had the evident contradiction implied in the attempt failed in preventing it the fearful abuses, the degrading idolatrous superstitions, which have resulted from its application to that beautiful yet awful article of the Christian faith, the unbroken unity of the triumphant with

---

16. The word *heretofore* appears twice in the paragraph; in the context in which Coleridge used it, it implies "before the philosophy of Samuel Taylor Coleridge" (a statement he was not too modest to make) rather than "earlier in the work."

the militant church, or communion of Saints, form too palpable a warning not to have deterred me even from motives of common morality. (216–17)[17]

This passage is characteristic of Coleridge's introductory passages in his published works in that it is more literary and circumlocutive than practical. To demonstrate that these traits are characteristic the reader need only examine the opening passages of, for instance, any of the issues of *The Friend* or *The Watchman*, either of the two Lay Sermons, *On the Constitution of the Church and State*, the *Biographia Literaria*, or for that matter any other published work of Coleridge's. But what is more important still is that this is the only chapter of any of the fragments that contains a general introduction; *all* the other chapters refer to an antecedent discussion.[18] If one accepts the order of the fragments as they are printed within the *Opus Maximum*, one must account for this substantial break in tone and rhetoric; there is no reason to believe that Coleridge would have broken his rhetorical practice within the work to introduce a subject that he had discussed already throughout fragments 1 and 2 (will and God as the Absolute Will). This passage was meant to be the opening of a work.

Coleridge next identifies his project: "In what I am about to deliver I have but one end in view, that of presenting an intelligible though not comprehensible idea of the possibility of that which in some sense or other is, yet is not God nor One with God" (217)—in other words, an idea that is intelligible to the reason but not comprehensible to the understanding. Later in the same paragraph Coleridge subtly but clearly indicates that he is creating a vitalist system of philosophy:

freed from the phenomena of time + space + seen in the depth of real being no longer therefore a nature, namely a That which is not but which is for ever only about to be, reveals itself to the pure reason as

---

17. Whenever quoting fragment 3, I use my own transcription of the holograph; the page numbers in Coleridge, *Opus Maximum*, where the McFarland/Halmi transcription appears are provided.

18. See below for a discussion of the antecedent references, especially in the outset of fragment 1.

the actual immanence. . . . Are we struck at beholding the cope of heaven imaged in a dew-drop? The heart of the animalcula to which that dew drop is an ocean presents an infinite problem, of which the omnipresent is the only solution. . . . The philosophy of nature can remain philosophy only by rising above nature, and by abstracting from nature. . . . (217–18)

In the second paragraph of the work he moves on to a discussion of the encountered world and the Divine Will as the means of creation (or, as he puts it, "causative of reality").

The Will, the absolute Will, is that which is essentially causative of reality, essentially + absolutely that is boundless from without + from within. This is our first principle, this is the position, contained in the postulate of the reality of Will at all. Difficult we have never attempted to conceal from ourselves, is it to master this first idea or could it be otherwise, in as much as an insight into its truth is not possible and we are perforce constrained to the only necedaneum [sic], the sense of the necessary falsehood of the contrary. We affirm it not because we comprehend the affirmation, but because we clearly comprehend the absurdity of the denial. But in this affirmation it is involved that what is essentially causative of all possible reality must be causative of its own reality. It is not the cause of all reality because it is causative of its own but it is necessarily causative of its own reality because it is essentially causative of all possible reality. These however are so far one, that the act being absolute and infinite, *such must the reality be[;] consequently the absolute will itself realized must in its own reality include the plentitude of all that is real as far as it is absolutely real, that is as far as the reality is actual + not merely possible.* (220–21; emphasis mine)

On these two principles hangs his entire theological system.

The concept of the will and God as the Absolute Will permeates fragments 1 and 2. During the discussion of reason as the *Imago Dei* in chapter 9, for instance, Coleridge writes, "If there be that in man, which is one with the universal reason, it cannot but coincide with or be congruous with, the absolute Will" (88). Or again later in fragment 2: "In Man the will as Will first appears, enough for him that he hath a Will at all; for this is the condition of his responsibility of his humanity. In the

<possession of a> responsible Will his creator has placed him, with all means and aidances to boot, to its growth and evolution. With these, in the possession of a Free-Will he is to place himself—that he may be in the divine humanity even as the divine humanity, that 'God may be all in all'" (144). It is this free will, the ability to choose to act rationally in accordance with the Divine Will, for instance self-sacrificially or altruistically, to proceed on the basis of reason rather than the understanding, that demarcates humanity as separate from the remainder of creation— which also contains the vital animating power of the Divine Will. Coleridge makes clear that will is free will only when it is exercised using reason.

An important passage at the beginning of chapter 15 makes this clear. "Still less dare we predicate personality of the single beast or plant. Why not? Of a fox, for instance? Here equally as in a man there is a unity of life in an organized whole. <Equally with> man <the fox is found to possess> vital power, instinct, perception, memory, recognition; and as far as we mean by 'understanding' the faculty of adapting means to ends according to varying circumstances, it is most undeniable that the fox possess understanding" (166–67). So the fox possesses understanding, but not reason. As Coleridge writes: "We withhold the name of person from the higher order of animals [because they do not possess] Reason and the responsible Will" (167). For Coleridge the will is inseparable from personeity: "That of a Will, personeity is an essential attribute, we have cleared from all objections" (166–67). From the perspective of personeity Coleridge will build his own presentation of an economic trinity:[19] "This divine reciprocation in and by which the Father attributeth his self to another, and the Son beholdeth and knoweth himself in the Father, is not and cannot be contemplated otherwise than as an act— as an act, therefore of the divine Will, which is one in both and therefore an act . . ." (205). Throughout the entire text of fragments 1 and 2, throughout every doctrine from the procession of the Son from the Father, to that of freedom in humanity, to that of the distinction between man and beast, the reference point is always the will, and reference is always made to the Absolute or Divine Will. The premise that Coleridge laid down in his first chapter runs through the entire work like a

---

19. *Economic* is used in its patristic meaning, merely indicating a trinity that has intellectual commerce among the three persons.

rhetorical spine. God as the Absolute Will is never far from the surface of any discussion Coleridge undertakes.

Now that the premises Coleridge outlined in the first sentences of fragment 3 have been shown to both permeate and bind the sixteen chapters as a whole, there remains one subject that could produce a possible counterargument to this view: the question of internal antecedent references within the fragments. Perhaps the clearest example comes in the second paragraph of chapter 15: "If we are to speak of the reason not as it is one with the Will—that is, not of the absolute Will, which is one with the Supreme Reason, but of the Reason in its relations to the finite and responsible will—the reply is obvious: it has been clearly demonstrated in a former chapter, in our disquisition on the nature of Faith and Conscience, that Reason is incompatible with individuality, or *peculiar* possession" (167). This is a clear reference to a chapter of fragment 1 that Coleridge both numbered and named, and it is a perfectly accurate reference to the contents of that chapter (see 72–77), specifically to Coleridge's statement that "REASON implies an insight into the necessity and universality of relations, and may be defined as power of drawing universal and necessary conclusions from individual forms or facts, ex.gr. from any three-cornered object or outline we conclude that in all triangles the two sides <conjointly> are necessarily greater than the third" (77). So there is an indisputable reference within fragment 2 to fragment 1. One instance, probably the only instance, of *antecedent* reference that could be used to argue against placing the fragments in the order 3, 1, 2 is the antecedent reference in the second paragraph of chapter 3.[20] The clear transition of subject matter, namely the nature of science as a practice of the understanding and hence science's inability to demonstrate the existence of God, has already been remarked upon, but the following antecedent reference must be sourced:

---

20. An argument could be made for the current ordering of the fragments based on the fact that within the final five pages of ch. 16, 208–13, the term *the Divine Ideas* is used several times and that a discussion of Plotinus is promised (and one takes place, though at insubstantial length) in the first chapter of fragment 3. But this argument is not only threadbare but wrongheaded. The use of the term *the Divine Ideas* is a grand conclusion to the work as a whole: Coleridge has concluded with a discussion of Christology within his view of the Trinity, the point from which he began, and in doing so brings his argument full circle to come to a conclusion with his title.

"It has likewise been shown that the power of withholding and, indirectly at least, of refusing our assent to the necessary foundation of an intellectual superstructure forms the essential difference between the moral and sciential systems. The assent having been given, this difference ceases, and moral positions both may and ought to be treated as sciences subject to the same universal logic as those of number and measure" (6). This reference does match the transition between the two chapters of fragment 3. The first is in large part concerned with theodicy and the existence of evil within the world in which God operates as an animating principle in the form of the Absolute Will; it is therefore a discussion of moral issues. Between pages 236 and 250 the issue of how moral evil can arise is the focus of Coleridge's argument. In Coleridge's system (as in Kant's) evil is moral evil, a rebellion against the Divine Will—which we come to know through reason. Coleridge's point throughout fragment 3 is that any proof of the existence of God must be made a priori and that science as a method dependent on the faculty of understanding cannot demonstrate the existence of God because it would have to rely upon a posteriori observations. All the above quotation is arguing is that Coleridge has previously demonstrated that an a priori (or moral) demonstration of the existence of God is the live option, an interpretation reinforced by the final sentence of this very short chapter:

> In one concluding sentence: there are several positions, each of which might be legitimately assumed and each of which might stand on its own grounds as a postulate of humanity, and á fortiori, therefore, of every code of religion and morality. But the one assumption, the one postulate, in which all the rest may assume a scientific form, and which granted we may coercively deduce even those which we might allowably have assumed, is the Existence of the *Will*, which a moment's reflexion will convince us is the same as *Moral Responsibility*, and that again with the reality and essential difference of <moral> *Good* and *Evil.* (11)

The chapter is unquestionably, and specifically, referent to the subjects immediately previously discussed in the first two chapters; Coleridge has simply introduced the term *moral* in opposition to *scientific*.

On the Divine Ideas is a systematic theology beginning with the chapter of that name, and its internal references demonstrate this.

Ramifications of the Systematic Theology
for Church and State Relations

The implications of this systematic theology for the question of Coleridge's relationship with the Church of England, and their dovetailing with the positions he advocates in other mature works, are valuable for piecing together the overall picture. What emerges in an inchoate way is that Coleridge produced a "catholic" theology both in the sense that he himself identified it as "catholic" (see below) and in the sense that the theology was Catholic as opposed to Protestant in its *methodology*— it worked off philosophical premises and postulates instead of biblical citations. This identification and this methodology both begin at a very early point in the work.

After setting out the ramifications of the existence of evil, Coleridge moves directly into a comparison of his "system" (his own word) with Plotinus and Plato. Here some real evidence of a High Church outlook begins to emerge. The specific argument he seeks to employ is that the doctrine of the Trinity has no parallel in any Platonic philosophy or in any other religious system (this is the bulk of the chapter); he begins by attempting to refute long-standing suggestions that Plotinus and Plato were essentially precursors of the Christian doctrine as it was received.

> Compare our system hitherto concerning Deity and the possible origin of Evil consistently with the idea of God with *[sic]* some scheme of preceding philosophers that shall seem to bear the nearest resemblance to the present, and from which, at first sight, it might have the appearance of having been borrowed. For this purpose I know of no one having the same claims with the doctrines of the Eclectic or Egypto-Grecian Philosophy or more definitely the Dogmas of Plotinus. It has indeed been long familiar with the learned to affirm or deny the identity of the supposed Platonic Trinity with that of the Christian Church and if it were reasonable to found a decision on so momentous a subject on a single fragment of Speusippus, and this comprized in one short sentence, I should be inclined to the affirmative: but I am well aware that however well calculated a single passage might be to confirm other proof it would be highly unsatisfactory if advanced as the proof itself. The writings of Plato are indeed still extant and sufficiently voluminous, but independent of Plato's

own assertion in an epistle the authenticity of which I see no reason for doubting that he never had nor ever would commit to writing his conviction on this subject, the origin of mysterious nature of the Supreme Being and the origin of Evil in consistence with the admission of a perfect Goodness, independently of this, I say I have long convinced myself that it was no part of Plato's aim or purpose in the works which he made public, + which are still extant to teach or unfold his own philosophy or indeed any philosophy in the strictest + Platonic sense of the word. (my transcription, 17)

It is significant here that although Coleridge is advocating an orthodox position—that the Trinity is a purely Christian doctrine—he advocates it not on the basis of the special revelation of the Son of Man but on purely philosophical grounds. That is, he is using Plato's works (or rather his interpretation of them, as he does not actually quote Plato) to refute the charge that Plato's trinity influenced the Christian Trinity. But although he admits that his own convictions on the subject are grounded in occasional passages and incidental observations found throughout Plato, the reason Coleridge believes them incompatible with the Christian doctrine of the Trinity is that the Platonic writings seem irreconcilable with the Christian doctrine of emanation. Now, earlier in the work Coleridge has used the doctrine of Creation ex nihilo to get himself out of the rhetorical jam of appearing to ascribe the origin of evil to the Divine—ex nihilo is the linchpin of his distinction between *created* and *begotten.* In other words, Coleridge is willing and able to use both models of Creation to suit his purposes, and here he is using the doctrine of Creation through emanation to refute the charge that the Trinity is derivative of Greek philosophy; this is a fairly sophisticated commentary on ancient philosophy.

This refutation of possible pre-Christian Trinitarian philosophical influences continues for some 3,500 words; it rambles through a discussion of the operation of the concepts of good and evil within Greek philosophy, highlighting differences between the Greek and Christian systems. The final conclusion Coleridge reaches is that the resemblance is "merely verbal."

Thus that the Alexandrian philosophy from Plotinus to Proclus, bears no other resemblance to the doctrine respecting the tri=unity of the Deity, or the unity of the Tri-personal God, than what it derives from the phrases, borrowed by these philosophers from the Jewish + Christian Church, or the imperfect traditions of the earliest ages, is evident. It is evident that the resemblance of the doctrines is merely verbal. Whether more than this is true of the esoteric philosophy of Plato himself, + of his immediate successors, may perhaps be rendered more or less probable but cannot be proved. In like manner respecting certain tenets, that seem to bear on this doctrine, in the scanty records of the Same Thracian mysteries, it will be sufficient to say that they are parts of a system clearly pantheistic, of a system in which the World is God. The resemblance therefore must be superficial only. (my transcription, 24)

From this point he will go on to argue that a properly triune, Christian, model of deity is the only form in which God can exist. This argument will be addressed shortly, but first it is important to examine several comments Coleridge made earlier in the text at the outset of this argument. It is extremely significant that he chose to describe the Christian tradition by the term *catholic.* He could easily have used *Christian,* which would have been the more likely choice for a theologian putting forward a traditional English Protestant agenda.

And here instead of selecting the passages in which a divine Trinity is asserted, much less enlarging their number from works later than the time of the Emperor Julian, the authors of which purposely coloured their language and selected their terminology with the view of setting up a religion of philosophy, now as a rival of christianity, + now as including the christian faith, I will give the substance of their principles or rather the grounds + primary principles, on which their doctrine rested + therein its fundamental + inherent diversity from the doctrine evolved in the preceding chapters, a diversity which no succeeding approximations to the language of the catholic church, nor real resemblance to the arguments +explications of the catholic article uttered in the writings of the Fathers can remove or diminish in opposition then to the position laid down or neglectful of the warning given by Speusippus, the most faithful organ of original Platonism. (my transcription, 19)

By using the word *catholic* (though granted, with a lowercase "c") in counterpoint to Greek systems, Coleridge is effectively defining it as the legitimate position of Christian Trinitarianism. Although this is exactly what the word means in its most pure etymology (and other statements by Coleridge about to be quoted suggest that he is employing here this pure, rather than Roman, meaning of *catholic*), the word had acquired a tremendous amount of ideological baggage, even when used with a lowercase "c," by the time Coleridge wrote. If Coleridge was indeed writing as a part of the Church of England, and by this time there is little question that he was, then effectively to define the word *catholic* as the orthodox and correct interpretation of the Christian doctrine is immensely significant because he was effectively making a claim that the Church of England was a catholic church. Such a claim was proleptic of the Tractarian position that would emerge just over a decade later.

The claim that Coleridge viewed the Church of England as a catholic church on the basis of these few lines would be tenuous were it not also supported by other statements. The most glaring example comes from his *Table Talk*. On April 29, 1823, Coleridge spoke at length about the question of catholicism. These are two of his three comments in full:

> The preset adherents of the church of Rome are not, in my judgement, Catholics. We are the Catholics. We can prove that we hold the doctrines of the primitive church for the first three hundred years. The Council of Trent made the Papists what they are. A foreign Romish bishop has declared, that the Protestants of his acquaintance were more like what he conceived the enlightened Catholics to have been before the Council of Trent, than the best of the latter in his days. Perhaps you will say, this bishop was not a *good* Catholic. I can not answer for that. The course of Christianity and the Christian church may not unaptly be likened to a mighty river, which filled a wide channel, and bore along with its waters mud, and gravel, and weeds till it met a great rock in the middle of its stream. By some means or other, the water flows purely, and separated from the filth, in a deeper and narrower course on one side of the rock, and the refuse of the dirt and troubled water goes off on the other in a broader current, and then cries out, "*We* are the river!" ...
>
> A person said to me lately, "But you will, for civility's sake, *call* them *Catholics*, will you not?" I answered, that I would not; for I would not tell a lie upon any, much less upon so solemn an occasion. The adherents of the church of Rome, I repeat, are not *Catholic* Christians. If they are, then it follows that we Protestants are

heretics and schismatics, as, indeed, the Papists very logically, from their own premisses, call us. And *"Roman* Catholics" makes no difference. Catholicism is not capable of degrees or local apportionments. There can be but one body of Catholics, *ex vi termini.* To talk strictly of *Irish* or *Scotch Roman* Catholics is a mere absurdity.[21]

What is remarkable about both these quotations is that between them they make clear that Coleridge was deeply concerned with presenting the Church of England as a catholic church, in fact according to *Table Talk,* the *true* Catholic Church. Though he did not place the Tractarians' characteristic emphasis upon the apostolic succession, and though he was more hostile to Roman Catholics than the Tractarians were—sounding more like Jewell in his argument than Newman or Froude—the very fact that he was concerned with presenting the Church of England as a catholic church is tremendously significant. This is true because it was neither an eighteenth-century concern nor an early nineteenth-century (i.e., ante-Tractarian) concern. Divines of the early English Reformation had employed the argument that the Church of England was the true Catholic Church after the split from Rome, but such arguments became less common as the Church of England became more and more aggressively Protestant under Cranmer during Edward's reign, and still less common under Elizabeth's reign. The fact that Coleridge was concerned with raising it at all demonstrates that he was an extremely High Churchman for his time.

---

21. Samuel Taylor Coleridge, *Specimens of the Table Talk of the Late Samuel Taylor Coleridge,* in *Complete Works,* 6:268–69.

9

On the Constitution of the Church and State
The Christian Nature of Society

ON THE CONSTITUTION OF THE CHURCH AND STATE IS, WITH THE
partial exception of the *Lay Sermons,* the text in which Coleridge most
overtly used Hooker to reconstruct a Tory position on church and state
in reaction to Warburton. It is not, however, any less prolix or capricious
than other Coleridge texts, and it suffers from his characteristic attempt
to accomplish several things within a single published work. Furthermore, as Coleridge makes clear at the very outset, it discusses an "ideal,"
a situation devoid of historical context. This should be viewed as a teleological perspective rather than an idealist one; and, indeed, the teleological theological perspective is a traditional one for Christianity.
Coleridge's strategy of describing an ideal outside of time is especially
important because it is similar to the perspective from which Warburton
claimed to be writing when he constructed the argument of *The Alliance.*
The latter stages of this chapter will argue that the first half of book 8 of
The Laws of Ecclesiastical Polity and the first chapters *On the Constitution of the Church and State* both contain systems that might broadly
(if imprecisely) be called contract theory. The term *contract theory* is
imprecise because it was the conscious basis of Warburton's model of
the church and state relationship, but Warburton claimed to be partially
influenced by Hooker in his employment of eighteenth-century philosophical contract theory (a precarious claim on his part, as discussed in
chapter 4). Hooker's and Coleridge's model may be better described

as one of tacit acceptance or acclamation of the state church on the part of the populace—giving the royal governorship of the church an almost democratic legitimacy from the grassroots. This hard parallel will be used as a foundation upon which to build the direct link of influence that (it is argued) exists between the two works. The basis of this parallel is that Hooker built a system that shifted the authority of the church from a traditional divine right model to a model in which the monarch's authority as a supreme governor of the church rested on tacit acclamation or acceptance by the populace at large—a sort of national *placet*. This suggests an English Reformation that was popular in nature and came into existence from the ground up—a picture of the English Reformation that was extremely consistent with the view Elizabeth's court wished to propagate.[1] In Hooker's system Elizabeth derived her authority as governor of the church because "England" desired her to hold that authority. This shift in the focus of authority from classical divine right to right by acclamation of the populace was what prompted Tory church theorists to claim that the text of the posthumous book 8 of *The Laws* had been tampered with, when in fact it had not. Interestingly, this was a charge that Coleridge refused to accept in a very early (A cut) annotation to Walton's *Life of Hooker* in the Ashley folio:

> It is a strange blind story of the three last books, and of Hooker's live relict, the Beast without Beauty instead of Beauty + the beast. But Saravia?—If honest Isaac's account of the tender, confidential, even confessional, friendship of Hooker and Saravia be accurate, how chanced it that H did not entrust the manuscripts to his friend who stood beside him in his last moments? At all events, Saravia must have known whether they had or had not received the author's last hand. Why were not Mr. Charke and the other Canterbury parson called to account, or questioned at least as to the truth of Mrs. Joan's story? Verily, I cannot help suspecting that the doubt cast on the

---

1. Whether one believes Christopher Haigh's "propaganda argument," and whether Hooker was influenced by court sources in the writing of book 8 of *The Laws*—and he almost certainly was not—are irrelevant. This is so because, regardless of whether the court *created* this view, they certainly actively disseminated it.

authenticity of the latter books by the high church party originated in their dislike of the contents.—In short, it is a blind story, a true Canterbury tale, dear Isaac! STC[2]

Though his refusal to believe that Hooker's text had been altered may have sprung from his radical political stance of the time (which made him skeptical of any charge that was levied by Tories), it still shows considerable insight, at a very young age, into the bibliography of Hooker's works.

Hooker's shift in the transmission of authority from God to the monarch also allowed Warburton to dupe readers by originally appearing to give homage to Hooker in the early editions of *The Alliance*, even though his theoretical paradigm demanded a refutation of Hooker if it was to be cogent.[3] Coleridge, in turn, sought to abrogate participatory social contract theory (such as Warburton's system relied on) by arguing that the simple existence of the idea of a social contract proved that society functioned through acclamation of the populace. In other words, no contract had been entered into; consent of the populace was implicit because acclamation was implicit in all society. Both Hooker's and Coleridge's systems stressed acceptance or acclamation rather than theoretical contracts drawn by *church* and *state*. The end result was an almost identical product, even if it was packaged differently by being discussed in the dialogues of the contemporary periods.

ON THE CONSTITUTION OF THE CHURCH AND STATE CONSIDERED ON ITS OWN

On the Constitution of the Church and State is confusingly eclectic. It contains twelve chapters followed by three independent sections: "Idea of the Christian Church" (which is in four subsections described as the

---

2. See chapter 4 above. Table identifying annotations to the Ashley folio, HNC [Henry Nelson Coleridge], identification number II.

3. See chapter 4 above. Bolingbroke rightly pointed this out and thereby caused Warburton to write the final section of chapter 5, book 2 of *The Alliance*— where he attempted a *refutatio* of Hooker.

four characters of the church), "On the Third Possible Church" (which deals with Coleridge's conception of the Church of the Antichrist), and "Second Part: or, Aids to a Right Appreciation of the Act Admitting Roman Catholics to Sit in Both Houses of Parliament, &c &c." This last section is followed by an appendix consisting of a letter to an unnamed recipient and a "Glossary to the Appended Letter"—which actually precedes the letter. There are three independent projects here. The first two are interlinked: they are (1) the twelve chapters discussing the idea of the English constitution (and its tripartite system of government under legislature, church, and monarch) and (2) the sections on the idea of the Christian Church and the Church of the Antichrist. The second project follows logically from the first, and there is logic to its inclusion and placement. The third section, which discusses the question of Catholic emancipation, does not follow from the two preceding sections; because Catholic emancipation challenged the idea of a Protestant state there is some logic to including it within the work as a whole, but its inclusion is not rhetorically well executed. The fact that the discussion of Catholic emancipation appears as an appendage to a more cogent work raises the question of whether the entirety of the text was actually prompted by a decision to write a tract upon the subject of Catholic emancipation. Coleridge always maintained that this was the case, but a careful examination of the structure of *On the Constitution of the Church and State* suggests that this is unlikely to have been more than legend. From the structure of the work one can see that the first twelve chapters (the only part of the work that is divided into chapters) are a work in and of themselves; they discuss state theory and the English constitution. Moreover, the full title of the work as it appears on the flyleaf of the book lends weight to this interpretation; there it is "On the Constitution of the Church and State, According to the Idea of Each with Aids toward a Right Judgment on the Late Catholic Bill." The fact that the "Advertisement" for the work addresses the question of the bill in the form of a preface, and even more so the fact that only the first two paragraphs of chapter 1 mention the bill at all (after which substantive discussion of the subject is dropped entirely until the later sections) constitute strong evidence in the form of higher criticism to believe that the discussion of Catholic emancipation was fastened on to a preexisting work or a work in progress. That conclusion is further supported by the fact that the heading of chapter 1 reads, "Prefatory

Remarks on the true import of the word, IDEA; and what the author means by 'according to the Idea,'" a heading that describes the content of the chapter perfectly—but only if the chapter is taken to begin at the third paragraph. This is not the first instance where examination of textual evidence has brought a different conclusion from the purported "truth" delivered by Coleridge discussing the creation of his own works. *On the Constitution of the Church and State* should, then, be taken to be a discussion of the English constitution, and it should be taken to begin with the third paragraph of the first chapter.

Though Coleridge makes an immense display of defining the term *idea,* in fact what he means by it is fairly straightforward. When used within the context of this work, it simply means a utopian form of the church or a utopian form of the state: that is, an ideal form separate from the travails of history. Coleridge puts his point uncharacteristically clearly when he writes: "By an *idea,* I mean, (in this instance) that conception of a thing, which is not abstracted from any particular state, form, or mode, in which the thing may happen to exist at this or at that time; nor yet generalized from any number or succession of such forms or modes; but which is given by the knowledge of *its ultimate aim.*"[4] Coleridge has in mind to distinguish between an idea and a conception, and the distinction is again straightforward: that which is contemplated objectively (outside the mind—existing) is a law (or conception), such as gravity, and that which is contemplated only subjectively is an idea, such as beauty (13). Coleridge moves on from this distinction to use the idea of a social contract as an example; this choice is important on its own ground (as mentioned earlier) because he uses both the general concept of a social contract and his repudiation of that social contract on the grounds that it is a conception rather than an idea, as the avenue into his discussion of the English constitution. Clearly his plan was to begin the discussion of an English constitution from the position of its existence by acclamation of the people. But lacking a written document such as the Constitution of the United States of America (which incidentally

---

4. Samuel Taylor Coleridge, *On the Constitution of the Church and State,* ed. John Colmer, vol. 10 of *The Collected Works of Samuel Taylor Coleridge,* Bollingen Series 75 (Princeton: Princeton University Press, 1976), 12. Subsequent page citations to this work are given parenthetically in the text.

is a conception rather than an idea, since it exists in history), Coleridge must place himself on firm footing by showing that the *idea* of an English constitution, extant through acclamation of the people, exists even if a *conception* of one extant in time does not. The point of this is to show tacit acclamation of the monarch as head (or governor) of the church in order to place the church in an elevated position by its very nature. Coleridge argues this in order to be able to give the idea of a clerisy educating the working classes of society the imprimatur of both the monarchy and democracy through the idea of acclamation. To illustrate this point further, Coleridge adopts the Kantian perspective of the innate belief that a person should be treated as an end and never as a means:

> But if instead of the *conception* or *theory* of an original social contract, you say the *idea* of an ever-originating social contract, this is so certain and so indispensable, that it constitutes the whole ground of the difference between subject and serf, between a commonwealth and a slave-plantation. And this, again, is evolved out of the yet higher idea of a *person*, in contra-distinction from *thing*—all social law and Justice being grounded on the principle, that a person can never, but by his own fault, become a thing, or, without grievous wrong, be treated as such: and the distinction in this that a thing may be used altogether and merely as the *means* to an end; but the person must always be included in the *end*. (15)

The employment of Kantian language is probably not by itself significant—nor does it appear that Coleridge is attempting to construct a Kantian foundation for his discussion of the constitution (had he done so, the discussion would have necessarily followed the lines of a fairly straightforward duty-theory ethical system, with illustrations drawn from history to show how the English constitution ensured that a given person would follow his duty to his fellow man—and thus would have proceeded along the lines of what he saw as a conception rather than an idea). Instead Coleridge is using Kant's philosophical theology as a point of departure for discussing, in the following two pages, the moral (as opposed to ethical) nature of the current political climate. Here he argues that although the workers may not be possessed of an intellectual understanding, through contemplation, of Kant's truth that a person should never be used solely as a means to an end, they are innately possessed of the idea: "No man, who has ever listened to laborers of this rank, in any alehouse, over the Saturday night's jug of beer, discussing the injustice of the present rate of wages, and the iniquity of their being paid in part out of the parish poor-rates, will doubt for a moment that they are fully possessed by the idea" (16). The route by which Coleridge moves from this Kantian position to a discussion of the English constitution is by discussing moral freedom, a difficult transition for anyone but Coleridge to see the point of; in fact, it lasts only a short paragraph and includes an attack on the philosophy of necessitarianism. His point seems to be that the idea of moral freedom is innate—as he will also argue that the idea of a constitution is innate—but difficult or impossible to define through specific examples (he quotes Augustine's definition of time, which he purports to be "I know it well enough when you do not ask me: taken from *Confessions*: 11.14" [18]). Clearly, the point of the discussion of moral freedom is meant to introduce an element of human responsibility within the (Christian) scheme of government that he is about to discuss as an innate idea. To use this as a transition from the position that persons must be treated as ends to the idea of a constitution is, however, confusing. The only logical bridge is that the responsibility for implicit acclamation comes through moral freedom, the freedom not to acknowledge governmental authority.

Finally, in the latter two pages of chapter 1, Coleridge comes to the point he has been attempting to make: that the idea of a constitution is innate and arises out of the very idea of a government:

> But a Constitution is an idea arising out of the idea of a state; and because our whole history from Alfred onward demonstrates the continued influence of such an idea, or ultimate aim, on the minds of our fore-fathers, in their characters and functions as public men; alike in what they resisted and in what they claimed; in the institutions and forms of polity which they established, and with regard to those, against which they more or less successfully contended; and because the result has been a progressive, though not always a direct, or equable advance in the gradual realization of the idea; and that it is actually, though even because it is an *idea* it cannot be *adequately*, represented in a correspondent scheme of means really existing; we speak, and have a right to speak, of the idea itself, as actually existing *i.e.*, as a *principle*, existing in the only way in which a principle can exist—in the minds and consciences of the persons, whose duties it prescribes, and whose rights it determines in the same sense that the

sciences of arithmetic and of geometry, that mind, that life itself, have reality; the constitution has real existence, and does not the less exist in reality, because it both *is* and *exists as,* an IDEA. (19)

Clearly, Coleridge writes all this circumlocution to solidify the fact that the English constitution exists, through both tradition and the idea, even though no written constitution (such as that in America) exists in fact. Here again he goes to great pains to make the redundant point that an idea is different from a conception: a conception is drawn from a generalization constructed through many concrete examples of one thing, while an idea exists innately through the mind—a point that he has covered before. He also takes pains to demonstrate that the English constitution is not a conception in order to clarify it as an idea—in other words, making an apophatic argument. It is likely that he goes to such didactic lengths to establish that when he calls the English constitution "*Lex Sacra, Mater Legum*" (here he purports to be quoting "an old writer," though he gives no citation) he means to imply, not that the English constitution is a nexus of laws drawn together (which is the essential form of English common law), but rather that it is a guiding principle behind *all specific laws*—the idea of law. On the whole these are simple points, but Coleridge manages to complicate them tremendously.

The Constitution of England and Its Church

The second chapter is well described by its heading: "The idea of a State in the larger sense of that term, introductory to the constitution of the state in the narrower sense, as it exists in this Country" (23). Interestingly, in the first edition the chapter heading was simply "Concerning the Right Idea of the Constitution." But it is important to note, as Coleridge does not, that implicitly extant within this argument is the fact that (though he places the English constitution in history by saying "as it exists in this country") he is safe from the accusation that he is now in the realm of conceptions because the British constitution remains an idea—since it is not locatable in one place. It is not only indiscrete but perpetually in flux, given that no parliament can bind its successors.

   In this second chapter Coleridge, having established that the constitution exists, gives a more technical definition of what he believes it to be. He begins by quoting Spinoza:

A Constitution is the attribute of a State *i.e.* of a body politic, having the principle of its unity within itself, whether by concentration of its forces, as a constitutional pure Monarchy, which, however, has hitherto continued to be *ens rationale,* unknown in history (*B. Spinozae Tract. Pol. Cap. VI De Monarchia ex rationis praescripto*),—or—with which we are alone concerned—by equipoise and interdependency: the *lex equilibrii,* the principle prescribing the means and conditions by and under which this balance is to be established and preserved, being the constitution of the state. (23)

The important section of this quotation is the idea of the *lex equilibrii,* which Coleridge immediately goes on to define as a binary pair: permanence and progression. He places these in historical context by stating that the dialectic of the two in English history is represented by the landowning classes for the force of permanence and the new mercantile classes for the force of progression. The functions of these two forces he terms *agricultural* and *distributive*—terms used interchangeably with *permanence* and *progression* respectively. Coleridge describes the legislature as composed of an upper house of the "major barons," representing the interests of the agricultural section of the population, and a lower house of the "minor barons" or "franklins," who over time have changed from small landowning gentry to mercantile businessmen. This is his commercial interpretation of the constitution with the monarch as the apex of a triangular system of government. His most concise statement of this interpretation is as follows:

> But whether this conjecture be well or ill grounded, the *principle* of the constitution remains the same. That harmonious balance of the two great correspondent, at once supporting and counterpoising, interests of the state, its permanence, and its progression: that balance of the landed and the personal interests was to be secured by a legislature of two Houses; the first consisting wholly of barons or landholders, permanent and hereditary senators: the second of the knights or minor barons, elected by, and as the representatives of the remaining landed community, together with the burgesses, the representatives of the commercial, manufacturing, distributive, and professional classes,—the latter (the elected burgesses) constituting the major number. The king, meanwhile, in whom the executive power is vested, it will suffice at present to consider as the beam of

the constitutional scales. A more comprehensive view of the kingly office must be deferred till the remaining problem (the idea of a national church) has been solved. (29–30)

Coleridge makes clear that the preceding scheme is his illustration of the constitution of the *state,* as opposed to the constitution of the *nation,* and this precise discrimination between state and nation brings up the issue of a national church. His overall point on the subject is simple, but again the argument is expressed rather disjointedly. He declares that the two poles of permanence and progression are operative within his scheme of the constitution of the state, not the constitution of the nation as a whole. To demonstrate his theory of the constitution of the nation, the constitution in the broader sense of the word, he shows a larger scheme, in which the separate pole of the national church acts in a dialectic with the pole of the state. In other words, the idea of the British constitution exists on two levels: the permanent (the constitution of the nation) and the transient or progressive (the constitution of the state). Only the latter deals with things that "moth and rust may corrupt."

Chapters 3, 4, and 5 deal with Coleridge's discussion of the national church. Chapter 3 discusses the idea of the church from the perspective of history. It is extremely short and concerns the delineation of religion and law. This is essentially a distinction between the spirit and the letter. It is an error, he states, to believe that the Levitical law was not only a part of an inspired wisdom giving laws for the state to administer the day-to-day life of the nation but also part of a revealed religion. He wishes to distinguish religion from law by highlighting religion as spiritual and contra-distinguished from temporal and political concerns. As he puts it: "It is enough to say, that not the principle itself, but the superior wisdom with which the principle was carried into effect, the greater perfection of the machinery, forms the true distinction, the *peculiar* worth of the Hebrew constitution" (34). Chapter 4 reiterates the themes of Jubilee and benevolence that Coleridge discussed in such great detail in *The Lectures on Revealed Religion.*[5]

Chapter 5 contains the heart of Coleridge's theories of the national church—as its heading indicates: "Of the Church of England, or National Clergy, according to the Constitution: its characteristic ends, pur-

---

5. See chapter 3 above.

poses and functions: and of the persons comprehended under the Clergy, or the Functionaries of the National Church" (42). Coleridge describes the church as the third estate, in the same way that he has called the House of Lords the first estate and the House of Commons the second; its function is the erudition of the nation.

> Now, as in the former estate, the permanency of the nation was provided for; and in the second estate its progressiveness, and personal freedom: while in the king the cohesion by interdependence, and the unity of the country, were established; there remains for the third estate only that interest, which is the ground, the necessary antecedent condition, of both the former. Now these depend on a continuing and progressive civilization. But civilization is itself but a mixed good, if not far more a corrupting influence, the hectic of disease, not the bloom of health and a nation so distinguished more fitly to be called a varnished than a polished people: where this civilization is not grounded in *cultivation,* in the harmonious development of those qualities and faculties that characterise our *humanity.*
> The Nationality, therefore, was reserved for the support and maintenance of a permanent class or order, with the following duties. A certain smaller number were to remain at the fountain heads of the humanities, in cultivating and enlarging the knowledge already possessed, and in watching over the interests of physical and moral science; being, likewise, the instructors of such as constituted, or were to constitute, the remaining more numerous classes of the order. This latter and far more numerous body were to be distributed throughout the country, so as not to leave even the smallest integral part or division without a resident guide, guardian, and instructor; . . . The object of the two former estates of the realm, which conjointly form the STATE, was to reconcile the interests of permanence with that of progression—law with liberty. The object of the National Church, the third remaining estate of the realm, was to secure and improve that civilization, without which the nation could be neither permanent nor progressive. (42–44)

Coleridge is unwilling, however, to use the term *church* in his nationalistic discussion—he would rather the word be used only in the greater sense of the "Church of Christ." Here he is instead discussing what he believed to be a social order of men, the clergy, and his scheme provides the clergy as an educated set of guardians for civilization. He notes that *clerk* has always been the term used to describe educated men, and from it he will coin the word *clerisy*. This term refers to the profession-als, or officer core, of the national church: those for whom the church is a vocation. Another focus of the chapter is Coleridge's reinforcement of the intellectual basis for terming all educators clerisy; on the purely philo-sophical level it argues that all the arts and sciences (*science* was then a new word and still by and large a natural philosophic enterprise) study a set of information that is teleological in nature and will lead to the dis-covery of what was pure and good in both humanity and nature. This teleology then displays the creating force behind those qualities—God. Coleridge's purpose here is to explain why he has cast theologians in the role of educators; the argument is, however, unnecessary on a practical level because at that time all fellowships in the two ancient universities of England required the holder to be an ordained priest in the Church of England. Perhaps for this very reason Coleridge spends virtually the entirety (and all the relevant sections) of chapter 6 reiterating that he is discussing the idea of a national clerisy and not the church (he has al-ready made clear his reservations about the use of that word in any his-torical context) in England at the time.

THE CLERISY AND EDUCATION

Chapter 7, "Regrets and Apprehensions," chapter 8, "The Subject Re-sumed," and chapter 9, "Practical Conclusion: what unfits; and what ex-cludes from the National Church," should be viewed as a three-unit set. The subject is the role of the national church in education—a role that Coleridge saw as administrative and "governing" (in the sense of "school governors"). Though chapter 7 is a bit of a rant against the Church of England for having fallen away from its true roots and the form designed for it by the Elizabethan divines in allowing education to be entrusted to persons other than Anglicans, it is important because it introduces the material that culminates in his coining of the word *clerisy* in chapter 9.[6] Coleridge's overall point is summed up in chapter 8:

---

6. See chapter 6 above. This section is reminiscent of the section of the *Lay Sermons* where he uses the Lancaster-Bell debate as an example of the need for the Church of England to maintain its hegemony over national education.

I have no better way of taking up the thread of my argument, than by restating my opinion, that our Eighth Henry would have acted in correspondence to the great principle of our Constitution if having restored the original balance on both sides, he had determined the nationality to the following objects: 1st. To the maintenance of the Universities and the great liberal schools. 2ndly. To the maintenance of a pastor and schoolmaster in every parish. 3rdly. To the raising and keeping in repair of the churches, schools, &c., and, Lastly: To the maintenance of the proper, that is, the infirm, poor whether from age or sickness: one of the original purposes of the national Reserve being the alleviation of those evils, which in the best forms of worldly states must arise and must have been foreseen as arising from the institution of individual properties and primogeniture. If these duties were efficiently performed, and these purposes adequately fulfilled, the very increase of the population ... would have more than counterbalanced those savings in the expenditure of the nationality occasioned by the detachment of the practitioners of law, medicine, &c., from the national clergy. (71)

The passage is illuminating on a number of points. Clearly it demonstrates that Coleridge saw the role of the church as primarily didactic, but equally importantly it demonstrates that his mature position on the concept of property was that property and its consequent ramification (the English law of primogeniture) would inevitably create inequality (and in some cases poverty). The church, however, was a national reserve that could compensate for the inequality created by the private holding of property. Finally, Coleridge's High Churchmanship and anti-Erastian principles are manifested in his argument that although it was right for Henry to have nationalized the wealth of the church (in order to stop it from exiting the community and going to increase the already staggering wealth of the Vatican and the greater religious orders), that wealth should have gone to make up a national charitable reserve, rather than simply being diverted to the exchequer or to Henry's war chest.

That this transfer of the national reserve from what had become national evils to its original and inherent purpose of national benefits, instead of the sacrilegious alienation which actually took place—that this was impracticable, is historically true: but no less true is it

198 Coleridge's Mature Project

philosophically, that this impracticability,—arising wholly from moral causes, that is, from loose manners and corrupt principles— does not rescue this wholesale sacrilege from deserving the character of the first and deadliest wound inflicted on the constitution of the kingdom: which term, constitution, in the body politic, as in bodies natural, expresses not only what has been actually evolved from, but likewise whatever is potentially contained in, the seminal principle of the particular body, and would in its due time have appeared but for emasculation or disease. (72)

The church ought to be both national and Protestant, but it should also be self-endowed and independent from the state. A freestanding corporate body composed of the same members as the state, it should not be reliant on the state for enforcement of its entitlements and should have no alliance with the state to employ the latter's law courts, for example. Unlike Warburton, Coleridge did not believe the clergy should be justices of the peace.

One of the church's functions is to relieve the misery collaterally created by the necessary economic actions of the state. But charity and the alleviation of destitution, though important, are clearly subsidiary to the church's pedagogic role. In Coleridge's dialectical understanding of English history, the pole of progression, which is eventually represented by the mercantile classes, was once represented by the church.

But during all this period of potential existence, or what we may call minority of the burgess order, the National Church was the substitute for the most important national benefits resulting from the same. The National Church presented the only breathing hole of hope. . . . To the Church alone could the nation look for the benefits of existing knowledge, and for the means of future civilization. Lastly let it never be forgotten, that under the fostering wing of the church, the class of free citizens and burgers were reared. To the feudal system we owe the *forms*, the church the *substance*, of our liberty. (72)

The medieval church was the repository of knowledge and the progress which that knowledge could bring. That circumstance was nigh on ideal for Coleridge—certainly the church was for him the ideal repository of knowledge.

The transitions between chapters 8 and 9, and chapters 9 and 10, are choppy but are key to a clear understanding of the work. The chapters are short, and it is wise to see them as one train of thought consisting of four parts: (1) the church is the depository of knowledge; (2) its priests should be seen as a professional class known as the clerisy; (3) the king, as governor of the church, is guardian of this national trust of knowledge; and (4) consequently the king is the "Head of the National Church, or Clerisy, and the Protector and Supreme Trustee of the NATIONALITY: the power of the same in relation to its proper objects being exercised by the King and the Houses of Convocation, of which, as before of the State, the King is the head and the arm" (83).

So the monarch's simultaneous position as head of the church and head of the state should be seen as a microcosm of the organic union exercised by members of society on the macro scale, who are simultaneously members of both church and state (acting as parts of the two together); church and state are not conceived as separate institutions and societies that act to help each other through contract. The unity of the two entities is paramount:

> The first and most indispensable qualification and pre-condition, that without which all others are null and void,—is that the National Clergy, and every member of the same from the highest to the lowest, shall be fully and exclusively citizens of the state, neither acknowledging the authority, nor within the influence of any other State in the world—full and undistracted subjects of this kingdom, and in no capacity, and under no pretences, owning any other earthly sovereign or visible head but the king, in whom alone the majesty of the nation is *apparent*, and by whom alone the unity of the nation in will and in deed is symbolically expressed and impersonated. (77)

This clearly had relevance to Catholic emancipation, by its implicit suggestion that Roman Catholic citizens of the state had an allegiance to another visible sovereign or head of their church in the person of the pope. In other words Coleridge seems to have been arguing, at least in the first twelve chapters of the book, that although Catholic emancipation was a moral necessity because Catholics held sufficient property to make them interested members of the society, it was not a danger to the nation because they were unfit to be members of the national clerisy—which, through its role as the national depository of knowledge, and the role of the monarch as its head with his constitutional powers of veto, acted as a protective influence and power for the nation.

THE MONARCH

The role of the monarch is important in this scheme. Colmer has remarked on this at some length in *Coleridge, Critic of Society.*

> Wisely, in his opinion, the protection of the Church had been entrusted to the King. That it was a sacred trust was officially recognized in the Coronation Oath. Should Parliament do anything therefore to endanger the safety of the Church it became the King's duty to use his constitutional veto. It might be thought that Coleridge was here evolving a theory of the constitution to suit the circumstances arising out of the problem of Catholic Emancipation, but this was not so; all the evidence of his published political writings and of the jottings in the Notebooks proves that he had the utmost horror for any doctrine concerning the omnipotence of Parliament. Wherever he discussed the constitutional balance between Crown and Parliament he laid special emphasis on the importance of the Crown. In one Notebook jotting he refers to the King as "the natural Magnet" of society, in another he asks how it is possible to place with safety "the revenues of this Country, its Functionaries, Armies, Fleets & Colonies in any other Man or Min," and in a letter to William Sotheby in 1831 he declared that though neither Whig nor Tory he was enough of the latter to honour the King, "as ordained of God—i.e. as no Reflection or Derivative from the (pretended) Sovereignty of the *People,* but as the lawful Representative, the consecrated Symbol of the Unity and Majesty of the *Nation.*" . . . [T]he chief charge that he brought against the Whigs was that they were unable to think of the function of the Crown except in terms of the man. "The Whig habit of Thought and Feeling is to know the Man only in the King, that of the Tory to find the King in the Man." . . . But, whatever view he put forward at any time, it always implied the right of the King to limit the power of Parliament.[7]

---

7. Colmer, *Coleridge,* 162–63.

These quotations show that in the notebooks Coleridge was hugely capricious, one reason why this book has been based on edited and published works. It is unwise to believe anything Coleridge ever said about himself. There is no question but that Coleridge was an ideological Tory at this point. (If anything, he was carping at the "new liberal" nature of the parliamentary Tory party—bitter that he had been unable to affect the party's recreation in the classical image).[8] As Coleridge's own friends were well aware, his ideology was Tory. In fact Colmer pointed this out four pages earlier by remarking on a statement of Henry Crabb Robinson's: "'He [Coleridge] exposes himself to the charge of being desirous to appear more of a Tory than he really is, leaving an opening to back out when assailed by his Liberal friends,' he [Crabb Robinson] declared. To the latter he could always explain that the present subordination of Church to State was no necessary part of the idea. Robinson complained that in his enthusiasm for tracing the 'idea' of a National Church Coleridge did not 'stay to enquire whether the actual Church be according to the idea.'"[9] As this quote shows, Coleridge's contemporaries viewed him as a Tory, though likely as a moderate one, and as someone seeking to create a Tory identity for church and state that was more ideological than "historically accurate." Crabb Robinson's criticism was not altogether fair, however, because Coleridge went to extreme lengths to reiterate that it was the idea of a national church he was discussing and not the actual functioning of the Church of England in Hanoverian England.

This stress on the role of the monarch, a Tory position, was consistent with Hooker's system in every way. The first two chapters of book 8 of *The Laws of Ecclesiastical Polity* deal directly with the role of the monarch: the first is entitled "State of the Question between the Church of England and its Opponents regarding the King's Supremacy" and the second "Principles on which the King's modified Supremacy is grounded." Hooker's point is straightforward: by whatever means kings come to power, they do so by God's imprimatur, and the monarch is owed honor because of divine authority:

> Some multitudes are brought into subjection by force, as they who being subdued are fain to submit their necks unto what yoke it

---

8. See chapter 5 above.
9. Colmer, *Coleridge*, 158.

pleaseth their conquerors to lay upon them; which conquerors by just and lawful wars do hold their power over such multitudes as a thing descending unto them, divine providence itself so disposing. For it is God who giveth victory in the day of war. And unto whom dominion in this sort is derived, the same they enjoy according unto that law of nations, which law authorizeth conquerors to reign as absolute lords over them who they vanquish.

Sometime it pleaseth God himself by special appointment to choose out and nominate such as to whom *Dominion* shalbe *[sic]* given, which thing he did often in the *Common-wealth* of *Israel*: They who in this sort receive power have it immediatelie from God by meer divine right, they by humane on whom the same is bestowed according unto mens discretion when they are left free by God to make choise of their owne governoure. By which of these meanes soever it happen, that *Kings* or governours be advanced unto their seates, we must acknowledg both their lawfull choise to be approoved of God, and themselves for *Godes Liuetenantes* and confess their power his.[10]

Hooker seems to have had in mind the final paradigm to apply to England—and this is not altogether surprising, considering that the attempt to alter Tudor succession by Edward VI and Northumberland was defeated by a popular uprising driven by anger at the arguably illegal alteration of Henry VIII's will;[11] the idea that a Roman Catholic movement defeated Northumberland could not stand, as Mary did not mention religion until she reached London, so the people of England had to have chosen the succession of the two sisters over Lady Jane Grey as "Godes Liuetenantes" and effectively confessed their power his.

For Hooker the unity of the two societies was also extremely important to their functioning as a nation:

We hold that seeing there is not any man of the *Church of England*, but the same man is also a member of the *Commonwealth*, nor any

---

10. Hooker, *Folger Library Edition*, 3:334–35 (emphasis in original).

11. Penry Williams has made the strongest attack on the legality of Edward and Northumberland's actions. See his *The Later Tudors: England, 1547–1603*, New Oxford History of England (Oxford: Oxford University Press, 1995).

man a member of the *Commonwealth* which is not also of the *Church of England,* therefore as in a figure *triangular* the base doth differ from the sides therof, and yet one and the self same line, is both a base and also a side; a side simplie, a base if it chance to be the bottome and underlie the rest: so albeit properties and actions of one kinde doe cause the name of Commonwealth, qualities and function of an other sort the name of a *Church* to be given unto a multitude, yet one and the self same multitude may in such sort be both and is so with us, that no person appertayning to the one can be denied to be also of the other.[12]

And later: "In respect of these differences therefore the *church* and the *Commonwealth* may in speech be compared or opposed aptly enoughe the one to the other, yet this is no argument that they are two independent societies."[13] Hooker also believed that the English constitution had happily provided the best system of government possible: a limited monarchy (exactly the same paradigm for the perfect form of government that Coleridge would offer some 230 years later). For Hooker the limits on royal authority came from the overarching system of English law; for Coleridge they had evolved into a system of constitutional law producing a stronger parliament than had existed in Hooker's lifetime. This in turn acted as a check on the king's power, though royal assent was still required and Coleridge still envisioned its withholding as an occasional necessity. He made this clear in an earlier passage where he demonstrated that Catholic emancipation was necessary because some Catholics met the freehold voting threshold: the morality of the country would not be jeopardized because (1) the clerisy would still control a national scheme of education and (2) the monarch's ultimate veto through royal assent would still be required for every act of Parliament. The role of the monarch as head of the church had become a moral "check and balance" on a parliament where the Test and Corporation Acts were repealed. The monarch's role as the head of the clerisy was seen by Coleridge as a sort of "moral insurance policy" providing a mechanism for the actions of the state to receive the assent of the head of the clerisy.

---

12. Hooker, *Folger Library Edition,* 3:319 (emphasis in original).
13. Hooker, *Folger Library Edition,* 3:327 (emphasis in original).

Hooker concluded his discussion of the commonwealth and the church as follows.

> Concerning therefore the matter wherof we have hitherto spoken, lett it stand for our finall conclusion that in a free *Christian* state or kingdome where one and the self same people are the *Church* and the *Commonwealth,* God through *Christ* directing that people, to see it for good and weightie considerations expedient that their Soveraigne *Lord* and Governor in causes civill have also in *Ecclesiasticall* affayres a supreme power, for as much as the light of reason doth lead them unto it, and against it, Godes own revealed law hath nothing; surely they doe not in submitting them selves thereunto any other than that which a wise and religious people ought to doe.[14]

Coleridge concluded his discussion of the constitution of the church and state this way:

> The right idea of a STATE, or Body Politic; "State" being here synonymous with a *constituted* Realm, Kingdom, commonwealth, or Nation, *i.e.* where the integral parts, classes, or orders are so balanced, or interdependent, as to constitute, more or less, a moral unit, an organic whole; and as arising oft of the Idea of a State I have added the Idea of a Constitution, as the informing principle of its coherence and unity. But in applying the above to our own kingdom . . . it was necessary to observe . . . that the Constitution, in its widest sense as the Constitution of the Realm arose out of, and in fact consisted in, the co-existence of the Constitutional STATE (in the second acceptation of the term) with the King as its head, and of the CHURCH (*i.e.* the *National* Church), likewise the King as its head; and lastly of the King, as the Head and Majesty of the whole Nation. (107–8)

The two paradigms are at root the same. Coleridge modeled his own explication of the idea of church and state on Hooker's.

Two brief points remain to clinch the argument. The first is utterly simple but extremely important. First, Warburton did not treat the role

---

14. Hooker, *Folger Library Edition,* 3:355–56 (emphasis in original).

of the monarch as head of the two societies with anywhere near as much emphasis as Coleridge and Hooker did. Warburton's paradigm stressed the role of the "Magistrate" as the paradigmatic operative of the state. The monarch's role as head of the two societies was a question that simply did not arise in Warburton. Therefore, when Coleridge chose to make the monarch the focus of his discussion on the question (after rereading Hooker) he was unquestionably actively departing from Warburton's entire structure, let alone Warburton's arguments and conclusions. He could have chosen to engage Warburton on the ground that Warburton himself had set up: the role of the Magistrate in the protection of the church's interests. He did not choose to do so, but instead recreated an older paradigm of Hooker's—the person of the monarch—and added his own emphasis to it.[15]

The second point is equally straightforward. Tories have always questioned Hooker's commitment to the question of divine right and have precariously claimed that he supported the divine right of kings, an arguable point at best (and equally possibly a completely misguided one). This is why they have traditionally been uneasy with Hooker's book 8 (and have suggested that there might have been posthumous tampering with the text because of their unease on this question). But Coleridge clearly chose to use Hooker's paradigm as part of his Tory ideology. His contemporaries, such as Crabb Robinson, recognized that he was a Tory—and even suggested that his system in *On the Constitution of the Church and State* went so far as to appear more Tory than his beliefs actually were. In any case, Coleridge's paradigm was certainly a departure from the orthodox Court Whiggism of his time, given its most pervasive and pure voice by Warburton.

---

15. See chapter 11 below.

10

Confessions of an Inquiring Spirit

Interpretation of the Scriptures

CONFESSIONS OF AN INQUIRING SPIRIT (1840) IS THE SHORTEST work that Coleridge prepared for publication; it was, apparently, originally intended as an appendix, or appendage, to *Aids to Reflection*, and because of these two facts it does not suffer from the characteristic Coleridgean flaw of attempting to accomplish more than one thing within a single work. It is uncharacteristically accessible in its prose style and straightforward in its argument. Because it is written in the form of seven separate letters, each of which encapsulates a separate section of the argument, Coleridge was forced to be concise in his discussion and clear in his rhetoric. In his excellent introduction to the Fortress Press edition, David Jasper summarizes the history of the work in progress:

> On 7 May 1825, Coleridge wrote to J. A. Hessey, of Taylor and Hessey, the publishers of *Aids to Reflection* (1825), concerning six "disquisitions," all except one of which are mentioned in *Aids to Reflection* as to be published in a "small supplementary volume." . . . According to a letter Coleridge wrote to J. Blanco White on 20 July 1825, the manuscript of this work was apparently with the publisher for more than a year, having been intended as a part of *Aids to Reflection* but omitted on account of its length. In further letters to Hessey in 1825, and in the notes and letters throughout the rest of his life, Coleridge continued to comment upon this "disquisition."[1]

---

1. David Jasper, introduction to *Confessions of an Inquiring Spirit*, by Samuel Taylor Coleridge (Philadelphia: Fortress Press, 1988), 8.

The most informative further comment upon the "disquisition" comes in letter no. 1466, written on May 23, 1825. It is worth quoting this letter at some length because it is the closest thing to an author's introduction that Coleridge provided—which is not surprising given that the work was published posthumously by Henry Nelson Coleridge on Coleridge's behalf. Coleridge wrote to Hessey (the bracketed passages are those crossed out in the manuscript):

> Since I left you, I have been *moiling* for an appropriate and inviting Title for, and instead of, the six Disquisitions. . . . Two only have occurred to me—or rather the same in two forms—both suggested by real incidents—the first, Conversations on Stainmoor (n.b. the dreariest and longest Waste-land in England) the second—[The young Chaplain and the Grey-headed passenger: or Conversations on Shipboard—or Convers. During a Voyage to the Mediterranean—or Cabin Conversations on subjects of moral and religious interest—supplemental of the AIDS TO REFLECTION—or lastly thus—]
>
> The Grey-headed Passenger: or Conversations on Ship-board during a voyage to the Mediterranean, supplemental of the AIDS TO REFLECTION by S. T. Coleridge.—
>
> My supposed fellow-passenger a young Clergyman, newly ordained who had subscribed [to] the 39 Articles, on the principles of Paley as mere Articles of Peace, quite satisfied in conscience that he should never preach counter to them as he should never trouble himself or his flock about them. He should keep to the *morality* of the Gospel & simply teach his Hearers to do as they would be done by.—In short, his Divinity would consist of two chapters—first, that Honesty is the best Policy; and, second, if you don't find it so here, you will hereafter. But notwithstanding this very compendious, convenient and portable faith, I find him a young man of fine intellect, and generous feelings, a good classic & an enthusiastic lover of Nature &c—The conversations are supposed to take place during the latter half of the Voyage—the first indeed at Gibraltar—& to have been preceded by a long series of discussions, which had ended in convincing him of the hollowness of the ground on which he had hitherto stood, of the cheerlessness, vulgarity and common-place character of the mechanical philosophy, and Paleyian Expedience— but still more in impressing him with the superior *power* and ampler

command given by the habit of seeking for the first principles of all living & effective truth in the constitution and constituent faculties of the Mind itself. He is roused and affected by an animated portraiture of the Life and Labors of a Minister of the Gospel, who is at the same time a Philosopher and a Christian and who finds the consummation and most perfect form of Philosophy in Christianity—and declares his determination to set about the building up of the philosophic mind in himself—but is mortified by the doubts which the Grey-headed Passenger expresses as to his perseverance in the task—and in the irritation occasioned by this unexpected Check avows his contempt and detestation of all quackery and mystery, and asks indignantly—If this Philosophy be true and important and agreeable to the Reason, Moral Being, and all the contra-distinguishing Attributes of Humanity, what should make it of such difficult acquirement for any man of education, and tolerable strength of intellect?—And with the answer to this question the Conversations commence: and after the two first that he begins to read the Aids to Reflection.[2]

Of course the "Grey-headed Passenger" is Coleridge himself (already forty-nine years of age at the point this letter was written). The text obviously underwent some substantial revision between the time this letter was written and Coleridge's death nine years later; seven letters make up the text of *Confessions of an Inquiring Spirit,* not six, and there is no formal argument with the Paleyian position in the text as it was published by Henry Nelson Coleridge. Furthermore, this letter, or introduction to the project, made no mention of Trinitarian philosophy, a major subject of the work as it stands.

Pneumatology

To be properly understood, *Confessions of an Inquiring Spirit* must be seen as a work about pneumatology. Though it places this subject within the context of a discussion of biblical hermeneutics and the doctrine of divine intelligence passed to the biblical authors (i.e., the interpretation

---

2. Coleridge, *Selected Letters,* 5:464–65. The brackets are Griggs's.

Table 2. The Pentad of Operative Christianity

Prothesis

Christ, The Word

Thesis	**Mesothesis**	*Antithesis*
	Or "The Indifference"	
The Scriptures	The Holy Spirit	The Church

Synthesis

The Preacher

The Scriptures, The Spirit, and the Church, are co-ordinate; the indispensable conditions and the working causes of the perpetuity, and continued renascence and spiritual life of Christ still militant. The Eternal Word, Christ from everlasting, is the *Prothesis,* or identity;—the Scriptures and the Church are the two poles, or *Thesis* and *Antithesis,* and the Preacher in direct line under the Spirit but likewise the Point of Junction of the Written Word and the Church, is the *Synthesis.*

This is God's Hand in the World

Source: Adapted from Coleridge, *Confessions of an Inquiring Spirit,* 19.

that the authors were not divinely inspired but that the divine intelligence passed into them while writing, thus making everything they wrote infallible and entirely reconcilable with the remainder of the texts and narratives within the canon), the underlying subject is the operation of the Holy Spirit through the faculty of the reason in the reader. This is clear at the outset because, as a preface to the entire work, Coleridge placed a diagram, entitled "The Pentad of Operative Christianity," that was followed by an explanatory passage (table 2).

The Pentad is an important key to understanding Coleridge's intention and underlying argument within the work as a whole. It is dropped in as a sort of preface without explanation, but the fact that he identified the "Preacher" as the synthesis of the dialectic, the point at which the scriptures, the Holy Spirit, and the church become one, makes the Pentad a coded précis of the spine of his argument that extends through the work. The Pentad is preceded on page 17 by two epigraphs. The first, significantly, is from Hooker: "Being persuaded of nothing more than of this, that whether it be in matter of speculation or of practice, no untruth can possibly avail the patron and defender long, and that things most truly are likewise most behovefully spoken.—*Hooker.*"[3] The second epigraph reads:

> Any thing will be pretended rather than admit the necessity of internal evidence, or acknowledge, among the external proofs, the convictions and experiences of Believers, though they should be common to all the faithful in every age of the Church. But in all superstition there is a heart of unbelief; and, *vice versa,* where a man's belief is but a superficial acquiescence, credulity is the natural result and accompaniment, if only he be not required to sink into the depths of his being, where the sensual man can no longer draw breath.—*Literary Remains.* (17)

The second passage is clearly by Coleridge himself; it was most likely taken by Henry Nelson Coleridge from a notebook entry and appended to the front of the work. In no other instance did Coleridge use a quotation from his own work as an epigraph to a published work, and it seems most logical to conclude that Coleridge chose the passage from Hooker to be an epigraph to the work and that Henry Nelson Coleridge added this passage from his uncle's remains because he felt it illuminated the text. Coleridge provides his own prose to introduce the project on the facing page to the beginning of letter 1:

> SEVEN Letters to a friend concerning the bounds between the right, and the superstitious, use and estimation of the Sacred Canon; in which the Writer submissively discloses his own private judgement on the following Questions:—

---

3. Coleridge, *Confessions,* 17. Subsequent page citations to this work are given parenthetically in the text.

I. Is it necessary, or expedient, to insist on the belief of the divine origin and authority of all, and every part of the Canonical Books as the condition, or first principle, of Christian Faith?

II. Or may not the due appreciation of the Scriptures collectively be more safely relied on as the result and consequence of the belief in Christ; the gradual increase—in respect of particular passages—of our spiritual discernment of their truth and authority supplying a test and measure of our own growth and progress as individual believers, without the servile fear that prevents or overclouds the free honour which cometh from love? *I John* iv. 18. (22)

(The text of 1 John 4:18 reads: "There is no room for fear in love; perfect love banishes fear. For fear brings with it the pains of judgment, and anyone who is afraid has not attained to love in its perfection.")[4]

Taking as read that one of the seven letters that make up the text of *Confessions of an Inquiring Spirit* must have been written later than 1825, it seems clear that this is letter 1: first, because letter 2 formally sets out Coleridge's disagreement with the doctrine that divine intelligence proceeded through the pen of the biblical writers (i.e., it sets out the major thesis for the work), and second, because letter 1 is as close as Coleridge ever came to giving an explanation of the Pentad. But it is also clear that some substantial revision of the other six letters took place between 1825 and Coleridge's death. This is most obvious in letter 2, because, during the explanation of his disagreement with the doctrine, Coleridge employed the language of catholicity, much as he had done in *On the Divine Ideas*:

And this Doctrine, I confess, plants the vineyard of the Word with thorns for me, and places snares in its pathways. These may be delusions of an evil spirit; but here I so harshly question the seeming angel of light—my reason, I mean, and moral sense in conjunction with my clearest knowledge—I must inquire on what authority this Doctrine rests. And what other authority dares a truly catholic Christian

---

4. The translation here is from *The New English Bible, with the Apocrypha,* Oxford study ed., gen. ed. Samuel Sandmel (New York: Oxford University Press, 1970).

admit as coercive in the final decision, but the declarations of the Book itself,—though I should not, without struggles and a trembling reluctance, gainsay even a universal tradition? (28)

Language describing good Christians as "catholic" does not appear in the text of *Aids to Reflection*. Furthermore, the text of *Confessions of an Inquiring Spirit* contains many references to Protestantism and to the Church of England as a Protestant enterprise. All of this suggests that the original manuscript for *Confessions of an Inquiring Spirit* was revised and added to as Coleridge developed both his idea of the Pentad and his interest in presenting the Church of England as a catholic church. His letter to Hessey makes clear that he envisioned the project of *Confessions of an Inquiring Spirit* to be a work in which the young clergyman finds himself to be a philosopher and Christianity to be the most perfect philosophy, and this idea of Christianity as the one perfect and true philosophy is the avowed subject of *On the Divine Ideas*, which was written around 1826.

So to the text of the seven letters themselves: early in letter 1 Coleridge says, regarding his approach to the scriptures, "Like certain plants, I creep towards the light, even though it draw me away from the more nourishing warmth. Yea, I should do so, even if the light had made its way through a rent in the wall of the Temple" (23). Clearly the light is a metaphor for reason, and nourishing warmth a metaphor for comfortable unquestioning acceptance of the Bible. He goes on to outline his faith in a fivefold creed, which he purports to be common to all the "Fathers of the Reformation—overlooking, as non-essential the differences between the several Reformed Churches—according to the five main classes or sections into which the aggregate distributes itself to my apprehension. I have then only to state the effect produced on my mind by each of these, or the *quantum* of recipiency and coincidence in myself relatively thereto, in order to complete my Confession of Faith" (24).[5] The five credenda correspond to the Pentad of Operative Christianity. It is important to note, though, that Coleridge is taking the Hookerian position on the Eucharist here. Hooker describes the Eucharist in a manner that he sees as common to all the Reformed churches,

---

5. All five of the positions that I am about to summarize are to be found on 24–25.

but in fact Hooker also suggests that his presentation of the doctrine includes material held in common with the Roman Catholic Church as well, though obviously not the Catholic position in toto. Here Coleridge adopts a position that he claims is common to all Reformed communions, but at the beginning of letter 2 he invokes the language of catholicity, giving an overall impression that he seeks to present the Church of England as a catholic Reformed communion (again consistent with his statement in the *Table Talk* that the Church of England was the real catholic church).

Though the five credenda correspond with the Pentad, as with so much of Coleridge this is not entirely straightforward. The first credendum is clearly identical to the first part of the Pentad: in the Pentad the prothesis is defined as "Christ, The Word," and the first credendum is described as "The Absolute; . . . whose transcendant *[sic]* I AM, as the Ground, *is* whatever *verily is:*—The Triune God, by whose Word and Spirit . . . *exists* whatever *substantially* exists . . . Stasis." This is straightforward. The second credendum is more complex, however. The Pentad lists the thesis as "The Scriptures," while the second credendum is defined (entirely) as "The Eternal Possibilities; the actuality of which hath not its origin in God: *Chaos spirituale*:—Apostasis"; here the correlation seems to break down, but it is important to remember that the remainder of the book will be spent arguing against divine dictation of the scriptures. Also, the clear correspondence of the other four credenda to the Pentad suggests that here Coleridge is presenting the scriptures as a source of infinite possibilities. The mesothesis of the Pentad is defined as the Holy Spirit, and this clearly corresponds to the third credendum, which is defined as (among other things) "The Creation and Formation of the heaven and the earth by the Redemptive Word . . . Regeneration:—Faith:—Prayer:—Grace: Communion with the Spirit: . . . Metastasis—Avastasis." So clearly the third element is the Spirit. Likewise, the fourth credendum and the antithesis of the Pentad are both clearly the church; the fourth credendum presents it as grace in the context of community and history, "a providence, a preparation, and a looking forward to Christ." The fifth credendum is defined as the Bible, while the synthesis of the Pentad is the preacher. But Coleridge makes it clear that his Bible is a living process:

> I will not leave it in the power of unbelievers to say that the Bible is for me only what the Koran is for the deaf Turk, and the Vedas

for the feeble and acquiescent Hindoo. No; I will retire *up into the mountain,* and hold secret commune with my Bible above the contagious blastments of prejudice, and the fog-blight of selfish superstition. . . . And what though *my* reason be to the power and splendour of the Scriptures but as the reflected and secondary shine of the moon compared with the solar radiance; . . . There is a Light higher than all, even *the Word that was in the beginning:*—the Light, of which light itself is but the shechinah and cloudy tabernacle; the Word that is light for every man, and life for as many as give heed to it. If between this Word and the written Letter I shall anywhere seem to myself to find a discrepance, I will not conclude that such there actually is; nor on the other hand will I fall under the condemnation of them that would *lie for God,* but seek as I may, be thankful for what I have—and wait. (25–26)

There are two ways to reconcile the five credenda with the Pentad, and each has good reason behind it. The first, as has recently been suggested, is to see the scriptures as a source of infinite possibility coming through the work of the human authors divinely inspired but not divinely informed. The second is to view the fifth credendum as a metaphor for the preacher, endlessly striving through his reason to bring the true meaning of scripture out of the text through communion with the Spirit (pneumatology). This second, more simplistic, and perhaps stronger approach concludes that the second credendum corresponds to the synthesis of the Pentad and the fifth credendum to the thesis of the Pentad. This perhaps reconciles the two presentations better because it allows the fifth credendum to be taken at face value (scripture) and the second credendum (infinite possibilities) to be the preacher—indicating that there are infinite possibilities of interpretation other than the face value of the particular historical accounts in the Old Testament as well as the New Testament ethic. This is a point Coleridge will emphasize through the rest of the work as a whole, and were the second and fifth credenda not listed in numerical order (i.e., introduced by roman numerals) one would have no trouble concluding that he had simply listed the five parts of the Pentad in an order different from that of the diagram. Either way, however, the fact that three out of the five correspond exactly makes it clear that he intends the credenda as an expanded presentation of the Pentad.

BIBLIOLATRY

Letter 2 explicates the doctrine of divine intelligence in the scriptures, which Coleridge argues is illicit, and letter 3 attempts to define an alternative approach to the Bible.

> The doctrine in question requires me to believe, that not only what finds me, [in the Bible], but that all that exists in the sacred volume, and which I am bound to find therein, was—not alone inspired by, that is, composed by men under the actuating influence of the Holy Spirit, but likewise—dictated by an Infallible Intelligence;—that the writers, each and all, were divinely informed as well as inspired. Now here all evasion, all excuse, is cut off. An Infallible Intelligence extends to all things, physical no less than spiritual. (27)

Coleridge argues that there are three possible languages for truth—sense, science, and philosophy—and that the doctrine of divine intelligence holds that all passages of the Bible would be consistent with all three of these. He makes the point that Jewish scholars held the doctrine to be true only of the Pentateuch—which (he also argues) they viewed as issuing from a single author. This doctrine, however, if applied to the entirety of the Old and New Testaments, will not stand. "I say that this is the doctrine which I reject as superstitious and unscriptural. And yet as long as the conceptions of the Revealing Word and the Inspiring Spirit are identified and confounded, I assert that whatever says less than this, says little more than nothing. For how can absolute infallibility be blended with Fallibility? Where is the infallible criterion? How can infallible truth be infallibly conveyed in defective and fallible expressions? The Jewish teachers confined this miraculous character to the Pentateuch" (30). The Bible and Christianity are their own sufficient evidence (31). The Bible should not need such a doctrine to support it. Coleridge draws the analogy of biographers writing of Bacon and Thomas More; there are, he stipulates, no grounds, internal or external, to doubt their work or to doubt the moral, intellectual, or circumstantial competence of them (34). But although these biographers took all possible steps to practice the art of history properly and conscientiously, "No Man in his senses!" would suppose that every anecdote and every extract from the subjects' papers was dictated by either Bacon or More (35).

Yet such an acceptance *is* required in the case of the Bible if the doctrine of divine intelligence is to stand. A great deal of the evidence against the doctrine of divine infallibility that Coleridge provides throughout the text takes the form of demonstrating, over and over again, the difficulty of correlating passages from the Old Testament with the ethic of Jesus presented within the books of the New Testament—the latter of which clearly must take precedence. This is in a great part the crux of his rejection of the doctrine. The first example he gives is the Book of Job.

> As you proceed, try to apply the tenet: try if you can even attach any sense or semblance of meaning to the speeches which you are reading. What! Were the hollow truism, the unsufficing half-truths, the false assumptions and malignant insinuation of the supercilious bigots, who corruptly defend the truth:—were the impressive facts, the piercing outcries, the pathetic appeals, and the close and powerful reasoning with which the poor sufferer—smarting at once from his wounds, and from the oil of vitriol which the orthodox *liars of God* were dropping into them—impatiently, but uprightly and holily, controverted this truth, while in will and in spirit he clung to it;—were both dictated by an infallible Intelligence?—Alas! If I may judge from the manner in which both indiscriminately are recited, quoted, appealed to, preached upon, by the *routiniers* of desk and pulpit, I cannot doubt that they think so,—or rather, without thinking, take for granted that so they are to think;—the more readily, perhaps, because the so thinking supercedes the necessity of all afterthought. (38)

Having set out the problem posed by the doctrine in letter 3, Coleridge goes on to reiterate the problems posed by the task of correlation in letter 4. In addition he brings in theological arguments to buttress the purely negative argument that total correlation was impossible. Rational examination, he writes, will lead to the recognition that the statement "The Bible contains the religion revealed by God" does not mean "Whatever is contained in the Bible is religion, and was revealed by God" (41). The counterposition put forth by Coleridge is that the Bible is "the appointed conservatory, an indispensable criterion, and a continual source and support of true Belief" (44). In other words, it contains the religion of Christians; it is not the Christian religion (45). It is at this point that

Confessions of an Inquiring Spirit becomes a work on pneumatology, because for Coleridge's system of interpretation to be genuine, the Holy Spirit must work through the pious interpreter—by acting through the human faculty of reason.

> But if . . . you admit the cooperation of a divine Spirit in souls desirous of good, even as the breath of heaven works variously in each several plant according to its kind, character, period of growth, and circumstance of soil, clime, and aspect;—on what ground can you assume that its presence is incompatible with all imperfection in the subject—even with such imperfection as is the natural accompaniment of the unripe season? . . . It was not for its thorns but for its sweet and medicinal flowers that the rose was cultivated; and he who cannot separate the husk from the grain, wants the power because sloth or malice has prevented the will. (46)

The motivation for proclaiming this revised doctrine of biblical authority was pastoral. Coleridge wished to give the young pastor the facility to solace members of his congregation who, in an emerging climate of rationalism and scientific enquiry, were finding their faith irreconcilable with the traditional doctrine of biblical authority. He wished to demonstrate that allowing the Holy Spirit to flow through such men's reason (so as to bring them to a comfortable understanding of the biblical canon consistent with their rational knowledge of the world and their moral beliefs garnered from the New Testament) was the proper way to ensure that their understanding and faith would be consistent with their beliefs.

Coleridge ends letter 4 with a recap of his argument presented to a skeptical friend who, through commitment to neo-rational scruples, finds his ability to believe in the Bible razed. The answer, he contends, is to see the Bible as *containing* the Christian religion revealed by God, and *not* as the Christian religion *directly dictated to the biblical authors* by God:

> Thenceforward, therefore, your doubts will be confined to such parts or passages of the received Canon, as seem to you irreconcilable with known truths, and at variance with the tests given in the Scriptures themselves, and as shall continue so to appear after you have examined each in reference to the circumstances of the Writer or Speaker,

the dispensation under which he lived and the purpose of the particular passage and the intent and object of the Scriptures at large. Respecting these, decide for yourself: and fear not for the result. I venture to tell it you beforehand. The result will be, a confidence in the
judgement and fidelity of the compilers of the Canon increased by
the apparent exceptions. (49)

THE PREACHER AS THE SYNTHESIS OF THE PENTAD

Letter 5 is extremely short—two paragraphs. It is, however, Coleridge's
introduction of the synthesis of the Pentad of Christianity. It is written
in a homiletic voice (likely because Coleridge was discussing the role
of the preacher). The inconsistencies of scripture must be reconciled
through the institution of the church and the Christian community, and
the most accessible level of the church is, of course, the pastor. Coleridge describes how he himself would present the scriptures to someone who had "a desire to believe, and a beginning love of Christ":

> "There are likewise sacred Writings, which, taken in connection
> with the institution and perpetuity of a visible Church, all believ-
> ers revere as the most precious boon of God, next to Christianity it-
> self, and attribute both their communication and preservation to an
> especial Providence. In them you will find all the revealed truths,
> which have been set forth and offered to you, clearly and circum-
> stantially recorded; and, in addition to these, examples of obedience
> and disobedience both in states and individuals, the lives and actions
> of men eminent under each dispensation, their sentiments, maxims,
> hymns, and prayers;—their affections, emotions, and conflicts;—in
> all which you will recognise the influence of the Holy Spirit, with a
> conviction increasing with the growth of your own faith and spiritual
> experience." (51)

The Spirit does not operate only in the original inspiration of the biblical authors; it is operative eternally in the inspiration of the interpretation of the biblical literature. The reader is inspired to find the substantive truth extant in the Christian religion through his reason, and
it is the Holy Spirit's inspiration of this interpretation, in its prompting

"the desire to believe," that will lead the pastor to teach the truth to his flock.

Letter 6 is entirely redundant. Coleridge suggests that it re-encapsulates the argument in a form that learned Christians can and will accept—the first five presentations of the argument, he writes, have been presented in a form designed to convince a Deist. The arguments themselves are not changed, and the main point of departure is still the irreconcilability of passages of the Old Testament with the Christian ethic. What is important here is that again Coleridge concludes his argument by stressing the importance of the catechetical structure of the visible church—again the position of the pastor is integral to a sound understanding of and faith in the Bible.

> With respect to [the] Christian generally, I object to the consequence drawn from the doctrine rather than to the Doctrine itself;—a consequence not only deducible from the premises, but actually and imperiously deduced; according to which the very man that can but read is to sit down to the consecutive and connected perusal of the Bible under the expectation and assurance that the whole is within his comprehension, and that, unaided by note or comment, catechism or liturgical preparation, he is to find out for himself what he is bound to believe and practice, and that whatever he conscientiously understands by what he reads is to be *his* religion. For he has found it in his Bible, and the Bible is the Religion of Protestants! (60)

In other words, Coleridge is absolutely opposed to those communions that teach biblical literalism and the ability of each Christian to find a particular truth relevant to him or her in his or her own reading of the Bible. The community is integral to Coleridge's presentation of biblical authority and interpretation; he implies that without the community of interpretation, with the pastor at its head (i.e., the community led by the clerisy), a proper understanding of the Bible is impossible. The pastor is the only way that the synthesis of the Pentad can be achieved—he unites the scriptures and the church through the mediation of the Holy Spirit.

In the next and final letter of the volume Coleridge directly attacks the concept that the Bible is sufficient to provide the Christian religion on its own; he calls this "idolatry" Bibliolatry. Here he is objecting to equating the Bible with Christianity. (This equation is in essence what twenty-first-century historians of religion would see as an Islamic perspective on the sacred text, in which the Qur'an is analogous to Christ rather than to the Bible.) Coleridge opens the letter:

> You are now, my dear Friend, in possession of my whole mind on this point,—one thing only excepted which has weighed with me more than all the rest, and which I have therefore reserved for my concluding Letter. This is the impelling principle, or way of thinking, which I have in most instances noticed in the assertors of what I have ventured to call Bibliolatry, and which I believe to be the main ground of its prevalence at this time, and among men whose religious views are anything rather than enthusiastic. And I here take occasion to declare, that my conviction of the danger and injury of this principle was and is my chief motive for bringing the Doctrine itself in question; the main error of which consists in the confounding of the two distinct conceptions, revelation by the Eternal Word, and actuation of the Holy Spirit. (61)

Here is, finally, indisputable proof that the *Confessions of an Inquiring Spirit* is a work about pneumatology. The lack of "actuation of the Holy Spirit" involved in biblical literalism leads Coleridge to see this as idolatry. Without the fluid and eternal participation of the Spirit in interpretation—that is, without the participation of the Divine in the Bible every time it is read—the Bible itself becomes an idol, a false conception of Christianity. He makes the point even clearer in a discussion of Bibliolatry in a historical context:

> The final resource was to restore what ought never to have been removed—the correspondent subjective, that is, the assent and confirmation of the Spirit promised to all true believers, as proved and manifested in the reception of such decision by the Church Universal in its rightful members.
>
> I comprise and conclude the sum of my conviction in this one sentence. Revealed Religion (and I know of no religion not revealed) is in its highest contemplation the unity, that is the identity or coinherence, of Subjective and Objective. It is in itself, and irrelatively, at once inward Life and Truth, and outward Fact and Luminary. But as all Power manifests itself in the harmony of correspondent Op-

posites, each supposing and supporting the other,—so has Religion
its objective, or historic and ecclesiastical pole, and its subjective, or
spiritual and individual pole. . . .

Lastly, in the Scriptures . . . and in the mind of the believing and
regenerate Reader and Meditater, there is proved to us the reciprocity,
or reciprocation, of the Spirit as subjective and objective. . . . (63)

The correspondence of opposites is, of course, a reference to the scheme
of the Pentad. At the two edges of the diamond, the thesis and the antithesis (the scriptures and the church), the Christian religion flows down
through the mediation of the mesothesis (the Holy Spirit) into the vessel
of the pastor: the synthesis. The Holy Spirit is the active reagent within
the Pentad, and the Bible is the portal to the activity of the Spirit; only
through the Spirit accessed by the scriptures and actualized through the
church in the form of the synthesis (the pastor) can the prothesis (Christ)
be brought to the individual Christian in the pew. Attempts to access
the prothesis through the thesis are idolatry: Bibliolatry.

In his last theological work, *Confessions of an Inquiring Spirit,* Coleridge discussed the scriptures, the same subject as he had discussed in
his first theological work: *Lectures on Revealed Religion.* Forty years
on, his conclusions were not so very different. In the *Lectures* he had
portrayed the scriptures as freestanding—to be interpreted only on the
lines of their own internal authority—and had concluded that they provided no evidence for the existence of a Triune God. But he argued that
to be understood they must be read critically. In *Confessions of an Inquiring Spirit* he concluded that proper interpretation of the scriptures
was impossible without the fluid, eternal participation of the Spirit.
Though he had moved a great distance in forty years, and though the
two works make an illuminating set of framing brackets to his life's project and theological progression, he stressed critical interpretation of the
Bible in both. From the position that the Holy Spirit did not exist he had
traveled to the position that without its active and imminent participation through the pastor (and the Christian's participation in the church)
a true understanding of the Christian religion was impossible.

Part Four

The Soul of Toryism

II

Coleridge in a Tory
Historical Context

IN ORDER TO UNDERSTAND COLERIDGE'S POLITICAL THEOLOGY in context, and to place it in its proper tradition, it will be appropriate to refer to two famous assize sermons preached from the pulpit of St. Mary's University Church in Oxford by fellow Tories. One of these is, of course, John Keble's *National Apostasy* (which has already been discussed). It helped to provoke W. E. Gladstone's *The State in Its Relations with the Church* (1838)—a work that made use of Coleridge's arguments in *On the Constitution of the Church and State*. (The second half of this chapter is devoted to Gladstone's book.) The other assize sermon is, however, no less important. Titled *The Nature and Mischief of Prejudice and Partiality*, it was preached by Henry Sacheverell in 1704—seventy years before Coleridge's birth—and its importance was that it led to Sacheverell's being invited to preach a similar sermon titled *The Perils of False Brethren, Both in Church and State* at St Paul's in London. Because *False Brethren* was a Tory sermon preached during a time of Whig ascendancy in 1709, its content led to Sacheverell's being tried for "high crimes and misdemeanours" by Parliament—a Whig project that failed overall, though it did in the end produce a guilty verdict.

The Sacheverell trial is important for understanding Coleridge's views on church and state because it was the point at which the two different theories of church and state relations that would dominate eighteenth- and nineteenth-century debate received their first public hearing in an adversarial manner. These two theories could be summed up as the contract or "alliance" theory and the notion of an organic unity of church and state, with the church ultimately supplying the imprimatur for the authority of the state. Sacheverell's impeachment by the House of Commons would prove, if not a disaster for the Whig party, such a hollow and Pyrrhic victory for the government that it is generally classed as a defeat—both for the government's credibility and, far more substantially, for the Whig ideology of contract theory. This defeat of the Court Whig ideology was a major contributing factor behind Warburton's project of setting out an exhaustive and elegant presentation of contract theory within the text of *The Alliance*.

In other words: Coleridge's intellectual war with Warburton was fought on a field that had originally been blooded by Sacheverell's combat with Walpole, Lechmere, and Sir Joseph Jekyll, and the same field would again see engagement between Gladstone and Chalmers soon after Coleridge's death. To be sure, Gladstone's and Chalmers's engagement was less vitriolic and bloody than Coleridge's with Warburton, but when Gladstone disputed with Chalmers he employed the Hookerian paradigms revoiced for the nineteenth-century mind by Coleridge. The key point here is that, though the ground was identical, the tactics used upon the terrain were vastly different: where Sacheverell had gone straight up the middle, using only his own authority and quoting no other Anglican divine, Coleridge flanked Warburton and deployed substantial artillery support in the form of Hooker's *Laws of Ecclesiastical Polity*. Gladstone also chose to use artillery to win his battle with Chalmers, using (among other writers) Richard Hooker and Samuel Taylor Coleridge, and like Coleridge he cited Hooker as his starting point. In other words, Gladstone could not have come to his own plan of attack had it not been for Coleridge.

In trying to follow the Tory tradition of church and state, one cannot get from Sacheverell to Gladstone except via Coleridge. In fact one cannot get from Sacheverell to Gladstone at all. One really must begin with Coleridge and then examine the neo-Tory position that relies on Hooker. In Sacheverell's era Hooker was distrusted by High Churchmen, but by Gladstone's time he was considered a sound foundation. This was, of course, largely because Keble had published an edition of Hooker's complete works, but also (as *The State in Its Relations with the Church* demonstrates) because Coleridge had employed Hooker in his battle with Warburton. Nowhere in any surviving work, notebook, collection of *Table Talk,* or annotation does Coleridge discuss Sacheverell or Sacheverell's works. This would seem to indicate that Warburton was successful over the long run in his attempt to wipe out the early eighteenth-century Tory position of church and state as Sacheverell had presented it.

The Sacheverell Trial: A Skeleton Sketch of the Tory versus Whig Position on Church and State during Queen Anne's Reign

Sacheverell was the *enfant terrible* of the High Church faction of the Tory party during the reign of Queen Anne. His heritage was one of pure Toryism; Sacheverell was an Ultra Tory if there ever was one.[1] John Kenyon describes him as follows: "Sacheverell was a man detested by most of his contemporaries, even by many who shared his views, and posterity. . . . But this does not mean that we can dismiss, or even diminish, the enormous influence he exerted on his times. . . . He was certainly no original thinker, but he was a brilliant polemicist. . . . His enemies, at least, had no illusions about his importance; they gave him full credit for launching the whole campaign against the Dissenters in 1702."[2] Sacheverell fiercely rejected the idea of the church playing a supportive role. Instead he took the classic Tory position on the church: he saw it and its role in politics and society as equal to the state's. He gave the most concise presentation of his position in his book *The Political Union: A Discourse Showing the Dependence of Government of Religion in General: And of the English Monarch on the Church of England in Particular.* "The *Civil* and *Ecclesiastical* State are the Two Parts and Divisions, that Both United make up One entire compound Constitution, and Body Politick, sharing the same Fate and Circumstances, Twisted and Interwoven into the very Being and Principles of each Other, Both

---

1. *Ultra* is a term I have avoided using because I feel it is vague; I have instead used the phrase *High Tory,* but in the case of Sacheverell *Ultra* is both precise and accurate.

2. J. P. Kenyon, *Revolution Principles: The Politics of Party, 1689–1720* (Cambridge: Cambridge University Press, 1977), 91–92.

alike jointly Assisting and being Assisted; Defending and Defended, Supporting and Supported, in the same Vital Union, Intercourse and Complication. . . . They are . . . at present, Cast under the same Lot and Condition, and, like the *Philosopher's Twins,* Communicate their Mirth or Sorrow, equally Suffer or Rejoyce."[3] Sacheverell may be called an Ultra because he aggressively pursued party factionalism in an era when a majority in Parliament sought to portray a spirit of concord and unity given the arguably vulnerable foundations of royal claims following the Glorious Revolution. He was certainly not alone in this; however, he encountered significant partisan opposition from the Whig peers, and was prosecuted by those leaders earlier identified as the Junto Lords (who were claiming Parliament's ultimate supremacy following the Glorious Revolution by promoting an assertive version of original contract theory). Sacheverell's drawn-out battle with the Junto over the source of licit monarchical authority was to prove arguably the most contentious partisan political squabble of Queen Anne's reign, and the Junto's failure successfully to destroy Sacheverell's position through impeachment by Parliament was, as stated above, a major contributing influence to Warburton's decision to write *The Alliance.*

The partisan combat of the first decade of the eighteenth century centered on what Kenyon has argued were two neuroses: the Whigs' infatuation with buttressing the Revolution and the Tories' "hysteria" about toleration.[4] The Tories foolishly attempted to place an amendment attempting to obliterate "occasional conformity" (i.e., the practice of Dissenters attending Church of England services in their parish just frequently enough to avoid prosecution under the law) by tacking it onto a finance bill in the winter of 1704–5. Coming a mere five months after Marlborough's historic victory at Blenheim, this made them appear to be attempting to derail the supply line of a successful military campaign for what were at best inferior (and at worst trivial) concerns on the domes-

---

3. Henry Sacheverell, *The Political Union: A Discourse Shewing the Dependance of Government on Religion in General: And of the English Monarchy on the Church of England in Particular* (Oxford: Printed by Leonard Lichfield, for George West, and Henry Clements, 1702), 9–10. Subsequent page citations to this work are given parenthetically in the text.

4. Kenyon, *Revolution Principles,* 127.

tic front. It also made their obsessive concern about conformity and the ultimate source of monarchical authority look more like an infatuation than a legitimate and loyal concern. In any case, this foolish miscalculation by the politicians was a contributing factor in Sacheverell's decision to attempt to articulate the Tory position on church and state more elegantly in his assize sermon that spring. The assize sermon was well received by the conservative Oxford community, and being published (as was the custom), it acquired a fairly wide audience over the next few years. As a result, Sacheverell was invited to give several other assize sermons around the Home Counties and the Midlands. In an odd way his attempt to articulate the Tory position was too successful, because on November 5, 1709 (Bonfire Night), he delivered a sermon to "The Lord Mayor, Alderman and Citizens of London" entitled *The Perils of False Brethren, Both in Church and State.* The engineering of this invitation proved to be a tactical mistake for the Tory hierarchy because of the trial that followed, but in one of those odd quirks of history the tactical error produced a subtle strategic victory for the Tories—prompting Warburton to set down the Whig position once and for all in *The Alliance.*

The idea of trying Sacheverell for treason or sedition was a flawed project from the beginning. There was certainly enough precedent in English law for his supporters to expect an acquittal in the High Court— an expectation that must have had good grounds, as the prosecutors from the Whig camp never even made a move in the direction of the courts. Having apparently ruled out the courts, the Whigs had three options left: Sacheverell could be imprisoned by the House of Commons under its own authority, the House could order the sermon to be publicly burned by the number one executioner, or Sacheverell could be prosecuted. The first was ruled out because the Commons could imprison Sacheverell under its judicial authority only for the remainder of the current term of session. The second option was out because it was likely to boost sales of the sermon exponentially. This left only the third and weakest option. Accordingly, an action of impeachment was lodged against Sacheverell for "high crimes and misdemeanours."[5]

Considering that the only avenue apparently available to the Whig leaders was the weakest of the three, and considering that Sacheverell

---

5. Kenyon, *Revolution Principles,* 131.

had been promulgating identical views to those in *False Brethren* for at least seven years, one must ask: Why did the Whig party choose to attack Sacheverell on an emaciated charge that could produce at best a weak penalty, and in particular why did they choose to do it at a time when they were in the ascendancy and so had the most to lose? Somers, for instance, had doubts about the possibility of success of the impeachment and about the project as a whole. But most of the Junto probably felt that they had no choice but to respond to the gauntlet Sacheverell had thrown down, virtually in front of the entire Parliament, by preaching at St. Paul's in London. In other words, Sacheverell's venue necessarily created a substantial feeling of outrage in ordinary Whig party members and placed the Junto under immense internal pressure to move against him.

In the end the impeachment for high crimes and misdemeanors was at best a hollow success. In order to prove that "high crimes and misdemeanors" had taken place, the Whigs had to show that Sacheverell had directly implied within the sermon that the Glorious Revolution was somehow illicit and had therefore indirectly attacked the legitimacy of Queen Anne's reign. This they attempted to do by arguing that Sacheverell was suggesting in his sermon that the Glorious Revolution had faced resistance from James II and had therefore been wrong, on the grounds that if James had resisted, the Revolution would by definition have attacked his divine right (in the full Laudian sense of the term). This they did basing their claim on, among others, the following passage of Sacheverell's sermon:

> The *Grand Security* of our *Government,* and the very *Pillar* upon which it *stands,* is founded upon the *steady Belief* of the *Subject's Obligation* to an *Absolute* and *Unconditional Obedience* to the *Supreme Power,* in *All* things *Lawful,* and the utter *Illegality* of *Resistance* upon any *Pretence* whatsoever. But this *Fundamental Doctrin [sic],* not withstanding its *Divine Sanction* in the *Express Command* of *God* in *Scripture,* and without which, it is impossible any *Government* of any *Kind,* or *Denomination* in the World, should *subsist* with safety, and which has been so long the *Honourable,* and *Distinguishing Characteristic* of *Our Church,* is now, it seems quite *Exploded,* and *Redicul'd [sic]* out of Countenance as an *Unfashionable, Superannuated,* nay (which is more wonderful) as a *Dangerous*

Tenet, utterly *Inconsistent* with the *Right Liberty,* and *Property* of the P E O P L E; who as our *New Preachers,* and *New Politicians* teach us, (I suppose by a *New,* and *Unheard* of *Gospel,* as well as *Laws*) have in Contradiction to *Both,* the *Power* Invested in *Them,* the Fountain and *Original,* of it, to *Cancel* their *Allegiance* at pleasure, and call their *Sovereign* to account for *High-Treason* against his *Supreme Subjects,* forsooth! Nay to *Dethrone,* and *Murder* Him for a Criminal, as they did the *Royal Marty [sic]* by a *Judiciary* Sentence. And what is almost Incredible, presume to make their *Court* to the *Prince,* by maintaining such *Anti-monarchical Schemes.* But God be Thanked! Neither the Constitution of Our Church or *State,* is so far *Alter'd,* but that by the *Laws of Both,* (*still* in Force, and which I hope *for ever* will be) these *Damnable Positions,* let 'em come either from *Rome,* or *Geneva,* from the *Pulpit,* or the *Press,* are condemn'd for *Rebellion* and *High-Treason.* Our Adversaries think they effectually stop our Mouths, and have Us Sure and Unanswerable on this Point, when they urge the *Revolution of this Day* in their *Defence.* But certainly They are the Greatest *Enemies of That,* and His *Late Majesty,* and the most *ungrateful* for the *Deliverance,* who endeavour to cast such *Black* and *Odious* Colours upon Both. How often must they be told, that the *King Himself* solemnly *Disclaim'd* the Least Imputation of *Resistance* in his *Declaration*; and that the *Parliament* declar'd, That they set the *Crown* on his Head, upon no other *Title,* but that of the *Vacancy of the* Throne? And did they not Unanimously condemn to the Flames, (as it justly Deserv'd) that *Infamous Libel,* that would have *Pleaded* the *Title of Conquest* by which *Resistance* was suppos'd? So *Tender* were they of the *Regal* Reights, and so averse to infringe the least Title of Our *Constitution!*[6]

According to Kenyon, the main thrust of article 1 of the impeachment, which accused Sacheverell of impugning the right and justice of the

---

6. Henry Sacheverell, *The Perils of False Brethren, Both in Church and State; Set Forth in a Sermon Preach'd before the Right Honourable the Lord-Mayor, Aldermen, and Citizens of London, at the Cathedral-Church of St. Paul, on the 5th of November, 1709* (London: Printed for Henry Clements, at the Half-Moon in St. Paul's Church-Yard, 1709), 12–13.

Revolution, was inconclusive in a most inconvenient way for the Whig party.[7] To demonstrate Sacheverell's guilt, they would have to prove that there had been resistance in 1688, or that contract theory had affected the outcome of the Comprehension Bill of 1689, or, preferably, both, but they could conclusively demonstrate neither. In fact, according to Kenyon, they were driven into a very difficult position by a twist of logic: because they were unable to demonstrate either that force had been used or that the abdication had involved the slightest modicum of coercion, they were forced into a utilitarian argument. Robert Eyre, the solicitor general, argued that "if resistance at the Revolution was illegal, the Revolution settled in usurpation and this Act can have no greater force and authority than an Act passed under a usurper."[8] This basic argument was seconded by John Smith, Chancellor of the Exchequer, who argued that all the acts of settlement of the Crown depended upon the legality of the Revolution. Stanhope put the Junto position in its strongest terms:

> If they be in the right, my lords, what are the consequences? The queen is not queen; your lordships are not a House of Lords, for you are not duly summoned by legal writ; we are no House of Commons, for the same reason; all the taxes which have been raised for these twenty years have been arbitrary and illegal and extortions; all the blood of so many brave men who have died (as they thought) in the service of their country, has been spilt in defence of a usurpation, and they were only so many rebels and traitors.[9]

Kenyon rightly argues that this was the point at which the tide in the trial turned against the Whigs because they had shifted their own position to apply contract theory to the Revolution. Kenyon's interpretation is that from this point on Sacheverell's defense was watertight. Because Sacheverell and his advocates "admitted that they, too, accepted and upheld the Revolution, their only quarrel with the Whigs being on the manner of its accomplishment and the justification for it, the Whigs were open to the accusation that it was they who were undermining the

---

7. Kenyon, *Revolution Principles,* 134–37.
8. Quoted in Kenyon, *Revolution Principles,* 135.
9. Quoted in Kenyon, *Revolution Principles,* 135–36.

constitution."[10] Simon Harcourt, Sacheverell's chief defense advocate, then clearly turned the "argument from contract" against the prosecution by saying:

> We are hearty well-wishers to the Revolution, and to the happiness of England that is in a great measure built upon it. We agree that the law of the land is the measure of the prince's authority and the people's rights; that in the case of the Revolution, when the laws were overturned, when popery was coming in upon us . . . the people of England being invited by his late Majesty did resort to the last remedy, that of necessity, and that necessity did induce resistance, and justify them in it, and upon that fact the Revolution succeeded.[11]

Kenyon argues that it is doubtful whether Sacheverell actually believed what Harcourt claimed for him. Furthermore, Kenyon suggests that Sacheverell deliberately muddied his actual position during his final address to the Commons because he was anxious to avoid imprisonment or the pillory—especially by his use of the phrase, "I neither expressly applied my doctrine of non-resistance to the case of the Revolution, nor had the least thoughts of including the Revolution under my general assertion."[12] Whatever the motivation, the defense worked. Harcourt's clever trick of placing the Whig theorists in a position where they themselves could be seen to be weakening the foundations of the constitution, combined with Parliament's very real fears of possible substantial general disorder if a stiff sentence was imposed (Sacheverell's trial had prompted two nights of rioting in the capital), resulted in a marginal conviction, only 69 in favor to 52 against. The sentence was merely a slap on the wrist: the common hangman was to burn a copy of the sermon publicly, and Sacheverell was to refrain from preaching for three years.

Sacheverell's motivation throughout is, however, important. Kenyon's interpretation that Sacheverell deliberately made his position less clear during his defense is not necessarily accurate. It is quite literally true that within the text of *False Brethren* Sacheverell never did apply his

---

10. Kenyon, *Revolution Principles,* 136.
11. Quoted in Kenyon, *Revolution Principles,* 138.
12. Quoted in Kenyon, *Revolution Principles,* 138.

doctrine of nonresistance to the case of the Revolution. But Sacheverell hated Roman Catholics, and though Jacobitism is not to be identified solely with Roman Catholicism, one of the reasons the Revolution occurred *was* to protect the Protestant nature of the English line. Sacheverell's hatred of Catholics is abundantly clear from the opening paragraph of *False Brethren*:

> A Conspiracy! So full of the most Unheard-of *Malice*, most Insatiable *Cruelty*, most Diabolical *Revenge*, as only could be *Hatch'd* in the *Cabinet-Council* of *Hell* and *Brought forth* in a Conclave of *Romish Jesuits*! Now, tho' the *History* of this Unparrall'd *Mystery of Inquity [sic]*, was *Design'd* against Us at such a *Distance* of Time, and the *Fact* so evidently *Acknowledg'd*, that the *Papists* themselves are so far from *Denying*, that they *Extol* it with the Highest *Panegyrics*; so that there needs neither *Proof* of the One, nor *Repetition* of the Other: Yet doubtless 'tis as much Our *Duty* as *Interest*, to keep up the *Annual Celebration* of this *Never-to-be-forgotten Festival*. For that the very Face, and Shadow of Our Church, and *Constitution*, is yet *Surviving;* That this *Good*, and *Pious Relict* of the *Royal Family*, Sits now Happily upon the *throne* of her Great *Ancestors*; That our *Hierarchy*, and *Nobility* was not finally *Extirpated*, and cut off; That Our *Country* was not made an *Aceldama*, a *Field of Blood, and a* Receptacle *of Usurping* Robbers; That we yet, without *slavery, superstition*, or *Idolatry*, enjoy the *Benefit* of our Excellent *Laws*, and most Holy *Profession* Undefil'd: in a Word, that God has yet *Vouchsav'd* Us *this Opportunity* of coming into his presence, to *Acknowledge* these Inestimable Blessings, is owing to his *Mercy* so signally shewn to Us, in Disappointing the *Barbarous Massacre* intended This Day.[13]

Now, the date of *False Brethren* is important: it was preached on Bonfire Night. Obviously a sermon at St. Paul's on the anniversary of the destruction of the Gunpowder Plot provided an opportunity for more invective than is usual (even for Sacheverell). But Sacheverell is careful to make clear Anne's legitimacy, even in the middle of his opening rant. Elsewhere within the text he compares Anne to Elizabeth I, a compari-

13. Sacheverell, *Perils*, 5.

son she was said to find flattering.[14] The fact is that *False Brethren* is a near-maniacal rant against toleration of *any* sort (a typical Bonfire Night subject for the early eighteenth century). Those confessing members of the establishment who sought to allow toleration, that is, dissent from the Church of England, were said to be "false brethren" and as bad as Dissenters themselves. Sacheverell held that the entire idea of toleration struck at the heart of the constitution of England and the society it protected. To the modern reader the sermon might appear absurdly vitriolic and logically naive, but it neither impugned Anne's title nor directly attacked the legitimacy of the Glorious Revolution. It was not a Jacobite work.

In fact, Sacheverell could be said to have protected himself from such a charge, and doubtlessly he was consciously doing so when he wrote the version for publication, by paying homage to Anne's monarchical function and linking her to the Tudor and Stuart lines. This link to the Stuart line, and the homage to Anne's rule, was made even more dramatically in the final paragraphs of Sacheverell's assize sermon at Oxford on March 9, 1704. The sermon, titled *The Nature and Mischief of Prejudice and Partiality,* is a much better reasoned and argued work than the St. Paul's sermon of 1709—which explains why he was invited to give the latter sermon in the first place. (The dean of St. Paul's would most likely have canceled the entire event had he received an advanced copy of *False Brethren.*) In *Prejudice and Partiality,* Sacheverell takes time to approach the concept of prejudice from an epistemological perspective, defines it as hinging on the use of will rather than understanding, then progresses through the consequences of prejudice for reason, law, and religion, before finally arriving at his actual point—which is, of course, that Dissent damages the English Church and therefore the English constitution. Unlike *False Brethren, The Nature and Mischief of Prejudice and Partiality* is a considered attack. Its major thrust is that Dissenting radicals perpetrated the Civil Wars of England and the Regicide, and that this was the unavoidable and logical end of Dissent and toleration. Sacheverell concludes the sermon:

Doubtless out of these *Schools* and *Nurseries* of *Rebellion,* have *Spawn'd* That Multitude of *Factious, Heterodox, Atheistical, Lewd*

---

14. Sacheverell, *Perils,* 19.

Books, and *Seditious* Libels, which are every day *Publish'd* against *Monarchy,* and the Established'd *Hierarchy,* and *Religion,* to the Encouragement of *Vice,* the Destruction of *Piety,* and the Scandal and Extirpation of Our *Law, Nation,* and *Government.* What *Church,* or *Kingdom* in the World would Patiently *Endure* to See It Self thus *Provokingly* Affronted? And the Memory of the BLESSED MARTYR, THE Greatest *Glory* and *Defender* of Both, made the Infamous Subject of Scorn and Drollery, whilst the *Last Branch* of the *Royal Family* is notwithstanding—*Yet,* God be Bles'd! *Flourishing* on the *Throne!* What can be the Meaning of Those *Justifications,* that are now every where Publish'd, of that *Horrid Rebellion,* both out of the *Press* (and, to Its Eternal Disgrace!) out of the *very Pulpit*; together with the Impudent *Burlesquing* the *Dismal Murder* of HER ROYAL GRANDFATHER, but to *Prepare* the Nation to *Act* over the *Same Bloody Tragedy* Agen? If an *Heathen* Republick wou'd not Suffer the *Mysteries* of a *False* Religion to be *Profan'd* What *Holy* Indignation, what *Zealous* Resolution, what *Ardent* Affection, Ought We to shew in the Defence of the Venerable *Mysteries* of Our *True Religion,* which is thus Openly Attack'd, with Reviling *Scoffs,* and Ridiculing *Blasphemy!* These are such *Crying Sins,* as are Enough to Sink Our *Place and Nation* into Everlasting Vengeance, if not Prevented by a Timely Execution of the *Law* upon such Enormous and Unheard-of Offences.

Consider therefore, MY LORDS, You that are the *Ministers of God, and Bear not the Sword in Vain,* that You are *Appointed as Revengers to Execute Wrath upon Those that do Evil.* Thus You may Avert the Judgements We have Just Cause to Fear, and Bring down a Blessing upon Our Government and Kingdom, and Establish Both in Peace, Happiness and Tranquility.[15]

Throughout both sermons, Sacheverell is clear that when he attacks revolution he is attacking the revolution against Charles I, not the Glo-

---

15. Henry Sacheverell, *The Nature and Mischief of Prejudice and Partiality Stated in a Sermon Preach'd at St. Mary's in Oxford at the Assizes Held There, March 9th, 1704* (Oxford: Printed by Leon. Lichfield, for John Stephens, Bookseller: And are to be Sold by James Knapton at the Crowne in St. Paul's Churchyard, London, 1704), 56–57.

rious Revolution, and throughout both sermons (and in his writings generally) he is careful to stress the legitimacy of Anne's succession back to the Stuart line. Sacheverell might have been aggressively intolerant to Dissenters but he was no Nonjuror; his entire theoretical approach to state authority would have collapsed had not Anne's claim been licit. Whatever Sacheverell was guilty of, he was not guilty of high crimes and misdemeanors against Queen Anne. In view of this the Junto was lucky to secure a conviction at all.

A much less furious and much more well-reasoned work than either sermon is Sacheverell's *The Political Union,* and it is a pity that *False Brethren* is the work for which he is remembered instead. It is important to examine *this* piece of Sacheverell's writing because it is the mature presentation of his position and a better exemplification of the Tory position that Warburton set out to refute in *The Alliance.* Likewise, because it is the clearest presentation of the tradition that Sacheverell embodied, it is also the most clear presentation of the tradition that Coleridge chose to revive in order to destroy Warburton's contract theory. Sacheverell represents the position Coleridge inherited before Coleridge built upon it so elegantly and made it his own.

The Political Union, like the two famous sermons that proceeded from it as well as several less famous ones (most notably a sermon titled *The Nature, Obligation, and Measures of Conscience,* which was delivered to the assizes in Leicester on July 25, 1706), is at its heart, like Sacheverell's other works, an attack on Roman Catholics, Dissenters, toleration, and occasional conformity. But in this work, unlike his later homiletic attacks, Sacheverell takes the time to prosecute his attack systematically. Here he begins the treatise by quoting Proverbs 8:15: "By Me kings reign and princes decree justice." This is his defining principle. He makes no real attempt at apologetics within the work; his hermeneutics are biblical throughout—assuming the position that he states in the first line as a postulate. The following statement is representative of his approach:

> A *Ruin'd Church* and *Prosperous Government* are Irreconcileable contradictions in Experience, Confronted and Confuted by the united, Universal, and Concurrent Testimony of all Ages, and Histories, Sacred and Prophane. Which Unanimously give in This, as their General *Verdict* and Eternal Truth, that the surest and most infallible Means to Strengthen, Support, and Establish the Civil Power,

is by Maintaining and Defending the True Worship of God, and the Exercise of His Genuine and Unmixt Religion, and the most ready, effectual, and never-failing Way to Destroy it, is by Ruining and Destroying That. (10–11)

In other words, because through God kings reign and princes decree justice the state cannot stand unless it is built upon the rock of the church. This position clearly includes the major premise that there is one society; that the two organs of this society are, essentially, one grand scheme of government; and that the church is the primary source of authority for the state. Sacheverell does not see the government, even the English constitutional government, as in any way distinct from the church. This is certainly a more Ultra Tory position than that taken by Coleridge, who saw church and state as separate societies that formed an organic unity, and it is one of the reasons why it is better to identify Coleridge as a High Tory rather than an Ultra Tory.

Sacheverell uses the first section, about the first twenty pages of the treatise, to cite incidental examples from history, mainly from the Old Testament, that support his position. He argues that whenever the Hebrew church fell into error the government of the Hebrews, and collaterally the Hebrew populace, suffered as a direct result. He then takes narrative history into the Christian era and through the medieval period to suggest that given the corruption in the papacy and superstition in the general church before the Reformation, the interdependence of the church and state at that time caused the state (meaning the Holy Roman Empire) to decay. Naturally he concludes this historical narration by presenting the Reformation as a cleansing event:

But then, by the good Providence of GOD, that in its due time *Awoke* out of this *Slumber,* to the Vindication of His Doctrine and Worship, the Dawn of Learning, after this long Night, Sprung forth in the West, and made way for the Light of the Gospel, and *The Sun of Righteousness to arise with Healing in his Wings.* Then the *Monkish* Ignorance began to vanish, the dark Errors and the vile Delusions of Popery put on their proper Colours, Reformation was Propagated apace, both in Church and State, Religion was purg'd from its Barbarous Corruptions, and Heathenish Depravations, and Government was brought out of its *Chaos,* and Moulded into a Regular

Form and Constitution, by wholesome *[sic]* Laws, Discipline, and Justice. It is very easy to pursue this Point downwards, through all Civil Divisions, that have infested Our own Church and Nation, but I shall forbear the ungrateful Reflection, and shall only leave this Remark, "That *Monarchy* and *Episcopacy,* the *Crown* and the *Mitre* have been always so mutually depending upon a Reciprocal Union and Support, that the fall of the One drew after it the Other, and the Government of the State was never known to Survive that of the Church." (16–17)

Sacheverell has set up the first of his paradigmatic enemies: Roman Catholics. He then spends a great deal of the central portion of the text harping upon the danger of his second paradigmatic enemy: Dissenters. But because Dissenters are Protestants they must be attacked on intellectual grounds rather than dismissed out of hand. So before he can commence his assault against them, he sets out his theoretical position.

Sacheverell's theoretical paradigm is that government has four pillars: justice, counsel, treasure, and religion. Of the four, religion is the supreme foundation; the other three are mere steadying columns that also need religion to function. This is fundamentally true because, while civil laws can control human behavior through fear of reprisal, they cannot reach the intellectual portion of human nature. The intellectual faculties of man are the most dangerous, as it is the intellect that can give rise to wicked acts or perverted decisions. Without religion, foolish and wicked acts can and will continue despite fears of reprisal, and the safety and tranquillity of the state and society are threatened:

Thus We see how Weak, Impotent and Unguarded Human Nature, and Human Government are Left, if Stript of that Support, Ornament and Defence *[sic]* that they receive from Religion. Nature, by itself, is a mere State of Anarchy and Confusion, a Ruine, Rapine and War; and tho' it be Regulated, Restrain'd, and Tyed up by *Political Laws,* yet These Reach not the *Intellectual Part,* the most Dangerous, Active, Busy, and Destructive part of Man. These take Cognizance only of *Evil in Act,* when it is brought forth and Produc'd: it must be Religion alone that can Stifle it in the Birth, and Destroy the Seeds and Original Causes of Impiety and Injustice. They may perhaps do the Office of *Bedlam,* keep a Man in Chains that is Mad, but This Alone must be the *Physick* to Curb, Correct, and Purge out the foul Distempers and Disorderly Passions of the Mind, and make Him fit to be let loose, and to Walk up and down, and Converse without Danger. (22–23)

First, Justice is founded on religion, for without religion there would be no confessions by criminals (as they would have nothing to gain by confessing to a crime that would send them to the gallows if they did not fear an eternal damnation worse than death). Furthermore, without Religion there could be no justice at all: for justice is God's to dispense. There could, therefore, be no true justice were not judges directly charged by God through the monarch (see the final passage of the Oxford assize sermon above) to deliver that justice. Sacheverell also argues that there would be no mercy attendant in that justice were not the judges Christians. Second, good counsel depends on religion, since it requires that counselors be religiously minded. War would be a far more common occurrence if they were not, and indeed it could not be legitimately prosecuted at all were not the ground of the monarch's claims to authority supported by religion. Third, without being bound by religious charity and temperance, treasure (or wealth), the third support of government, and a necessary functional system of government, would lead to concupiscence, and, as in the medieval period, the government would be consumed by corruption, interest, and bribery: "From All these Arguments Laid together, I hope it evidently appears, that the Whole Frame of Government, is Built, and Founded on *Religion,* and its Grand *Basis* and Support, that its Great Weight and Stress Depends upon it, that its Whole Welfare, Happiness, and Security is Owing to It, and that the Taking That away will Infallibly Bring Anarchy, Ruine, and Confusion into a Kingdom" (47).

Now, having demonstrated that all governments are founded upon religion, Sacheverell can demonstrate that the government of England is the most perfect form of government ever devised because the "Royal Throne and Divine Altar" are so inseparably joined and united in each other's interest and because the Church of England stands upon a "*Legal* Foundation Establish'd, and Distinguish'd, from All That Confus'd Swarm of *Sectarists,* that Gather about Its Body, not to Partake of Its Communion, but to Disturb Its Pease and Presume to Shelter Themselves under Its Character . . ." (49, 48). The state under the English con-

stitution openly professes and embraces the church as its foundation
and through that profession makes itself the logical end of government.

This, holds Sacheverell, is why Dissenters, and those who seek toleration for Dissenters, are so dangerous: they seek to undermine the
constitution that through law establishes the church and protects the lay
person from heresy. Dissenters in the Protestant tradition will tend to
attempt to use the mechanisms of the state because

> What Alters the Fundamental Constitution of the One, will Infallibly
> Destroy Both. *Presbytery* and Republicanism go hand in hand, They
> are but the Same Disorderly, *Levelling Principle,* in the Two Differ-
> ent Branches of Our State, Equally Implacable Enemies to *Monarchy*
> and *Episcopacy,* and if the Government does not Severely find This
> Truth in Their *Indulgence,* 'tis not Beholding to Their *Tenets.* It may
> be Remember'd, that they were the *Same* Hands that were Guilty
> Both of *Regicide* and *Sacriledge,* that at once Divided the *King's* Head
> and Crown, and made Our *Churches* Stables, and *Dens of Beasts, as
> well as Thieves.* (50–51)

Sacheverell's main perceived enemy in *The Political Union* is identical
to the perceived enemy in *False Brethren*: Dissenters. Dissent has led to
regicide in the past; and it should be avoided at all costs, and certainly
not formally and constitutionally tolerated.

The presentation of Sacheverell's ecclesiological position is much
more palatable in *The Political Union* than in *False Brethren,* or even
The Nature, Measure and Obligation of Conscience, though the latter is
certainly more palatable than the penultimate. But the position remains
fundamentally the same throughout all Sacheverell's works. Sacheverell
was fixated on stamping out both toleration and Dissent; the Glorious
Revolution was simply not a primary concern.

The Ultra Tory position that Sacheverell embodied was, then, one
that saw all legitimacy of government as coming directly from God. It
was Laudian divine right theory taken to an extreme. Sacheverell stead-
fastly refused to see the church and state as operating in tandem rather
than as an "intertwined" unity—a view that was (to a certain extent) vin-
dicated by the strategic loss the Whigs suffered through the Sacheverell
trial. It is little wonder that Warburton felt the need to articulate the
countertheory based on the emerging philosophical idea of original

contract, which had been so crudely put by the Junto prosecutors (who were considered, incidentally, to be the leading philosophical and legal intellectuals of the Whig party). This Ultra Tory position, as set forth by Sacheverell, was not deeply theological; it was more biblically oriented. Nowhere did Sacheverell quote by name previous divines of the Church of England in any of the three works discussed here. When Coleridge chose to revive the Tory position on church and state to confront Warburton, he received a rough-cut and inelegant piece of philosophy—a mere skeleton sketch of the Tory position. In contrast, Warburton's *Alliance* was rhetorically superb and well researched, and to dispute with it Coleridge had to take the skeleton of the Tory position and construct a body (to borrow imagery from Gladstone). To do this he went back to the source of Anglicanism: he went back to Hooker. It was through his combination of Hooker's elegant theology with his own clever use of contract theory that he forged the new Tory position presented in *On the Constitution of the Church and State.* This elegant presentation of the Tory position is what would be passed on to the young William Ewart Gladstone, who felt a need to articulate the High Church Tory position formally in response to Thomas Chalmers's presentation of the relationship between the church and state, which was too utilitarian to allow the state to take moral action.

Gladstone's Use of Coleridge in Disputation with Chalmers

Gladstone's "coming out party" as a theologian took place in the form of his first full-length book when he was already a member of Parliament: *The State in Its Relations with the Church,* which appeared in 1838, was a presentation of the High Church position on church and state written as part of the ongoing Tory revival. Heavily influenced by Coleridge, it was written in part as a rejoinder to Thomas Chalmers's "Lectures on the Establishment and Extension of National Churches," which were delivered in London in 1838 in an attempt to apply pressure to the Whig government to release substantial funds to the Church of Scotland for the building of new churches, both in the cities and in the countryside. Chalmers's primary concern was with the extremely rapid expansion of the cities, where Dissenting churches were growing exponentially as the population increased. His concerns were not, in this respect, entirely remote from those of the Oxford Movement, but his opinion on the role of the established church in society was, and this is where Gladstone was deeply dissatisfied with Chalmers's approach and felt the need to publicly put forth his own differing view.

A thumbnail sketch of Gladstone's early ecclesiastical biography will be useful. He was raised in a liberal Tory household by a merchant father who was a leading figure, both financially and politically, in the community of Evangelicals within Liverpool. His father also had links with the Clapham sect through the national concatenation of Evangelical communities. Gladstone's grandfather had been a practicing member of the Church of Scotland all his life and an elder of the North Leith Kirk, where, having had no sympathy for the moderate party then dominant in the Scottish Church, he had actively participated in "rooting out moral laxity and enforcing the strict Calvinistic discipline."[16] Gladstone's father, John, had to worship with other Scots in Benn's Garden Chapel because there was no Scottish Church in Liverpool for some years after his arrival there, but he was one of a group of Scots who eventually established a Scots Kirk in Oldham Street with a church-school beside it in 1792. When he married his second wife, Anne, in 1804, however, John Gladstone converted to the Church of England and paid 203 pounds for a pair of seats in the newly built St. Mark's Church.

A firm Evangelical, Anne Gladstone corresponded with and visited Hannah More, and when Thomas Chalmers visited Liverpool in 1817 he resided with the Gladstone family.[17] So Gladstone most probably knew Chalmers at least passingly, as a child. This seems all the more likely because when Chalmers came to Oxford to preach at the local Baptist chapel, Gladstone stayed out after the bell to hear his sermon.[18]

While up at Oxford Gladstone became involved with the St. Ebbes Evangelical community, led by Henry Bellenden Bulteel. Gladstone was at first fascinated by the charismatic elements of this new Evangelicalism, but he became revolted by the increasing departure from orthodoxy

---

16. Perry Butler, *Gladstone: Church, State and Tractarianism* (Oxford: Clarendon Press, 1982), 10.

17. Butler, *Gladstone*, 9–12.

18. Butler, *Gladstone*, 78.

of Bulteel's practices and by Bulteel's claim (in a book entitled *The Doctrine of the Miraculous Interference of Jesus on Behalf of Believers, Addressed to the Church of God at Oxford* [1832]) to have miraculously healed several chronically ill women. Like other men brought up in Evangelical households who became disillusioned with Evangelical practices but still believed deeply in the passion of worship, Gladstone became a High Churchman upon leaving the Bulteel set. He came to believe strongly in sanctification, sacramentalism, and the apostolic succession. Concurrent with his move to the High Church, and arguably partly because of it, Gladstone became a High Tory; this move to the right was also due, and perhaps especially due, to Gladstone's revulsion and fury at the riots sparked by Parliament's failure to pass the Great Reform Bill in 1831. On leaving Oxford in the summer of 1832 he had obtained his first seat as an MP from the Duke of Newcastle, who, like Sacheverell, can legitimately be called an Ultra Tory. It is difficult to overemphasize Gladstone's detestation of the riots, which was due in great part to his High Church conviction that the Christian subject could not take up arms against the government, since government derived its authority from God. For instance, he famously called the Reform Bill of 1832 the work of the Antichrist. The young Gladstone was also terribly opposed to any relief for Dissenters. Reading Keble's assize sermon in 1833, he must have felt that he had found a spiritual home, for the concerns Keble addressed in *National Apostasy* were close to his own: the rise in numbers of Dissenters, violence against the government in the working classes, and so on. It is important to keep this position in mind because the Oxford Movement south of the border and the Church of Scotland extensionists, led by Chalmers, north of the border in Scotland, had so many concerns in common. So when Gladstone engaged with Chalmers over the relationship of the church and state they shared a substantial middle ground, but they also fundamentally disagreed about the role the church had to play within the governance of the state.

One point on which Chalmers and Gladstone were diametrically opposed was the participation of the church in the electoral process. The Evangelical wing of the Church of Scotland had always held that it was inappropriate for its ministers to seek to influence the election of secular authorities in any way. Chalmers had been reminded of this in a painful way in 1836. By simply printing a letter in a Tory periodical, the *Edinburgh Advertiser,* to support the candidacy of his friend and fellow church extensionist Alexander Campbell, who was the Tory candidate in a parliamentary by-election (Chalmers's hope had been to demonstrate cross-party support for Campbell), he elicited a public protest that contributed substantially to Campbell's defeat. The reason for the public outrage was that Chalmers, even by this seemingly innocuous act, had violated what Stewart Brown has called

> a convention peculiarly sacred to the Evangelical party in the Church of Scotland—that is, the strict separation of Church and State in their internal government. According to this convention, while the Church as a body might petition Parliament, or even resist an unchristian monarch, it was not to interfere directly in the internal affairs of government. The lines separating legitimate from illegitimate uses of the Church's political influence were hazy; none the less, Church interference in a Parliamentary election was considered an unacceptable breach of convention.[19]

So when Chalmers came to defend the position of the established church, there was at least one fundamental difference in approach.

Yet the delivery of Chalmers's "Lectures on the Establishment and Extension of National Churches" in April and May of 1838 in a very real sense gave the lie to this entire convention of the strict separation of church and state in their internal government because, through their delivery, Chalmers sought directly to influence the Whig government. That government, returned in 1837, but with a pared-down majority of fewer than thirty, had originally led the Scottish church extensionists to believe that substantial monies would be made available to them in exchange for their support. Immediately after the general election these promises were radically scaled down to a proposal of simply making available unclaimed funds from lands originally belonging to the Crown to build churches in the Highlands; unclaimed monies in the possession of private landowners would be appropriated to expand church buildings in rural parishes where the existing facilities were no longer sufficient. This second offer of help entailed abandoning any monies for the urban

---

19. Stewart J. Brown, *Thomas Chalmers and the Godly Commonwealth in Scotland* (Oxford: Oxford University Press, 1982), 266–67.

parish renewal that Chalmers and the extensionists were most concerned with. Still later (and this is what led Chalmers to London to deliver his lectures) in late March the promises were reneged on altogether. The Whigs had good *realpolitik* reasons for doing this: most church extensionists, unlike Chalmers, were committed Tories and would never have switched allegiance over this issue alone. Thus the extensionist movement appeared linked with the Tory party—and the Whig government, with its now thinning majority, could not afford to alienate radical, independent, and dissenting members of Parliament by responding to its demands. Chalmers's motivation for giving his lectures is described by Brown:

> He had long threatened that if the Whig Government rejected the Church's request for the endowment grant after the completion of the Royal Commission's inquiry, he would mobilize the country against the Government. Now, he determined to act upon this threat. . . .
> His main purpose was to introduce the Church of Scotland's case to the English people.[20]

By doing so, he also hoped to raise a groundswell of popular support from the English population that would force the government to fund the expansion of the Church of Scotland. The lectures were on the whole well received and were widely printed immediately (within a year eight thousand copies had been sold).[21] Chalmers did not break new theological ground in their delivery; rather, he elucidated the Calvinist idea of the godly commonwealth (which the Scottish Evangelicals had been promulgating for decades) to an English audience largely unfamiliar with it and sought to demonstrate how this idea was best achieved through an established state church. Brown clearly and succinctly describes his interpretation of Chalmers's ideal in his introduction:

> When Chalmers referred to the ideal of the godly commonwealth, he meant essentially the sixteenth- and seventeenth-century Calvinist

---

20. S. Brown, *Thomas Chalmers*, 269. My narration of the political events following the general election of 1837 is also drawn from Brown; see 266–69.
21. S. Brown, *Thomas Chalmers*, 271.

social ideal, as it had been expressed in . . . basic documents of the
early Reformed Church of Scotland. . . . Church and State would cooperate in the elevation of the whole society for the glory of God—
the Church by disseminating the pure Word of God, the State by
enforcing God's laws for man as discerned from Scripture. Under
Christian discipline, people would learn to live in unison, sharing nature's bounty for the common welfare, suppressing usury and mandating a "fair price" for goods and services, practising benevolence
towards the sick and indigent poor, and cultivating their spiritual,
moral, and intellectual natures in the service of God. Where the pure
word was preached, it was believed, there would be consensus upon
the essential matters of faith, and society would not be divided by
faction or dissent. In short, the commonwealth would represent the
rule of God on earth.[22]

But this is not a fully prescriptive discussion: Chalmers was always a
difficult man to pin down,[23] and here Brown can be construed to be mis-
leading. Though Chalmers certainly believed in the charging of a fair
price for goods and services, he was also absolutely committed to, and a
theological champion of, the free market. Though he believed that the
"elite" (for lack of a better word) were certainly bound by their Christian faith to be charitable, he also believed that it was the responsibility
of the individual Christian to provide for himself in whatever circumstances providence had placed him. Chalmers was against central control of prices and wages by the state. He believed that the state should
provide for the sick (no individual responsibility could be attached to
illness), but he did not believe that the state should provide for the indigent poor. They had to provide for themselves by taking whatever work
was available—Chalmers had no tolerance for what he saw as laziness
in any incarnation. He believed that the free market would teach the
principles of frugality, fair pricing, and charity over time and that governmental control in mandating a price structure would only make the
poor self-detrimentally reliant on the elite. For Chalmers, the church
was to teach and aid in charity, but the state had to allow market forces

22. S. Brown, *Thomas Chalmers,* xv–xvi.
23. See below.

to teach frugality, diligence, and the need to accrue savings for the inevitable economic recessions that would occur during a person's lifetime.[24] (Note that this was an absolutely different perspective from that of both Gladstone and Coleridge, who believed that to act morally the state had to both provide central control over economic forces and oversee the welfare of the poor through its union, or relations, with the state church.) But this belief in the free market, and the mutual independent action of the state and the established church in Scotland, should not be seen to detract from the godly commonwealth that Chalmers certainly held as an ideal; his ideal of the godly commonwealth simply presented the state and the established church working independently in parallel rather than in tandem.

Chalmers presented these ideals in his lectures and berated the government for allowing the ideal of a parish community within either an urban neighborhood or a rural settlement to fall apart through the lack of a cohesive established structure. Though the government should not control the actions of the church through central administration, and though each parish should have its own independent governing authority, the state was still responsible for maintaining the establishment and for providing sufficient funds for the established church to be able to minister to the entirety of its flock. He pressed home the argument that "a religious Establishment of territorial churches and schools represented the highest aspirations of a nation, elevating it above the politics of self-interest and the shallow vision of utilitarianism."[25] He also prosecuted explosive attacks on the system of so-called "Voluntaryism," in which religion was dispensed on a supply and demand basis. This, he argued, produced an urban church where access to the establishment was the preserve of the wealthy who could afford high seat rents (the Scottish system of urban tithing) and neglected the state's duty to compel the attendance of the irreligious and ignorant. Worse still, it simultaneously neglected its obligations to provide establishment education and wor-

---

24. Chalmers is the archetypal "Malthusian Evangelical" of the paradigm described by Boyd Hilton in his study of Evangelicalism, *The Age of Atonement: The Influence of Evangelicalism on Social and Economic Thought, 1785–1865* (Oxford: Clarendon Press, 1991).

25. S. Brown, *Thomas Chalmers*, 270.

ship facilities for the religious poor, who were being forced to turn to Dissenting communions for access to education and worship. In short, by neglecting to expand the funding of the Church of Scotland, the British Parliament was actively standing in the way of the proper functioning of the godly commonwealth. Such a commonwealth was morally necessary because humanity's natural depravity would lead to sloth and irreligion, and the only functional way to combat this was through a vibrant established church, which would be sure to preach and educate in the tradition of the true word of God.

There were six lectures in all, with the following titles:

1. Statement of the Question respecting a National Establishment of Christianity; and exposure of the Misconceptions regarding it
2. Vindication of a Religious National Establishment, in Opposition to the Reasonings and Views of the Economists
3. Vindication of a National Religious Establishment, in Opposition to the views of those who allege the Sufficiency of the Voluntary Principle
4. On the Circumstances which determine a Government to select one Denomination of Christianity for the National Religion
5. On a Territorial Establishment, and the Reasons of its Efficacy
6. Circumstances which justify a Government, that has assumed one from among the several Denominations of Evangelical Protestantism, for the National Establishment, in abiding by the Selection which it has made[26]

The lectures contain a great deal with which Gladstone agreed, but it is not surprising that Gladstone felt spurred on immediately to write his own defense of the establishment in *The State in Its Relations with the Church*—a project that he clearly had had in his mind for some time.[27] He seems to have felt that the vindication of the establishment, especially the established Church of England, needed a second airing

---

26. Thomas Chalmers, *Lectures on the Establishment and Extension of National Churches* (Glasgow, 1838), 2. Subsequent page citations to this work are given parenthetically in the text.
27. See below.

immediately. Not only were Chalmers's substantive arguments too close to Warburton's contract theory, but the whole foundation of "his" establishment was too close to utilitarianism for Gladstone's liking. For instance, Chalmers writes in the first two paragraphs of lecture 1:

> There is a felt indisposition on the part of certain religionists to the question of an Establishment; and that just because it appears to them a mere question of machinery. . . .
> To meet their antipathy in this very general form, it might be perhaps enough to say, that, if acted upon or carried into effect, it were in utter violation of all the analogies both of nature and providence. In the business, for example, of agriculture, as well as of seamanship and the arts, do we behold processes of human contrivance, adapted to powers, that often, in their principle and mode of operation, are altogether beyond the reach of human comprehension. And certain it is, that the dependence we ought to feel on the Sovereign of our world, for the shower and the sunshine, and the various influences of the firmament above, does not supercede the diligence wherewith we ply the labours, and both devise and prosecute the schemes, of our well-arranged husbandry below. Here, then, we have a supernal influence in the hands of God, conjoined with the terrestrial economy in the hands of man. If nature withhold her part, there might be no valuable produce from the fields cultivated with whatever skill or whatever strenuousness. If we withhold our part, there might be a hundred fold less of valuable produce from the same fields lying waste and neglected, however genial the seasons, or with whatever benign an aspect the year may have rolled over us. (3)

Chalmers sets forth his belief in the free market and in the need for society to cooperate with God for its members' provision through the market by setting aside a part of the bounty God had provided for a period in which the bounty of God through nature might be less: a fallow year. But unless one is familiar with Chalmers's ideology before reading the *Lectures* it is difficult to understand exactly what he is arguing. To be fair to Chalmers, and to avoid the appearance of carping at him on stylistic points, these lectures were delivered towards the end of his career, so he could assume some familiarity with his own previous works; but then again, he was delivering them to an audience in London in order to win converts to the Scottish church extensionist movement, so he must have expected a substantial portion of his audience to be unfamiliar with the workings of and issues troubling the Church of Scotland. These are minor points, however, and the lectures were unarguably well received by Chalmers's large audience (even if they were unsuccessful in securing governmental funding for the extension).

The point where Gladstone began to have substantial disagreements with Chalmers's defense of the established church comes in the general conclusion of the first lecture. Here Chalmers makes clear the premise of his macro argument, that the establishment forms the most *effective and efficient* way of achieving the godly commonwealth, by using the image of a machine:

> Our distinct object is to demonstrate the power and the properties which belong to a National Establishment of religion, viewed as a machine; and, in regard to the working of it, we may at least state as our triumphant confidence, that, notwithstanding the exaggeration of its enemies, the evidence is every day growing, of its vast practical importance to the moral wellbeing of our nation. If it be an undoubted truth, that there is a distinct and decided improvement in the *personnel* of the Church of Scotland; if in England, the mighty instrument is passing into the hands of a more efficient clergy than before; if in Ireland, persecution, with its wonted influence is begetting a resolute and high-toned spirituality in the devoted ministers of that deeply injured hierarchy—is this, we ask, the time to wrest from the hold of its now more faithful and energetic agency, that engine which would enable them to operate with tenfold effect on the families of the land? The work of reformation was prosecuted more wisely in other days; when, notwithstanding the provocative of a grossly immoral and tyrannic priesthood, they but changed the agency and preserved the engine. And with our present agency, I trust we shall, by the blessing of Heaven, be enabled not only to preserve but to perfect the engine; and that, with enough of energy and conscientiousness and devoted zeal on the part of their ministers, all the menace and agitation by which they are surrounded will only rivet the three churches more firmly on their bases, and rally more closely around their common cause, the wise and the good of our nation. (15–16)

The choice of this image as the principal hermeneutic of the *Lectures* was unfortunate; it is easy to see how because of it Chalmers could be seen to be employing the argument from utility when he was actually employing an argument from efficiency. It is even easier to see how a young High Churchman like Gladstone would have found this mechanistic image an entirely unsatisfactory presentation of the relationship between church and state that weakened the church's position, since arguments from efficiency and utility did not allow actions to be taken based upon moral principles (which was, of course, Coleridge's premise for attacking Canning in *The Friend*).[28] In fact, taken in the context of the idea of the godly commonwealth, the image makes a great deal of sense theologically; however, the Church of England had never held the Calvinistic idea of the godly commonwealth as one of its principles, and consequently the image and the argument from efficiency seemed not only unnatural but inappropriate from the High Church perspective. This is why Gladstone said that Chalmers had laid down principles that were seriously detrimental to the cause of the establishment (see below). The argument from efficiency is continued in lecture 2, if anything more overtly; again the concluding paragraph is demonstrative:

> We have not yet, however, made good the conclusion, that a National Establishment is the best and fittest expedient for providing our general population with the lessons of Christianity, although we trust that it may soon appear, that it is not on the free trade principle, which is the principle of let alone, that we can most effectually secure this high interest. We may have scored off this from the list of expedients; yet other expedients for the religious education of the people may remain to be disposed of, besides that of an Establishment— and having now delivered our views on the scheme of the econonists *[sic]*, we shall proceed in our next Lecture to expound and to give our estimate of another scheme, which, though generally held to be identical with the former, is, in some material respects, distinct from it;— we mean the scheme of the voluntaries. (30)

Chalmers seeks to undercut all other arguments on the grounds of "expediency"—or efficiency—until he is left with the establishment as the "last man standing," so to speak. Again, the primary criterion of effi-

---

28. See chapter 5 above.

ciency would grate on Gladstone's own beliefs on church and state and seem to him damaging to the cause overall.

Chalmers attacked the English government strongly on the more general point of ignoring the lower social orders. He chose lecture 3 to begin this thrust (which continues through the final four lectures) partly because, at the halfway point, it was necessary to bring up the damage that the antiextensionist position was doing to the working class of Scotland. The demonstration of this damage was, after all, the primary reason why Chalmers had come to London in the first place. He argued that the reform bill of 1832 had enfranchised only the ten-pound freeholders, so that the refusal to fund extensionism in the Church of Scotland amounted to enfranchising only those who could afford the marginally substantial seat rent in the urban parishes. The government, Chalmers argued, was simply uninterested in the wishes of the great majority of the working class in Scotland (who he claimed supported the extensionist movement) simply because, having assets below the ten-pound freehold threshold, they were disenfranchised and therefore of negligible concern to MPs.

> The best recommendation I can give of their errand [the errand of the ministers of the Church of Scotland pleading for funding for the extensionist movement in London], is to state the class or description of persons for whom they are labouring,—and who are now shut from the benefits of moral and religious instruction, in virtue of the numbers in our land having increased, and the Establishment not having increased along with them. On whom is it that the burden of this calamity principally lights; and of what description in society are those sufferers, who are left without a church to humanise and elevate their spirits,—without a clergyman, who might be at once the friend and adviser of the families? They are the men who, finding no provision for them within the Church, are either not able or not willing to provide a ministration for themselves. The two requisite elements for this, are wealth and the will; and they who want either of these, or most generally both of them together, form the great class of our unhappy exiles from the habits and observances of a Christian land. (43)

Chalmers proclaimed that the church would not relinquish its advocacy of the poor, who would also *raise their voices loud enough for the legislature south of the border to hear their cries* (44, emphasis mine). This is a difficult threat (for lack of a better word: *threat* is not strictly accurate because Chalmers was not the sort of man who made threats) to unravel. Clearly at one level it was a reference to the riots during the Reform Bill agitation of 1831–32, but it is inconceivable that Chalmers would have advocated revolution: the lectures were delivered to save the church and to save society from revolution. It is probable that he was warning that the Kirk could eventually be put in the position of considering secession from the state to effect self-funding (taking the church into the free market, so to speak) if the money for extension was not forthcoming from Westminster: a point he would end the entire series of lectures by stressing in the closing paragraphs of lecture 6—and, of course, Chalmers did later lead a separatist movement away from the established Kirk in 1843. But it is also inconceivable that he was actively threatening Kirk secession in 1838.[29] His rhetoric is strong, but its exact meaning here is uncertain.

Lecture 6 returns to the argument from efficiency; here Chalmers essentially argues that the most efficient way of creating the godly commonwealth is for the government to choose one form of religion and to establish it as the only acceptable form of religion within the state (46–47). There is a very long discussion of how this is demonstrated by history, and Chalmers employs the classically Anglican paradigm of using the biblical example of the state of Israel as his foundation, but he ends with a convoluted (and nearly interminable) defense of the state's choice of Protestantism over Roman Catholicism on the grounds of its more democratic structure, which provides a more efficient church governmental structure for the state to enforce and deal with (51–53). He concludes with the argument that one way to demonstrate this in the contemporary context is the Church of Ireland: the answer is "not to abolish the Protestant Establishment of Ireland but rightly to patronize it" (54).

Lecture 5 is a vindication of the "Territorial Establishment" and the "Reasons of its Efficacy." The two parts of the title should really be reversed to read "Efficacy as the Reason for Territorial Establishment." Chalmers felt the need to demonstrate why it was necessary for the gov-

---

29. See below.

ernment to choose one sect of "Evangelical Protestantism" (58–59) from the several, or many, available to it, and to do this he returned to his image of the establishment as a machine (60). He revisits his main argument from lecture 1, using a large number of pseudohypothetical examples from contemporary culture. His argument is circular. The government can provide the machine for building the godly commonwealth, but machines are only as good as the men that operate them, and to have the most efficient machine for the governance of a Christian society, the state must establish within its territory one religion. Once this has been done, all men will be educated in that tradition, thereby providing the largest possible pool from which to choose men to run the machinery of government and church. In other words, the state should choose and establish one sect of Protestants because the establishment of that one sect will provide the best pool from which to draw operators, as all the best men will be of the one established religious tradition (65). To put it even more succinctly: the church should be established because adept men are needed to run the established church.

Lecture 6 is Chalmers's final plea for the extensionist cause. He argues that, having chosen to establish one form of Protestantism, the state has a responsibility to abide by that choice and to continue to act as the patron of that establishment. This is by far the most convincing portion of the series. Clearly his point is that by refusing to fund the extensionist movement within the Church of Scotland, Westminster is in effect acting to *dis*-establish it. This argument has substantial merit and contains some of the most subtle rhetoric in the entire series of lectures. An apparent peculiarity of the final lecture, though, occurs in the penultimate paragraph, where Chalmers, for the first time in the text, is very kind to Dissenters in both his rhetoric and his historical analysis. "But the best and highest sacrifice of all were by the Dissenters of England, those representatives and descendents of the excellent ones of the earth— the Owens, and Flavels, and Howes, and Baxters, and Henrys of a bygone age—who rejoiced to hear of all the Christianity which there was in the Church; and to see all which the Church did, if but done for the Christian good of the people" (74). This apparent change of direction actually makes perfect sense: the men he mentions here left the Church of England, though reluctantly, to establish a separate Presbyterian Church in England. In other words, they were reluctant separatists who were forced to take what they believed to be a final resort, and Chalmers is presenting them as being forced by the state into a position they neither wanted nor thought the optimal. So to most effectively drive his point home Chalmers should have said: "But the best and highest sacrifices of all were made by the Dissenters of England who because of the actions of Parliament were forced to act, under the pressure of their own consciences, for what they perceived to be the Christian good of the people."

Now, again this brings up the thorny issue of whether, in 1838, Chalmers knew that he would be or even thought that he might be forced to lead the separatist movement in the Kirk—which, of course, he eventually did in 1843 (three years before his death). It is a fact, however, that five years (and more importantly several rivers of water under the political bridge) passed between the delivery of the lectures and the great divide within the Kirk. Once again to be blunt: it is inconceivable that this ending to the lectures could legitimately suggest that Chalmers knew by 1848 that he would eventually be forced to split the Kirk. The lectures were written as a *defense* of the establishment; their entire focus was that establishment was the most efficient way to operate the Kirk. This alone is enough to demonstrate that in 1838 Chalmers wished entirely to preserve the establishment—he merely needed more money to do it. The preceding quotation might have been a warning to the nineteen prelates of the Church of England and the Westminster MPs in the room that *without money* the Kirk might *at some point* be forced to consider disestablishment (as subsequent history proved), but it was not a threat by Chalmers to begin such a movement. (In fact, the concept of disestablishment was not an entirely unusual subject for even High Churchmen to bring up: earlier in this book a discussion between Froude and Pusey on the subject has already been highlighted.)

That Chalmers had in mind disestablishment in 1838 is also inconceivable because of the amount of time in the lectures that Chalmers spent on discussing the danger that Dissenters posed to the church. Either Dissenters were a danger or they were not, and Chalmers made it clear that they were. So given his insistence throughout the lectures that Dissenters were a danger to the established church, and given his argument that by refusing to fund the extension of the Kirk the government was effectively disestablishing it, it makes perfect sense that in the penultimate paragraph of the last lecture he speaks highly of the *reluctant* seventeenth-century Dissenters as making the highest sacrifice (i.e., leaving the establishment). These men were not cradle Dissenters, they were men of the establishment who were forced outside of it—and they always maintained that they were still part of the Church of England.

It is also noteworthy that Chalmers closes the *Lectures* by emphasizing that he is speaking "not of the sin of schism . . . but the blessings of unity" (74). So there is no evidence that he had any inkling he would eventually be a part of disestablishment (let alone lead it). He was trying to save the establishment.

The lectures contain no argument from either justice or divine right. This is not surprising considering the Calvinist tradition from which Brown argues they were drawn, and (if Brown is correct) the fact that that Chalmers always had the ideal of the godly commonwealth before him rather than the teleological position of divine authority stretching down through the government to the individual Christian. But Chalmers was a difficult man to pin down: soteriologically he was an Arminian, and this suggests that Gladstone might have expected a heavier emphasis upon grace within the lectures—grace as a source of good government. So the young Gladstone, the High Churchman listening to Chalmers, would have been presented with a series of arguably convoluted and certainly verbose lectures that prosecuted an argument for the established church based on efficiency. Though it was not an argument from utility it was a close cousin to it, and though Chalmers spent more time than Warburton basing the argument in the constitution, Gladstone would have still found the overall picture unconvincing.

Gladstone probably agreed with a substantial amount of what Chalmers was arguing for. (Considering his family background, he most certainly would have supported the extensionist movement in the Church of Scotland.)[30] But much as he respected Chalmers he did not agree with Chalmers's argument or even find it acceptable. So in *The State in Its Relations with the Church*, Gladstone's opposition to Chalmers was not adversarial, like his opposition (following Coleridge) to Warburton, but rather corrective.[31] After all, Chalmers's lectures were meant to defend the establishment of the Church of Scotland, and whatever their form, they would have had some intrinsic divergence from Gladstone's arguments defending the Church of England. Gladstone's perception of the need for a new formal treatment of the question of church and state in

---

30. See above and below.
31. On his arguments against Warburton, see below.

England should therefore be seen to be a preexisting project that was spurred by Chalmers's lectures but not focused directly against them.

Even Gladstone's adverse reaction to Chalmers's presentation was couched in a respect for the man himself, as a letter of May 14, 1838, makes clear: "Such a jumble of Church, un-Church and anti-Church principles as that excellent and eloquent man Dr Chalmers has given us in his recent lectures, no human being ever heard."[32] So Gladstone's decision to write *The State in Its Relations with the Church* should be seen, not as a personal attack on Chalmers, but rather as a project of corrective education for the Church of England. Chalmers had indeed defended the establishment, but in a way Gladstone could not accept as relevant and "right-headed" for the Church of England. "Despite Chalmers's eloquent vindication of the establishment principle, his attack on the Voluntaryists and on the spiritual independence of the Church, Gladstone could not but lament the grave deficiency in theological outlook of a man who, as he put it, 'flogged, the apostolical succession grievously, seven bishops sitting below him: London, Winchester, Chester, Oxford, Llandaff, Gloucester, Exeter and the Duke of Cambridge incessantly bobbing assent.'"[33] Gladstone's purpose in writing was "to vindicate the idea of a National Church established by law, to show that despite recent events the Church of England was the only possible Church to be so established, and to commend this to the Tory party in the hope that it would provide them with a coherent set of principles on which to base their future ecclesiastical policy."[34] Or as Gladstone himself put it:

> There are others who, although they are themselves unshaken in their attachment to the principle, yet defend it upon grounds untenable for their purpose, and better fitted to be occupied as positions against them. . . .
>
> But besides the fact that we are more ignorant of our duty as citizens than as churchmen, in respect of the connection, we shall find another reason for instituting the investigation in the former capacity rather than in the latter. The unison is to the church a matter of sec-

32. Quoted in Butler, *Gladstone,* 78.

33. Butler, *Gladstone,* 78. The internal quotation is from John Morley's 1903 biography, *The Life of William Ewart Gladstone.*

34. Butler, *Gladstone,* 79.

ondary importance. *Her* foundations are on the holy hills. Her charter is legibly divine. She, if she should be excluded from the precinct of government, may still fulfill all her functions, and carry them out to perfection. Her condition would be anything rather than pitiable, should she once more occupy the position which she held before the reign of Constantine. But the state, in rejecting her, would actively violate its most solemn duty, and would, if the theory of the connection be sound, entail upon itself a curse. We know of no effectual preservative principle except religion; nor of any permanent, secure, and authenticated religion but in the church. The state, then, if she allow false opinions to overrun and bewilder her, and under their influence, separates from the church, will be guilty of an obstinate refusal of truth and light, which is the heaviest sin of man. It is of more importance, therefore, for our interests as a nation, that we should sift this matter to the bottom, than for our interests as a church. Besides all which, it may be shown that the principles, upon which alone the connection can be disavowed, tend intrinsically and directly to disorganization, in as much as they place government itself upon a false foundation.[35]

So what Gladstone had in mind was not only a disputation of the portions of Chalmers's theoretical foundations with which he disagreed but a new and encompassing defense of the doctrine of the established Church of England. In a very real sense his was the first public voice of the Oxford Movement—for while the Puseyites were still talking to each other and getting excited over tracts with print runs of no more than a few hundred, Gladstone issued a large book that undertook a highly successful defense of the apostolic succession and the established church. *The State in Its Relations with the Church* sold out five printings in its first twelve months of publication and was expanded and reissued two years later. Gladstone described the need for such a polemical work as follows:

It does not appear that our literature is well supplied with works which would meet the necessity above described, and furnish men

---

35. W. E. Gladstone, *The State in Its Relations with the Church*, 1st ed. (London: John Murray, 1838), 3–4. Subsequent page citations to this work are given parenthetically in the text.

with sound principles (axiomata summa) upon the fundamental conditions of the union between the church and the state. Bishop Warburton has written upon it with much acuteness and ability, but in the dry and technical manner of a man who lived in times when there was no strong pressure in one direction requiring to be warmly and feelingly met from another. Mr. Coleridge has dealt admirably with the subject in his "Idea of Church and State"; but he does not carry out his conceptions into detail, nor apply them to practice sufficiently to meet the wants of general readers. Dr. Chalmers has handled some points connected with this inquiry in a manner the most felicitous, but, in other parts of his recently published lectures, he has laid down principles, we fear, not less seriously detrimental to our cause. The work of Dr. Paley on Moral and Political Philosophy is a store-house of anything rather than sound principles. Hooker looked at the question under influences derived from the general controversy with the Puritans, and rather with reference to the terms than to the grounds of the connection. (6)

So, within four years of his death, Coleridge's work on church and state was included in a list of works on the subject by England's most prominent divines, and crucially Gladstone's introduction treated him more favorably than Warburton or even Hooker—let alone Chalmers. Further, Gladstone chose to carry on Coleridge's attacks against Warburton's alliance theory within the text of his work, and he chose Hooker's idea of the state as a metaphorical individual whose actions had moral consequences as the foundation of his model of church and state.[36] Coleridge's work in *On the Constitution of the Church and State* (and apparently *The Lay Sermons* as well; see below) was seminal for Gladstone. *The State in Its Relations with the Church* was not only Gladstone's coming out party as a theologian: it was Coleridge's coming out party as a theological authority.

So where and when did Gladstone encounter Coleridge's thought? The second half of this question is much easier to answer than the first. Thanks to Colin Matthew's masterful compilation of Gladstone's diaries, we know when for certain (table 3).

---

36. See below.

Table 3. Chronology for Gladstone's Reading of Coleridge's Works

Title of Coleridge Work	1st Reading	2nd Reading	3rd Reading
Schiller's *The Death of Wallenstein*	8/30/33	9/25/33	
A Lay Sermon (1839)	3/25/64		
Aids to Reflection (*1825*)	2/21/30	3/21/30	
Confessions of an Inquiring Spirit (1840)	1/30/41	1/26/90	
France: An Ode (1790)	1/1/69		
Letters to . . . Daniel Stuart (1889)	7/8/92		
Letters, Conversations and Recollections of STC (1836), ed. T. Allsop	2/8/39	2/18/40	
On the Constitution of the Church and State (1830)	8/20/37	10/30/37	10/31/37
On the Prometheus of Aeschylus: An Essay (1825)	5/3/47		
Osario: A Tragedy (1797)	3/15/74		
Poetical Works (1878)	6/5/79		
Seven Lectures on Shakespeare and Milton (1856)	8/4/64		
The Friend (1809)[a]	11/30/29		
The Rime of the Ancient Mariner (1798)	3/17/30		
The Three Graves (1818)	4/23/30		

Source: Compiled from the index to W. E. Gladstone, *The Gladstone Diaries*, vol. 14, ed. H. G. C. Matthew (Oxford: Oxford University Press; 1994), 342.

a. The date here is among the reasons that have led me to concentrate on *The Friend* of 1809 (see introduction to chapter 5). Clearly, the journal in a bound format circulated beyond its termination of publication. The expanded version was readily available some fifteen years before Gladstone read the work, and (assuming Matthew is correct in his delineation of the 1809 edition) Gladstone chose to read the journal instead of the one-volume edition—when, as his consistent acquiring of Coleridge texts shows, he could easily have chosen the alternative and expanded edition. Not only does the journal more clearly demonstrate the evolution of Coleridge's thought, but it had a circulatory life far surpassing 1809–10.

Clearly Coleridge was an author Gladstone read throughout the course of his life, and to whom he returned in his later years. Equally clearly, Gladstone read Coleridge prior to writing his own discussion of the church and state relationship. In fact, Coleridge would have been fresh in his mind while he attended Chalmers's lectures, as he had read *On the Constitution of the Church and State* a mere six months earlier.

The first of the diary entries, for Sunday, August 20, 1837, reads merely, "recommenced prayers—mg& evg: &reading service in aftn— with Sumner's Serm 16—very apposite. Read Newman—& Coleridge on Ch—Par Lost B. VII.—Fettn Ch. in mg."[37] Still more clear from the entry linking Coleridge with Newman is that Gladstone correctly understood Coleridge to be a High Church Tory theorist. Gladstone returned to Coleridge over the weekend of October 28–29, 1837. He read Coleridge over the Sunday, Monday, and Tuesday (the Sunday being the 29th); oddly Matthew has not included Gladstone's reading of Coleridge on the Sunday (only the Monday and Tuesday where *On the Constitution of the Church and State* is mentioned by name, but it is of little matter). Earlier in the month, on the first to be precise, he had been reading Newman—he finished the third volume of Newman's sermons that day; on the 24th of the month he read Blackstone on benefit of clergy; on the 29th he read E. Denison's *Sermons Preached before the University of Oxford* (1836).

From all of this it is clear that Gladstone was in the process of formulating a systematic approach to church and state before Chalmers delivered his lectures and that Coleridge was a substantial influence on that position. There is also good reason to conjecture that Gladstone linked Coleridge with Newman intellectually. The text of *The State in Its Relations with the Church* makes all of this (other than the conjectured link between Coleridge and Newman) even more clear.

Gladstone's history of the approaches to the relationship of church and state, like Coleridge's, begins with Hooker (7–9). That this is a coincidence seems unlikely, since if he were undertaking a step-by-step history he would have begun with at least Jewell—if not earlier. The point is that Gladstone has chosen to narrate the Tory position on church and

---

37. W. E. Gladstone, *The Gladstone Diaries,* vol. 1, ed. M. R. D. Foot (Oxford: Oxford University Press, 1968), 310.

state. His choice to begin with Hooker is probably due to Coleridge's influence. Indeed, like Coleridge, Gladstone uses a concept from Hooker as the font of his theoretical paradigm—the metaphor of the state as an individual: "There can be no doubt that it [book 9 of the *Ecclesiastical Polity*] teaches, or rather involves, as a basis and precondition of all its particular arguments, the great doctrine that the state is a person, having a conscience, cognizant of matter of religion, and bound by all constitutional and natural means to advance it. It is impossible not to recognize throughout the book a texture of thought such as pre-eminently distinguished the great man whose name it bears" (9). Gladstone also links the idea of the state as an individual with Coleridge.[38]

In his next paragraph, Gladstone begins a discussion of Warburton's work that seeks to refute Warburton's paradigm of alliance first on the grounds of Erastianism: "She [the Church] surrenders to the state her original independency *[sic]*, and subjects all her laws and movements to the necessity of the state's previous approval. If there be more than one such religious society or church, the state is to contract with the largest; to which will naturally belong the greatest share of political influence" (12–13). Then he raises a more important objection: "The greatest *moral* defect in this theory is that indicated by the concluding sentence. The state is to contract with the largest religious society. The adoption of a national church is then with it *[sic]* matter of calculation, and not of conscience" (13). Yet the most damning indictment of Warburton's theories comes in the next two paragraphs:

> The propositions of this work generally are to be received with qualification. It is a very low theory of government which teaches, that it has only the care of the body and bodily goods; and might seem besides to imply, that all physicians are more peculiarly statesmen. There was far more truth in the [eu zen] of Aristotle; under which we may consider that the state, bound to promote the general good of man, finds the church ready made to its hand, as the appointed instrument for advancing that department of human well-being which is spiritual, and contracts with it accordingly.

---

38. See below: he will bring in the concept of the state having a soul through Coleridge.

And there does appear to be something reasonable in the objection of Bolingbroke to the representation of the alliance in the light of a fact, on the ground that it is a fiction. (13)

Gladstone concludes that Warburton "appears to have adopted the views of Locke, and to have copied his representation of the alliance from the original compact" (14). Although Gladstone's work is prescriptive rather than proscriptive, it is clear from his first chapter that the focus of his attack, insofar as he is attacking anyone, is Warburton, not Chalmers. For instance, Gladstone chooses directly to attack Warburton in two of the last three paragraphs of chapter 1: "It remains to observe, before proceeding to the formal investigation of our subject, that, when we speak of the Church of England as having actually entered into connection with the State, we use a phrase which has more of historical truth, undoubtedly, than belongs to the celebrated original compact with which Bishop Warburton compares it" (22). And in the penultimate paragraph: "Alliance means too little: it puts too much out of view the Christian conscience of the state, and seems to suppose too great an original distance between the parties; whereas, in their personal composition, they very greatly mix; and when Warburton says the state will *ally* with the largest communion, because that will have most influence in the legislature, this should mean that the majority of persons composing the legislature will have such a conscience as will approve and establish that communion" (22). Gladstone, of course, prefers the term *relations* to *alliance, union,* and *connection,* each of which he professes to reject for various semantic reasons; the underlying reason, however, is that *relations* fits best with his metaphor of seeing the state as an individual that takes moral actions. Persons have relations with one another, they do not have alliances (which occur between groups) or connections, and Gladstone is too concerned about avoiding Erastianism through maintaining the church's independence to be comfortable with the idea of a "union" of church and state (which would indicate a marriage). Chalmers's lectures and their argument from efficiency may have spurred Gladstone's production of *The State in Its Relations with the Church,* but the theoretical position Gladstone wished to raze was clearly the utilitarian one of Warburton.

In contrast, Gladstone wears metaphorical kid gloves when discussing Chalmers's *Lectures,* though he gently criticizes Chalmers's arguably prolix presentation of the system ("The profuse and brilliant eloquence of Dr. Chalmers, and the warm heart from which its colouring is principally derived, have necessarily contributed to render the scientific development of his views less accurately discernible than it would have been had he written more apathetically"), he is careful to point out that according to Chalmers Christianity is the foundation of order and prosperity and that the efforts of individuals "without aid from government are insufficient to bring it [wealth] within reach of the whole population" (19). Even when he criticizes Chalmers outright, he qualifies his criticisms:

> It did not enter into the purpose of Dr. Chalmers to exhibit the whole subject, but even in these propositions he has, it may be apprehended, put forward much questionable matter. He appears by no means to succeed in showing, upon his own principles, that his territorial establishment must be of one denomination: he would probably find it impossible, upon stricter investigation, so to define Evangelical Protestantism as to make it an universal criterion for the guidance of governments: it might further be argued, that he has surrendered the condition without which all others fail, in omitting from his calculation the divine constitution of the visible church. . . . But no more: it is painful even to indicate points of difference from a man so distinguished, so excellent, so liberal—and one, too, who has studied and explained the machinery of a religious establishment with such admirable effect. (20–21)

No such respect is shown to Warburton, though Chalmers's arguments from efficiency owe more to Warburton's alliance paradigm than Gladstone would like to admit. The real crux of Gladstone's disappointment with Chalmers lies in what Gladstone calls Chalmers's "omitting from his calculation the divine constitution of the visible church." Without the constitutional establishment of a specific denomination *with the sovereign as its head or governor,* the state cannot act as a moral agent—and this is of course the paramount tenet of *The State in Its Relations with the Church.* Though Gladstone was disappointed with Chalmers's rhetoric in the lectures, which did not advocate a sufficiently Tory position for Gladstone's liking, he at worst reproaches Chalmers, whereas he attacks and refutes Warburton using the positions on church and state outlined by Hooker and Coleridge.

If Gladstone is respectful of Chalmers, he might be said to be almost flattering of Coleridge's contribution to the debate on church and state. He introduces Coleridge to the discussion as follows: "The argument of Mr. Coleridge 'on the Constitution of the Church and State according to the Idea of each' is alike beautiful and profound. He shows, from an analysis of the parts of the body politic, that, in order to its well-being, there must necessarily enter into its composition an estate, whose office it shall be to supply those governing and harmonising qualities of character, without which the remaining elements cannot advantageously cohere. . . . In the king, again, 'the cohesion by interdependence and the unity of the country were established'" (17). Gladstone's image is probably Pauline in its ultimate origin (see, e.g., Eph. 4:15): like Paul portraying Christ as the head of the body of the faithful, he portrays the populace of England as a microcosm of the church, and the monarch as head of the body politic. (In the passage omitted from this quotation Gladstone simply describes Coleridge's discussion of the different states that make up the population of England—or, in Gladstone's terminology, "the body politic.")[39] Because Gladstone takes as his hermeneutical starting point the state rather than the church, his discussion is always from the perspective of the state: but the moral nature of the action of the monarch and government as the head of the body politic is clear: "The acts of the national personality are those of the governing body, which is the organ of that personality; and the religion which is to sanctify it must be a religion of the governing body, which we have already once deduced from the responsibilities of the men composing it, as individuals and which we now once more infer as the natural attendant upon all agency which is truly national" (40). Theologically Gladstone relies on Coleridge's pattern, or paradigm, to make the body whole. If the king is the head of the body politic, then the soul of the body politic is the clerisy:

> There must be a soul, underlying and animating them all, *cultivation* of the inward man, which is the root, the corrective, and the safeguard of *civilisation*. The nourishment of this paramount ingredient of national life constitutes the function of a third great estate: living

---

39. See chapter 9 above.

on reserved property for more free devotion to its duties, and divided into two classes; a smaller number dwelling at the fountainheads of knowledge, guarding the treasures already acquired, opening new shafts and mines, and dispensing their acquisitions to their brethren; the *second* division of this estate, a far larger number distributed throughout the country, supplying for every spot a resident guide and teacher; and thus connecting each part of time and each part of the nation with the rest respectively. Such is the natural "clerisy" of a state. (17–18)

Gladstone does do some fine-tuning of Coleridge's discussion of his own paradigm of the first two "estates" of government—noting, for example, that the landed estate is not entirely permanent but also productive and progressive—but is careful to add that "these explanations in no way detract from the substantial truth of Mr. Coleridge's definition; and I [Gladstone] do not venture any further to encumber the masterly sketch which he has drawn" (19).

The State in Its Relations with the Church is best remembered within the corpus of Gladstone's work for being the text in which he first espoused his position that the actions of the state must be considered under the moral criteria of the actions of an individual. Within the text of the first chapter of the work he professes to have drawn the body from Hooker and the soul from Coleridge. And though he has attacked Warburton's "Whig" position of alliance through utility, he has yet to reveal the truly Tory nature of the work: this he begins to do in the final pages of the second chapter where he discusses the idea of a government in which no one religious creed is established. There he states that though perhaps there may be a situation, possibly in America or some of the British colonies, where "religious communions are so equally divided, or so variously subdivided, that the government is itself similarly chequered in its religious complexion, and thus internally incapacitated by disunion from acting in matters of religion; or, again there may be a state in which the members of government may be of one faith or persuasion, the mass of the subjects of another, and hence there may be an external incapacity to act in matters of religion," such incapacity, under any of these circumstances, is "*a social defect and calamity*" (73). This thread is continued in chapter 6, where Gladstone admits that although, because of Catholic emancipation, the propagation of the state religion by legislators is very much in jeopardy, the profession of the state religion is still a must:

> We are not yet ready to acquiesce in the proposal which has found an organ but not an echo in the House of Commons, that acts of worship should be discontinued in the great council of the nation. . . . As to the duty of active pecuniary support to the national church, that must depend upon our abilities. If we are absolutely precluded from its performance for the time, let it be considered as suspended. In that negative state with regard to *propagation,* so that we retain always the profession, we may acquiesce; but let us not be led into the fatal error of establishing all creeds, or affirm a false principle merely because we want power to carry out the true one. When the propagation has been generalised, can the unity of profession be long maintained? (230–31)

The state should formally participate in the worship of the national church within the walls of the palace of Westminster and should actively propagate the teachings of the state church at the expense of Dissenting creeds throughout the kingdom. At the very least the legislators must profess membership in the state church or the actions of their governance cannot be moral.

In chapter 7 he put the point perhaps most succinctly when discussing the difference between the established churches of England and Scotland: "The church membership of the sovereign, the worship of the state in her solemn assemblies, the terms of the writ, the parallel summons of the convocation, the participation of the bishops in legislative powers, all seems to show that the state, so far as it is a moral being, is still, in some special sense, of the communion of the English Church" (240). In other words, he has returned to his original point in chapter 1 (in his kid-gloved criticism of Chalmers), only from the reverse direction: here he is advocating the English system rather than noting how Chalmers's work does not quite bear up to examination if applied to the English situation. This is the Tory position on church and state, and it is once again being advocated publicly by politicians.

The Tractarian concerns, and among them their emphasis upon the Tory paradigm of church and state, might never have become an issue of the widest national importance if they had not been given political expression by a group of young High Church High Tories such as T. D.

Acland, J. P. Plumtre, and above all W. E. Gladstone. Gladstone's High Church theories of church and state mattered so much because they were at the center of contemporary debate about the need for a publicly financed system of national education. Central to this debate was whether that system should be administered and staffed by the state church (as Gladstone fervently believed it should be). The Tractarians were important to Gladstone in this regard as the most likely source for supplying high-minded young priests for fulfilling the role of the clerisy, as his 1838 dedication to *The State in Its Relations with the Church* makes clear: "Inscribed to The University Of Oxford; tried and not found wanting, through the vicissitudes of a thousand years; in the belief that she is providentially designed to be a fountain of blessings, Spiritual, Social and Intellectual, to this and to other countries, to the present and future times; and in the hope that the temper of these pages may be found not alien from her own" (vi). In the political application of Gladstone's Tory theory of the state as an individual, the soul of the body politic existed to animate the populace through educating them (a direct application of Coleridge's plan for the clerisy as national educators).[40] Without this political focus Oxford Tractarianism might never have developed into a national movement and could easily have remained a closed circle of backbiting dons speaking among themselves. It is not too much to say that Gladstone's book was the most important response to the call issued by Keble's assize sermon of 1833. While the Tractarians were producing works that had at most a circulation of a few hundred copies and rarely reached outside the confines of Oxford society in a meaningful way, Gladstone produced a book that went through multiple printings of several thousand volumes and was revised and expanded in further editions. Though he may not have been part of the Oxford Movement, he was first to voice its concerns to the general populace. It is therefore important that *The State in Its Relations with the Church* was written about a debate that went back a couple of centuries and relied on Coleridge and Hooker, rather than one focusing on the theological minutiae of the apostolic secession, the nature of the sacraments, or other technical theological issues argued at length within the tracts, which had little practical relevance or interest to the average churchgoer.

---

40. See chapter 9 above.

FINAL REMARKS

So, what the reader encounters upon examination of *The State in Its Relations with the Church* is indeed the first national voice of the Oxford Movement: neo-Toryism come of age out of what Colin Matthew called "the gathering forces of Toryism" that were coalescing during the 1820s. It was a system Gladstone professed to have built upon the foundation stones of Hooker and Coleridge, with the former providing the body and the latter the soul. In other words, within four years of his death Coleridge's work had been taken up by a leading young intellectual light associated with the Oxford Movement and used to profess the Tory principle of the necessity of a vibrant national church in answer to the second clarion call sounded from the pulpit of the University Church of St. Mary the Virgin: Keble's assize sermon.

That the vision would eventually fail, and that Gladstone would eventually abandon the project outlined in *The State in Its Relations with the Church* because it was unworkable, is not the issue. Gladstone abandoned the project (though he never repudiated the ideas central to the book) partly because Tractarianism itself failed. With the flight to Rome of Newman and others, Oxford (to which the book was dedicated) ceased to be a reliable "priest factory" producing the clerisy so central to Gladstone's project outlined in the book, and implementation became impossible. That he eventually disestablished the Church of Ireland and became actively and intimately linked with the Episcopal Church of Scotland rather than the established Kirk is not the issue either.[41] The former is explicable in that it was the specific issue upon which he was elected to form a government in 1868. The latter is explicable in that once Tractarianism had failed Gladstone became interested in promoting the High Church perspective any way he could, and it was not until the 1840s that Gladstone "discussed the need for high Church revival and greater zeal" in Scotland.[42] For instance, the earliest example of Gladstone seek-

41. See Peter Nockles, "Continuity and Change in Anglican High Church-manship in Britain, 1752–1850" (D. Phil. thesis., Oxford University, June 1982). For a full discussion of Gladstone's relations with the Episcopal Church of Scotland, see ch. 7, especially 546–58.

42. Nockles, "Continuity and Change," 548.

ing to promote High Church principles in Scotland comes in a letter to James Hope where he discusses the idea of establishing a High Church seminary, a project he believed would be of great benefit to "the Church in Scotland." As this was before the Great Divide, Gladstone may have thought such an educational institution could have benefited both the established Kirk and the Scottish Episcopal Church.[43] It should also be remembered that it is difficult, if not impossible, to trace a cogent thread of ideology throughout Gladstone's life; the simple fact is that the Grand Old Man was different from the young Hotspur in Peel's Tory party. Men change their minds over the course of their lives, and great men are no less apt to do this. Coleridge was a radical advocating the abolition of property in 1794 and a reactionary High Tory in 1834. Gladstone was certainly less capricious than Coleridge, but he was not necessarily less willing to change his position on a given matter (even a matter of the greatest possible importance to him) after giving it due consideration.

The real issue is that the first widely circulated answer to Keble's clarion call of 1833 professed Coleridge's principles as its soul.

---

43. Nockles, "Continuity and Change," 546.

BIBLIOGRAPHY

Primary Sources

Augustine. *City of God.* Trans. Henry Bettenson. London: Penguin Books, 1984.

Chalmers, Thomas. *Lectures on the Establishment and Extension of National Churches.* Glasgow, 1838.

Coleridge, John. *Miscellaneous Dissertations, Arising from the XVIIth and XVIIIth Chapters of the Book of Judges.* London, 1768.

Coleridge, Samuel Taylor. "Advertisement." In *Aids to Reflection in the Formation of a Manly Character on the Several Grounds of Prudence, Morality, and Religion . . .* London: Taylor and Hessey, 1825.

———. *Aids to Reflection.* Ed. John Beer. Vol. 9 of *The Collected Works of Samuel Taylor Coleridge.* Bollingen Series 75. Princeton: Princeton University Press, 1993.

———. *Biographia Literaria.* 2 vols. Ed. James Engell and W. Jackson Bate. Vol. 7 of *The Collected Works of Samuel Taylor Coleridge.* Bollingen Series 75. Princeton: Princeton University Press, 1983.

———. *Collected Letters of Samuel Taylor Coleridge.* 6 vols. Ed. Earl Leslie Griggs. Oxford: Clarendon Press, 1956–71.

———. *The Complete Works.* 7 vols. Ed. W. G. T. Shedd. New York: Harper and Brothers, 1853.

———. *Confessions of an Inquiring Spirit.* Ed. David Jasper. Philadelphia: Fortress Press, 1988.

———. *The Friend.* 2 vols. Ed. Barbara E. Rooke. Vol. 4 of *The Collected Works of Samuel Taylor Coleridge.* Bollingen Series 75. Princeton: Princeton University Press, 1969.

———. *Lay Sermons.* Ed. R. J. White. Vol. 6 of *The Collected Works of Samuel Taylor Coleridge.* Bollingen Series 75. Princeton: Princeton University Press, 1972.

———. *Lectures, 1795: On Politics and Religion.* Ed. Lewis Patton and Peter Mann. Vol. 1 of *The Collected Works of Samuel Taylor Coleridge.* Bollingen Series 75. Princeton: Princeton University Press, 1971.

———. *The Notebooks of Samuel Taylor Coleridge.* 5 vols. Ed. Kathleen Coburn. London: Routledge and Kegan Paul, 1957–2002.

———. *On the Constitution of the Church and State.* Ed. John Colmer. Vol. 10 of *The Collected Works of Samuel Taylor Coleridge.* Bollingen Series 75. Princeton: Princeton University Press, 1976.

———. *Opus Maximum.* Ed. Thomas McFarland with Nicholas Halmi. Vol. 15 of *The Collected Works of Samuel Taylor Coleridge.* Bollingen Series 75. Princeton: Princeton University Press, 2002.

———. *The Watchman.* Ed. Lewis Patton. Vol. 2 of *The Collected Works of Samuel Taylor Coleridge.* Bollingen Series 75. Princeton: Princeton University Press, 1970.

Coleridge, Sara. *Memoir and Letters.* 2 vols. Ed. Edith Coleridge. London: Henry S. King, 1873.

Frend, William. *An Address to the Inhabitants of Cambridge and Its Neighbourhood, Exhorting Them to Turn from the False Worship of Three Persons to the Worship of the One True God.* St. Ives: Printed by T. Bloom and sold by all the booksellers in Cambridge, W. Davis, Ely and the Printer, 1788.

Gladstone, W. E. *The Gladstone Diaries.* Vol. 1. Ed. M. R. D. Foot. Oxford: Oxford University Press, 1968.

———. *The Gladstone Diaries.* Vol. 14. Ed. H. G. C. Matthew. Oxford: Oxford University Press, 1994.

———. *The State in Its Relations with the Church.* 1st ed. London: John Murray, 1838.

Hooker, Richard. *The Folger Library Edition of the Works of Richard Hooker.* 7 vols. Ed. W. Speed Hill. Cambridge, MA: Harvard University Press, 1977.

———. *The Works of That Learned and Judicious Divine Mr. Richard Hooker, with an Account of His Life and Death by Isaac Walton.* 3 vols. Ed. J. Keble. Oxford: Oxford University Press, 1845.

Keble, John. *National Apostasy Considered in a Sermon Preached in St. Mary's, Oxford, before His Majesty's Judges of Assize.* Oxford: Printed by S. Collingwood Printer to the University for J. H. Parker, 1833.

Leighton, Robert. *The Whole Works of the Most Reverend Father in God, Robert Leighton, D.D., Archbishop of Glasgow: To Which Is Prefixed a Life of the Author by the Reverend John Norman Pearson, M.A.: A New Edition in 4 Volumes.* London: James Duncan, 1830.

Marsh, Herbert. "An Inquiry into the Consequences of Neglecting to Give the Prayer Book with the Bible, Interspersed with Remarks on Some Late Speeches at Cambridge, and Other Important Matter Relative to the British and Foreign Bible Society." Printed in Cambridge, 1812.

Sacheverell, Henry. *The Nature and Mischief of Prejudice and Partiality Stated in a Sermon Preach'd at St. Mary's in Oxford at the Assizes Held There, March 9th 1704.* Oxford: Printed by Leon. Lichfield, for John Stephens, Bookseller: And are to be Sold by James Knapton at the Crowne in St. Paul's Churchyard, London, 1704.

————. *The Perils of False Brethren, Both in Church and State; Set Forth in a Sermon Preach'd before the Right Honourable the Lord-Mayor, Aldermen, and Citizens of London, at the Cathedral-Church of St. Paul, on the 5th of November, 1709.* London: Printed for Henry Clements, at the Half-Moon in St. Paul's Church-Yard, 1709.

————. *The Political Union: A Discourse Shewing the Dependance of Government on Religion in General: And of the English Monarchy on the Church of England in Particular.* Oxford: Printed by Leonard Lichfield for George West, and Henry Clement, 1702.

Southey, Robert. *The Book of the Church.* 2 vols. London: John Murray, 1824.

————. *The Origin, Nature, and Object of the New System of Education.* London: Printed for John Murray, 32, Fleet-Street; Edinburgh: W. Blackwood; Dublin: J. Cumming, 1812.

————. *Vindiciae Ecclesiae Anglicanae.* London: John Murray, 1826.

Warburton, William. *The Alliance between Church and State.* Vol. 7 of *The Works of the Right Reverend William Warburton, D.D. Lord Bishop of Gloucester,* 12 vols., ed. Richard Hurd. London: Printed by Luke Hansard & Sons, near Lincoln's Inn Fields, for T. Cadell and W. Davies, in The Strand, London, 1811.

SECONDARY SOURCES

Avis, P. D. L. "Richard Hooker and John Calvin." *Journal of Ecclesiastical History* 32, no. 1 (1981): 19–28.

Avni, Abraham. "Coleridge and Ecclesiastes: A Wary Response." *Wordsworth Circle* 12, no. 2 (1981): 27–29.

Babbitt, Irving. "Coleridge and Imagination." *Nineteenth Century and After* 106 (September 1929): 383–98.

Baker, James V. *The Sacred River: Coleridge's Theory of Imagination.* Baton Rouge: Louisiana State University Press, 1957.

Barclay, Robert. *The Inner Life of the Religious Society of the Commonwealth: Considered Principally with Reference to the Influence of Church Organisation on the Spread of Christianity.* London, 1876.

Barfield, Owen. *Romanticism Comes of Age.* London: Anthroposophical Publishing, 1944.

————. *Romanticism Comes of Age.* New ed. London: Rudolf Steiner Press, 1966.

————. *Saving the Appearances.* London: Faber and Faber, 1957.

————. *What Coleridge Thought.* London: Oxford University Press, 1972.

————. *Worlds Apart: A Dialogue of the 1960's.* Middletown, CT: Wesleyan University Press, 1971.

Barth, John Robert. *Coleridge and Christian Doctrine.* Cambridge, MA: Harvard University Press, 1969.

———. *Coleridge and the Power of Love.* St. Louis: University of Missouri Press, 1988.

Bauckham, Richard. "Richard Hooker and John Calvin: A Comment." *Journal of Ecclesiastical History* 32, no. 1 (1981): 29–33.

Beer, John B. "Coleridge and Havel." *Wordsworth Circle* 22, no. 1 (1991): 40–46.

———. *Coleridge, the Visionary.* London: Chatto and Windus, 1959.

———, ed. *Coleridge's Variety: Bicentennary Studies.* London: Macmillan, 1974.

Blunden, Edmund, and E. L. Griggs, eds. *Coleridge: Studies by Several Hands on the Hundredth Anniversary of His Death.* London: Constable, 1934.

Brantley, R. E. *Locke, Wesley and the Method of English Romanticism.* Gainesville: University of Florida Press, 1984.

Bray, Gerald, ed. *Documents of the English Reformation.* Cambridge: James Clark, 1994.

Briggs, Asa. *The Age of Improvement, 1783–1867.* London: Longmans, Green, 1967.

Brooke, N. "Coleridge's True and Original Realism." *Durham University Journal* 22, no. 2 (1961): 58–69.

Brown, Ford K. *Fathers of the Victorians: The Age of Wilberforce.* Cambridge: Cambridge University Press, 1961.

Brown, P. A. *The French Revolution in English History.* London: Lockwood, 1918.

Brown, Stewart J. *Thomas Chalmers and the Godly Commonwealth.* Oxford: Oxford University Press, 1982.

Browning, Reed. *Political and Constitutional Ideas of the Court Whigs.* Baton Rouge: Louisiana State University Press, 1982.

Butler, Perry. *Gladstone: Church, State and Tractarianism.* Oxford: Clarendon Press, 1982.

Calleo, David P. *Coleridge and the Idea of the Modern State.* New Haven: Yale University Press, 1966.

Chambers, E. K. *Samuel Taylor Coleridge: A Biographical Study.* Oxford: Clarendon Press, 1938.

Chandler, David G. "Copenhagen, Bombardment of." In *Dictionary of the Napoleonic Wars,* 105. London: Arms and Armour Press, 1979.

Clark, J. C. D. *English Society, 1688–1832.* Cambridge: Cambridge University Press, 1985.

Coburn, Kathleen. *Inquiring Spirit: A New Presentation of Coleridge from His Published and Unpublished Prose Writings.* Toronto: University of Toronto Press, 1979.

Coleman, Deirdre. *Coleridge and "The Friend" (1809–1810).* Oxford: Clarendon Press, 1988.

Colmer, John. *Coleridge, Critic of Society.* Oxford: Clarendon Press, 1959.

Davies, H.S. *The English Mind: Studies Presented to Basil Wiley.* Cambridge: Cambridge University Press, 1964.

De Paolo, Charles. "Coleridge, Hegel, and the Philosophy of History." *Wordsworth Circle* 26, no. 1 (1995): 31–36.

———. "Coleridge's Theory of Distributive Justice." *Wordsworth Circle* 19, no. 2 (1988): 93–96.

———. "Kant, Coleridge, and the Ethics of War." *Wordsworth Circle* 16, no. 1 (1985): 3–14.

———. "The Lessons of Wisdom and Caution: Coleridge's Periodization of Western History." *Wordsworth Circle* 17, no. 3 (1986): 119–31.

Derrida, Jacques. *Dissemination.* London: Athlone, 1981.

Deschamps, Paul. *La formation de la penseé de Coleridge.* Paris: Didier, 1964.

Dickinson, H.T., ed. *Britain and the French Revolution.* New York: St. Martin's Press, 1989.

———. *Liberty and Property: Political Ideology in Eighteenth-Century Britain.* London: Weidenfeld and Nicolson, 1977.

Evans, A.W. *Warburton and the Warburtonians: A Study in Some Eighteenth-Century Controversies.* London: Oxford University Press, 1932.

Fritze, Ronald H. "Root or Link? Luther's Position in the Historical Debate over the Legitimacy of the Church of England, 1558–1625." *Journal of Ecclesiastical History* 37, no. 2 (1986): 288–302.

Fulford, Tim. "Coleridge and the Royal Family: The Politics of Androgyny." *Coleridge's Visionary Languages,* ed. Tim Fulford and Morton D. Paley, 67–82. Cambridge: Brewer, 1993.

———. "Coleridge and the Wisdom Tradition." *Wordsworth Circle* 22, no. 1 (1991): 77–78.

———. "Coleridge, Kabbalah, and the Book of Daniel." In *Coleridge and the Armoury of the Human Mind,* ed. Peter J. Kitson and Thomas N. Corns, 63–77. London: F. Cass, 1991.

Fulford, Tim, and Morton D. Paley. *Coleridge's Visionary Languages.* Cambridge: Brewer, 1993.

Gascoigne, John. "The Unity of Church and State Challenged: Responses to Hooker from the Restoration to the Nineteenth-Century Age of Reform." *Journal of Religious History* 21, no 1 (1997): 60–79.

Gatti, Hilary. "Coleridge's Reading of Giordano Bruno." *Wordsworth Circle* 27, no. 3 (1996): 136–44.

Gaull, Marilyn. "Coleridge and the Kingdoms of the World." *Wordsworth Circle* 22, no. 1 (1991): 47–52.

Gill, Frederick C. *The Romantic Movement and Methodism: A Study of English Romanticism and the Evangelical Revival.* London: Epworth Press, 1937.

Greaves, R. W. "The Working of the Alliance: A Comment on Warburton." In *Essays in Modern English Church History in Memory of Norman Sykes*, ed. Gareth V. Bennett and John D. Walsh, 163–80. London: Black, 1966.

Griggs, E. L. "Robert Southey's Estimate of S. T. Coleridge: A Study in Human Relations." *Huntington Library Quarterly* 9, no. 1 (1945–46): 61–94.

Haigh, Christopher. *Elizabeth I*. London: Longman, 1988.

———. *English Reformations: Religion, Politics, and Society under the Tudors*. Oxford: Clarendon Press, 1993.

———, ed. *The Reign of Elizabeth I*. London: Macmillan, 1994.

Halévy, Elie. *The Growth of Philosophic Radicalism*. London: Faber and Faber, 1949.

———. *A History of the English People in the Nineteenth Century*. 2nd rev. ed. 6 vols. London: E. Benn, 1949–52.

Halmi, N. "How Christian Is the Coleridgean Symbol?" *Wordsworth Circle* 26, no. 1 (1995): 26–30.

Harding, Anthony J. *Coleridge and the Inspired Word*. Kingston: McGill-Queen's University Press, 1985.

———. "Coleridge's College Declamation, 1792." *Wordsworth Circle* 8, no. 4 (1977): 361–67.

Hartley, David. *Observations on Man*. Poole: Woodstock Books, 1998.

Hayter, Alethea. *A Voyage in Vain: Coleridge's Journey to Malta in 1804*. London: RC London, 1993.

Hedley, Douglas. *Coleridge, Philosophy and Religion: "Aids to Reflection" and "The Mirror of the Spirit."* Cambridge: Cambridge University Press, 2000.

———. "Coleridge's Speculative Mysticism: Reflections on Dr Perkins's 'Logic and Logos.'" *Heythrop Journal* 35, no. 4 (1994): 421–39.

Hilton, Boyd. *The Age of Atonement: The Influence of Evangelicalism on Social and Economic Thought, 1785–1865*. Oxford: Clarendon Press, 1995.

———. *Corn, Cash, Commerce: The Economic Policies of the Tory Governments, 1815–1830*. Oxford: Oxford University Press, 1977.

Hinchliff, Peter B. *Benjamin Jowett and the Christian Religion*. Oxford: Clarendon Press, 1987.

———. *The One-Sided Reciprocity: A Study in the Modification of the Establishment*. London: Darton, Longman and Todd, 1966.

———. Sion College Lent Lectures, 1995, lecture 1. Typescript, author's files.

Hinde, Wendy. *Catholic Emancipation: A Shake to Men's Minds*. Oxford: Blackwell, 1992.

Hirst, Désireé. *Hidden Riches: Traditional Symbolism from the Renaissance to Blake*. London: Routledge and Kegan Paul, 1974.

Holmes, Geoffrey. *The Trial of Doctor Sacheverell*. London: Eyre Methuen, 1973.

Holmes, Richard. *Coleridge: Early Visions*. London: Hodder and Stoughton, 1990.

Horne, Alistair. *How Far from Austerlitz? Napoleon, 1805–1815.* London: Macmillan, 1996.

Jackson, James Robert de Jager. *Coleridge: The Critical Heritage.* Vol. 1. *1794–1834.* London: Routledge and Kegan Paul, 1970.

———. *Coleridge: The Critical Heritage.* Vol. 2. *1834–1900.* London: Routledge and Kegan Paul, 1991.

Johnson, David. "Amiens 1802: The Phoney Peace." *History Today* 52, no. 9 (2002): 20–26.

Katritzky, L. "Eighteenth Century German Literary Influences on Coleridge." *History of European Ideas* 20, no. 4 (1996): 295–305.

Kenyon, J. P. *Revolution Principles: The Politics of Party, 1689–1720.* Cambridge: Cambridge University Press, 1977.

King, E. H. "Beattie and Coleridge: New Light on the Damaged Archangel." *Wordsworth Circle* 7, no. 2 (1976): 142–53.

Kitson, Peter J. "Coleridge, Milton and the Millennium." *Wordsworth Circle* 18, no. 2 (1987): 61–66.

———. "'The Electric Fluid of Truth': The Ideology of the Commonwealthsman in *The Plot Discovered.*" In *Coleridge and the Armoury of the Human Mind,* ed. Peter J. Kitson and Thomas N. Corns, 36–62. London: F. Cass, 1991.

———. "'Our Prophetic Harrington': Coleridge, Pantisocracy and Puritan Utopias." *Wordsworth Circle* 24, no. 2 (1993): 97–101.

———. "The Whore of Babylon and the Woman in White: Coleridge's Radical Unitarian Language." In *Coleridge's Visionary Languages,* ed. Tim Fulford and Morton D. Paley, 1–14. Cambridge: Brewer, 1993.

Kooy, M. J. "The End of Poetry: Aesthetic and Ethical Investigations in Coleridge and Schiller." *Wordsworth Circle* 26, no. 1 (1995): 23–26.

Lang, Timothy. *The Victorians and the Stuart Heritage: Interpretations of a Discordant Past.* Cambridge: Cambridge University Press, 1995.

Lefebvre, Molly. *The Bondage of Love: A Life of Mrs. Samuel Coleridge.* London: Gollancz, 1986.

———. *Samuel Taylor Coleridge: A Bondage of Opium.* London: Gollancz, 1974.

Levere, Trevor H. "Coleridge and the Sciences." In *Romanticism and the Sciences,* ed. Andrew Cunningham and Nicholas Jardine, 295–306. Cambridge: Cambridge University Press, 1990.

Lovejoy, A. O. *Essays in the History of Ideas.* Baltimore: Johns Hopkins University Press, 1958.

Lowes, J. L. *The Road to Xanadu.* London: Constable, 1927.

MacCaffrey, Wallace T. *Elizabeth I: War and Politics, 1588–1603.* Princeton: Princeton University Press, 1992.

MacCulloch, Diarmaid. "Richard Hooker's Reputation." *English Historical Review* 117 (2002): 773–812.

Mahoney, J. L. "Theme and Image in Coleridge's Later Poetry." *Wordsworth Circle* 8, no. 4 (1977): 349–60.

Marshall, John S. *Hooker and the Anglican Tradition: An Historical and Theological Study of Hooker's Ecclesiastical Polity.* London: Black, 1964.

Mason, Michael. *The Making of Victorian Sexual Attitudes.* Oxford: Oxford University Press, 1994.

Matthew, H. C. G. *Gladstone, 1809–1898.* Oxford: Oxford University Press, 1997.

———. "Noetics, Tractarians, and the Reform of the University of Oxford in the Nineteenth Century." *History of Universities* 9 (1990): 195–225.

McVeigh, D. M. "Political Vision in Coleridge's *The Statesman's Manual.*" *Wordsworth Circle* 14, no. 2 (1983): 87–92.

Miall, D. S. "Coleridge on Emotion: Experience into Theory." *Wordsworth Circle* 22, no. 1 (1991): 35–39.

Modiano, Raimonda. *Coleridge and the Concept of Nature.* London: Macmillan, 1985.

Moffat, D. "Coleridge's Ten Theses: The Plotinian Alternative." *Wordsworth Circle* 13, no. 1 (1982): 27–31.

Muirhead, J. H. *Coleridge as Philosopher.* London: Allen and Unwin, 1930.

Newsome, D. *Two Classes of Men: Platonism and English Romantic Thought.* London: J. Murray, 1974.

Nichols, David. *Deity and Domination: Images of God and the State in the Nineteenth and Twentieth Centuries.* London: Routledge, 1989.

———. *God and Government in an "Age of Reason."* London: Routledge, 1995.

Nockles, Peter. "Continuity and Change in Anglican High Churchmanship in Britain, 1752–1850." D. Phil. thesis., Oxford University, June 1982.

———. "Our Brethren of the North: The Scottish Episcopal Church and the Oxford Movement." *Journal of Ecclesiastical History* 47, no. 4 (1996): 655–82.

———. *The Oxford Movement in Context.* Oxford: Oxford University Press, 1994.

Oberman, Heiko A. *The Impact of the Reformation.* Edinburgh: T. and T. Clark, 1994.

Ollard, S. L., and Gordon Crosse, eds. *A Dictionary of English Church History.* London: Mowbray, 1912.

O'Mera, John J. *Charter of Christendom: The Significance of the City of God.* New York: Macmillan, 1961.

Orsini, Gian N. G. *Coleridge and German Idealism.* Carbondale: Southern Illinois University Press, 1969.

Piper, H. W. *The Singing of Mount Abora: Coleridge's Use of Biblical Imagery and Natural Symbolism in Poetry and Philosophy.* Rutherford, NJ: Fairleigh Dickinson University Press, 1987.

Pocock, J. G. A. *Virtue, Commerce, and History: Essays on Political Thought and History, Chiefly in the Eighteenth Century.* Cambridge: Cambridge University Press, 1985.

Prickett, S. "The Living Educts of the Imagination: Coleridge on Religious Language." *Wordsworth Circle* 4, no. 3 (1973).

Purton, Valerie. *A Coleridge Chronology.* London: Macmillan, 1993.

Raine, Kathleen, and George Mills Harper, eds. *Thomas Taylor the Platonist: Selected Writings.* London: Routledge and Kegan Paul, 1969.

Ridley, Jasper. *Elizabeth I.* London: Constable, 1987.

Robinson, Henry Crabb. *On Books and Their Writers.* London: J. M. Dent and Sons, 1938.

Rudwick, M. J. S. *The Meaning of Fossils: Episodes in the History of Paleontology.* New York: Science History Publications, 1976.

Sanders, Charles Richard. *Coleridge and the Broad Church Movement.* Durham: Duke University Press, 1942.

Shaffer, E. S. "'Infernal Dreams' and Romantic Art Criticism: Coleridge on the Campo Santo, Pisa." *Wordsworth Circle* 20, no. 1 (1989): 9–19.

———. *"Kubla Khan" and the Fall of Jerusalem.* Cambridge: Cambridge University Press, 1975.

Snyder, Alice D. "Coleridge and Giordano Bruno." *Modern Language Notes* 42 (1927): 427–36.

Sommerville, M. R. "Richard Hooker and His Contemporaries on Episcopacy: An Elizabethan Consensus." *Journal of Ecclesiastical History* 35, no. 2 (1984): 177–87.

Stevenson, Warren. "Coleridge's Divine Duplicity: Being a Concatenation of His Surrogates, Succedaneums, and Doppelgangers." *Wordsworth Circle* 20, no. 2 (1989): 74–78.

Stott, Anne. "Hannah More and the Blagdon Controversy, 1799–1802." *Journal of Ecclesiastical History* 51 (2000): 319–46.

Sykes, Norman. *Church and State in England in the XVIIIth Century.* Hamden, CT: Archon Books, 1962.

Tagliacozzo, Giorgio, ed. *Giambattista Vico: An International Symposium.* Baltimore: Johns Hopkins University Press, 1969.

Taylor, A. "Coleridge, Wollstonecraft, and the Rights of Women." In *Coleridge's Visionary Languages,* ed. Tim Fulford and Morton D. Paley, 83–98. Cambridge: Brewer, 1993.

Taylor, Stephen. "William Warburton and the Alliance of Church and State." *Journal of Ecclesiastical History* 43, no. 2 (1992): 271–86.

Thompson, F. M. L. *The Rise of Respectable Society: A Social History of Victorian Britain, 1830–1900.* London: Fontana Press, 1988.

"Towards a Bibliometric Analysis of the Surviving Record 1701–1800." In *The Cambridge History of the Book in Britain,* vol. 5, *1695–1830,* ed. Michael F.

Suarez S.J. and Michael L. Turner, 39–65. Cambridge: Cambridge University Press, 2009.

Tulloch, John. *Movements of Religious Thought in Britain during the Nineteenth Century.* Leicester: Leicester University Press, 1971.

Vereker, Charles. *Eighteenth Century Optimism: A Study of the Interrelations of Moral and Social Theory in English and French Thought between 1689 and 1789.* Liverpool: Liverpool University Press, 1967.

Virgin, Peter. *The Church in an Age of Negligence: Ecclesiastical Structure and Problems of Church Reform, 1700–1840.* Cambridge: James Clarke, 1989.

Waldo, M. L. "Why Coleridge Hated to Write: An Ambivalence of Theory and Practice." *Wordsworth Circle* 16, no. 1 (1985): 25–32.

Wallace, C. M. "The Function of Autobiography in *Biographia Literaria.*" *Wordsworth Circle* 12, no. 4 (1981): 216–25.

Walsh, John, Colin Haydon, and Stephen Taylor, eds. *The Church of England, c. 1689–c. 1833.* Cambridge: Cambridge University Press, 1993.

Wand, J. W. *The Second Reform.* London: Faith Press, 1953.

Wante, Charles Etienne Pierre, and Frank Howard Warner. *The National Union Catalog; Pre-1956 Imprints.* London: Mansell, 1979.

Willey, Basil. "Coleridge and Religion." In *Writers and Their Background: S. T. Coleridge,* ed. R. L. Brett, 221–43. London: Bell, 1971.

———. *Nineteenth Century Studies: Coleridge to Matthew Arnold.* London: Chatto and Windus, 1949.

———. *Samuel Taylor Coleridge.* London: Chatto and Windus, 1972.

Williams, Penry. *The Later Tudors: England, 1547–1603.* New Oxford History of England. Oxford: Oxford University Press, 1995.

Wilson, D. B. "Coleridge and the Endangered Self." *Wordsworth Circle* 26, no. 1 (1995): 18–23.

Winch, Donald. *Riches and Poverty: An Intellectual History of Political Economy in Britain, 1750–1834.* Cambridge: Cambridge University Press, 1996.

Wordsworth, John. "The Infinite I AM: Coleridge and the Ascent of Being." In *Coleridge's Imagination,* ed. Richard Gravil, Lucy Newlyn, and Nicholas Roe, 22–52. Cambridge: Cambridge University Press, 1985.

Young, B. W. *Religion and Enlightenment in Eighteenth-Century England: Theological Debate from Locke to Burke.* Oxford: Clarendon Press, 1998.

Zall, P. M. "The Cool World of Samuel Taylor Coleridge: Joseph Lancaster's System." *Wordsworth Circle* 13, no. 2 (1982): 64–70.

INDEX

Luke Savin Herrick Wright

is a visiting scholar in the Corcoran Department of History,

University of Virginia.